The Michigan Historical Reprint Series

Reprints from the collection of the University of Michigan University Library

This volume is produced from digital images created through the University of Michigan University Library's preservation reformatting program. The Library seeks to preserve the intellectual content of items in a manner that facilitates and promotes a variety of uses. The digital reformatting process results in an electronic version of the text that can both be accessed online and used to create new print copies. This book and thousands of others can be found in the digital collections of the University of Michigan Library. The University Library also understands and values the utility of print, and makes reprints available through its Scholarly Publishing Office.

For access to the University of Michigan Library's digital collections, please see http://www.lib.umich.edu.

The Scholarly Publishing Office seeks to disseminate high-quality, cost-effective scholarly content through both print and electronic publishing. Information about the Scholarly Publishing Office can be found at http://spo.umdl.umich.edu.

The Scholarly Publishing Office
the University of Michigan
University Library

A WOMAN'S

FIRST IMPRESSIONS OF EUROPE.

BEING

WAYSIDE SKETCHES

MADE DURING A SHORT TOUR IN THE YEAR 1863.

BY MRS. E. A. FORBES.

NEW YORK:
DERBY & MILLER.

1865.

THOMAS, TYPOGRAPHER,
BUFFALO.

TO

Mr. and Mrs. Henry W. Rogers,

THE DEAR FRIENDS,

UNDER WHOSE PROTECTION LIFELONG DREAMS HAVE BECOME

REALITIES, THESE WAYSIDE SKETCHES OF SCENES

WHICH WE HAVE ENJOYED TOGETHER,

ARE AFFECTIONATELY INSCRIBED.

PREFACE.

THE writer of the following sketches cannot send them forth from their original domestic destination to the impertinence of print, without reminding any who may honor them with their notice, that an egotism in incident and a dogmatism in criticism, which would be insufferable, if intended for the public eye, are simply the shortest and easiest mode of recording one's personal impressions in a private journal.

To disentangle these elements from what remains, would prove a task altogether disproportionate to the value of the work; it is therefore commended to friendly indulgence, with an earnest disclaimer of these two worst vices of the literature of travel.

ERRATA.

Page 32, line 15, for "for" read *to*.
Page 148, line 10, for "Donneker" read *Danneker*.
Page 198, line 2, for "Glisshone" read *Glisshorn*.
Page 200, line 8, for "valley" read *gallery*.
Page 220, line 5, for "manor" read *manner*.
Page 247, line 11, for "the portico" read *a portico*.
Page 267, line 12, for "mysterious" read *mysteries*.
Page 268, line 19, for "Centi" read *Conti*.

CONTENTS.

CHAPTER IX.

CHAPTER X.

CHAPTER XI.

CHAPTER XII.

CHAPTER XIII.

CHAPTER XIV.

CHAPTER XV.

CHAPTER XVI.

CHAPTER XVII.

CHAPTER XVIII.

WAYSIDE SKETCHES.

CHAPTER I.

THE GREAT EASTERN.

New York to Liverpool.

We left Flushing yesterday, July 21st, 1863, at one o'clock P. M. It was blowing a gale, yet the great ship got under weigh without making us aware that she had left her moorings. She held on her course without perceptible motion until we left the Sound, and since, nothing beyond a slight roll reminds us that we are not upon terra firma.

This morning we passed one of our gunboats pitching and tossing upon the waves, and later in the day have seen a veritable whale spouting in the distance. The day is charming—and the deck resembles the street of a city. We find our state-rooms delightful. The time is apparently measured only by alternate seasons of eating and sleeping. We breakfast at eight, lunch at twelve, dine at five, and take tea at any later hour until ten. The lights are extinguished at half-past eleven. A trumpet is blown in each companionway to summon us to table, and a band discourses sweet music at intervals, winding up at night with God save the Queen. The number of passengers is said to be between two and three hundred.

July 23. The sea still smooth as a river—the day charming—no symptom of seasickness possible. The magnificent ship holds her stately way as if she were an island set adrift upon the waters. She is indeed a little world within herself. Her regular quota of officials is four hundred and eighty, and she registers twenty-five thousand tons.

We have been upon deck all the morning, and its size, and the multitudes of people every where astir, destroy entirely the effect of isolation which we usually connect with the idea of a ship alone in an amphitheatre of sea and sky. A programme of games among the sailors for this afternoon has been put aside for the funeral of a little child among the steerage passengers. My heart aches for the mother who leaves her baby in these lone waters. A ball announced for eight o'clock will probably be postponed also.

July 24. Another charming day. There is a stiff breeze, which, however, produces no perceptible effect upon the motion of the ship. For the last two days, we have made two hundred and ninety miles each, and our entire progress amounts to eight hundred and thirty-five miles since we weighed anchor in Flushing Bay. The ball came off, and lasted until nearly midnight. The postponed games are to be instituted this afternoon. Meanwhile, we enjoy the afternoon regulation nap; an unlimited capacity for sleep seeming to be among the legitimate effects of seagoing. This morning, as I looked out at the port-hole, I saw an oar floating by—perhaps borne away by the tide from the peaceful shore—perhaps only the relic of some nameless wreck, for whose return loving eyes have grown dim with watching—perhaps it was plied by some lone wanderer towards a hope of safety, until death unnerved his grasp, and he sank down to be drifted out to the mighty sepulchre, which enshrouds alike the wealth of past ages and the baby of yesterday.

July 25. I do not know two more incongruous personalities than a Yankee ashore and a Yankee at sea. It would be decidedly to the advantage of the "universal nation" if it could be set afloat, and learn to enjoy the delicious dreamy idleness of ship life. It seems impossible to settle one's self to any more intense mental activity than may consist with watching the lazy dip of the distant horizon as the great ship rolls gently from side to side. Occasionally a distant sail attracts universal attention, but for my own part, I should scarcely have believed it possible to spend so many days without a real thought.

This morning opened fair, with a strong breeze, but on going upon deck this afternoon, we found ourselves enveloped in a thick fog. The ship goes on with diminished speed, blowing a warning whistle at short intervals, with good reason, for we are on the banks, and have passed a fleet of fishing boats with their small craft out. Little chance for the unlucky vessel which fails to keep a good lookout for the Leviathan.

The amusements of yesterday and to-day have had the attraction of novelty at least. They have been foot races, sack races, steeple chases, hurdle races and cock fights. The last mentioned not being the inhuman sport of the feathered tribe, but a good natured set-to of the biped of more pretensions. It is conducted on this wise. Two men, having their hands tied, clasp their knees, and a stout stick is thrust under the knees and over the arms. Then, sitting upon the deck, face to face, they fight with the feet; the object of each man being to throw his opponent on his back, by inserting his toes under his feet. The match evidently requires much coolness and dexterity, and the last one was prolonged until the intensity of concentration and watchfulness on the part of the combatants became something painful. The winner is he who first throws his adversary three times.

The sack race is very amusing. The men are tied in sacks to their throats, feet, hands and all, and accomplish their progress by hopping within their limited accommodations—of course, the slightest mischance sends them rolling helplessly upon the ground. In addition to the interest common to all the spectators, the races have evidently gratified the English thirst for betting.

The weather grows cold, but is delightful and invigorating. I have not yet come to a realizing sense of being at sea, more than a thousand miles from home, and am half inclined to fancy that the vivid descriptions of self-consciousness which belong to the literature of the sea must be written after one has reached dry land.

July 29. The foregoing hiatus is chargeable to the account of Neptune and his angry nymphs, as I shall proceed to show.

On Sunday morning we came upon the wake of an old gale, which, having been perhaps baulked of the mischief for which it was brewed, proceeded to wreak its vengeance upon us innocent voyagers. We assembled in the grand saloon at eleven o'clock for divine service. The captain, having been up all night, declined his accustomed office of chaplain, which devolved, in consequence, upon a Presbyterian minister, who received private instructions in the purser's cabin upon the English service. The lessons were read by the Rev. Gordon Hall, son of the first American missionary to India, and the sermon preached by a Scotch minister from Toronto. The band led the music in the adjoining saloon. This was one of three services held at the same time in the enormous vessel.

For my own part, I soon became aware that the ship had added to her usual roll a peculiar lifting of her forefoot, producing a gastric complication by no means enviable, and I prudently seated myself near the door; where, having remained until the conclusion of the morning prayer, I found it expedient to beat a hasty retreat; and for a few moments my personal experience of the malady of the sea would have satisfied the wishes of my best medical advisers. But the disease is fatal neither to life nor spirits, and although I had missed the sermon, I stood at the port-hole, and the magnificent waves took to themselves a text and preached to me a solitary sermon upon the might of Him who has poured these resistless waters from the hollow of His hand, and yet has made of the sand a bound to the sea that it shall not pass over. I remarked, too, that the angrier the wave, the more beautiful was its crest, and I thought of His tender love, that outrides the billows of turmoil and pain, and brings, even out of their own depths, joy and peace by the light of His countenance.

But the gale freshened, and presently the moveables of our domain broke away and went adrift—chairs, tables and trunks performing gyrations after the most approved style of a modern waltz; while the peregrinations of the inhabitants were performed upon decidedly original principles. But the careful steward of the bed chamber soon made all fast; hooked up the tables, screwed up the port, made a barricade of the luggage before my sofa, confiscated one chair and made a chevaux-de-frise of the other, and left us all prostrate at the altar of the Tritons.

However, it is not to be supposed that we were so wanting to ourselves as to be absent from table, and the ludicrous scenes of the dining room abundantly compensated us for the effort. The guards prevented an escapade of the dishes, but not necessarily of their contents. The reckless wight who took soup took a good deal of it; my vis-a-vis ate his duck, but pocketed the olives: somersaults were in fashion, and the waiters scrambled about, distributing the viands impartially between the guests and the floor. A sudden lurch made a cataract of the china upon the sideboard, while the same blow sent the dessert flying about the kitchen floor. Nobody slept at night; some of the waves broke over our port, fifty feet above water level, and washed the boats at the davits. The only sight visible through the darkness was the window, like the great eye of Neptune, now staring at us from above, now peering at us from below. Among the rest of the unearthly noises of the night, was the flapping of canvas, as the sailors struggled to set the main topsail to steady the ship. The struggle was short, and the sail went by the board, with a report like the crack of artillery. The tattered remnants still cling to the heavy yard.

With all this, there was neither storm nor danger, but an experience which one would not miss, as a part of the legitimate routine of seagoing. Our cabin is a cozy home of our own, so arranged that it becomes at pleasure one room or two; my own domain especially comfortable, as, with my friends usual kind consideration for my comfort, I am bestowed where I am "rocked in the cradle of the deep," instead of playing at see-saw with my head and feet. We are especially favored with good ventilation, as, besides the port-hole, we have a window communicating through the deck with the outer air, and also with a tartarus of a fire-hole in the abyss below. It is curious to watch at night the weird effect of the grimy demon of those profound depths, as he stirs the raging fires, and eminently suggestive also of the potentialities hanging on his watchfulness.

On Monday and Tuesday we had a heavy sea, but we have crossed the gale, and are out of the rolling forties. Notwithstanding the roll, it has been delightful on deck, and we cannot sufficiently congratulate ourselves that we are established in such a stately palace of motion, and can enjoy the rough sea without being driven below by the waves.

It rains to-day, and we have taken refuge in whist. We have advanced many degrees towards the sunrising, and it requires a fresh calculation every day to follow home friends, God bless them, through home avocations.

Another death occurred on board yesterday,—that of a woman travelling to England to die. Her husband and children are with her. Her disease was a hopelessly advanced cancer, and the sickness of the rough night induced a hemorrhage, which hastened her sufferings to a close. She is to be taken to land for burial. I do not know that there is any thing very terrible in the thought of being consigned to this vast sepulchre of the dead, where no foot of mammon may disturb the long repose; where the solemn requiem of wind and wave rings ever above the spot, marked only by the eye of Him who knows where to find His beloved when the sea shall give up its dead.

July 30. The weather, rainy for some days, is making an effort at sunlight—the sea steady—but it is not a good day for the deck.

The event of yesterday was a musical soirée, for the benefit of the band which has contributed so largely towards our enjoyment on board. It was difficult to remember that we were on shipboard, thousands of miles at sea. The grand saloon, a splendid well lighted parlor, filled with well dressed people, the charming band, the amateur volunteers, both gentlemen and ladies, differed in nothing—except, perhaps, in their superiority—from a similar scene in the parlor of a fashionable watering place; while in the steady way of the great ship, there was nothing to remind us that we were ploughing the unstable waves. We had Italian music and ballads—some admirable performances upon the piano. A fine barytone gave us The Old Sexton, Rocked in the Cradle of the Deep, and Twenty Years Ago—the last mentioned going down straight into the depths of the heart. We had, in addition, some amusing feats of legerdemain and ventriloquism; wound up with the Marseillaise, the Star Spangled

Banner, and God save the Queen, and went home near midnight, highly gratified.

It is a matter of continual regret that the splendid ship, which we so much enjoy, should, in any respect, fail to deserve the suffrages of the travelling public. But, while in security, accommodations and pleasure it is inimitable, the table is unpardonably deficient. The viands are badly (not scantily) furnished, and worse cooked. It is a matter of comparatively little importance to me, but it is a pity that an establishment, otherwise so perfect, should fail in a point essential to general comfort and to the reputation of the vessel. However, I am willing to compound for its many advantages with the temporary discomfort of the table; and, undoubtedly, the mortification attendant upon the faults of the present trip will prevent their recurrence. We are to have races again this afternoon, and a dance this evening.

July 31. Once more a delicious day—the air bland with the soft south wind, and the sea quiet as a lake. Made the first land a little past one, and I can no more realize that we are actually running down the coast of Ireland, than if I had been making only a trip up the Hudson—moreover, we have had no tedium at sea, to make us hail the sight of land with any enthusiasm for the land's sake. Having never enjoyed a more delightful week in my life, I am in no haste to urge it to a close, and in no humor to lose the intensity of present enjoyment in visions of anticipation.

Yesterday was the Captain's dinner, and, as my first experience of a public dinner, I shall not readily forget it. The dinner was a handsome one, wine plentifully bestowed, and after the cloth was removed came toasts and speeches. The Captain led off by proposing with appropriate speeches the Queen, and the American Nation. Nobody taking upon himself the representation of either personality, the toasts were drunk with acclamation, and then came Mr. R., briefly but happily proposing the Captain. His speech was not only applauded, but afterwards warmly commended by the passengers. Capt. Paton's reply was very good, defining his position in a modest yet dignified manner, and taking the occasion to express the pain which the failure of his agents of supply in New York had caused him, in such a hearty earnest way, that every body felt there was nothing more to be said upon the subject.

The Surgeon, the Purser and the first officer were then called out. The ladies made their acknowledgments by the mouth of some English gentleman. Afterwards came other speeches and toasts, prolonging the affair a trifle beyond the limits of good taste, and concluding with the Captain's speech in behalf of Mrs. Paton. It was all quite exciting to me, and had, besides, the charm of novelty.

The evening was spent in the ball room. I wish I could picture the scene to home eyes, by way of contrast to the commonly received ideas of even pleasant life on shipboard. Here was an elegant room, about sixty by thirty feet in extent, brilliantly lighted by chandeliers and gaily decorated shades, and adorned with banners, filled with gay dancers and a merry host of spectators, officers, waiters with trays of ices, &c., all moving about at perfect ease, and in utter oblivion of the unstable element upon which we were floating; our single world probably the sole tenant of the horizon. We looked into each other's faces to exclaim "Can this be the sea?" Success to the stately ship, the wonder of the seas. We shall all leave her with real regret, and with kindly remembrances of her commander. I hear, at this moment, the merry shouts on deck. They are finishing the races of the trip with a grinning match. To-morrow night we expect to sleep on shore. If our tour should end here, I should be the happier, for the rest of my life, for the pleasure of the last fortnight.

Aug. 1. One more entry at sea. We are running up St. George's Channel this morning, and have already passed Holyhead, the grand headland of North Wales. And now I feel, for the first time, the awe of treading the threshold of the Old World — that long desire of a lifetime. The very air we breathe is redolent of past ages — the soil we seek to tread rich in classic memories. We come to lay hold of tangible links in the chain that binds the Present to the immutable Past, and must, at every step, kindle a torch of remembrance, whose light shall shine amid the lengthening shadows of our lifelong path

—an Aladdin's lamp, whose touch shall bring to light visions which put to shame the fairy dreams of Arabian lore.

CHAPTER II.

FIRST IMPRESSIONS.

Liverpool—Chester—Eaton Hall—Bangor—Caernarvon—Llanberis—Dublin—Belfast—Giant's Causeway.

AUG. 2. On shore at last. The great ship came to anchor yesterday about five o'clock, too late to cross the bar. A tug took off all the passengers who desired to land, among whom we were not: the prospect of a twenty miles' sail at night in an open steamer, not proving enticing. The band played Auld Lang Syne as the tug moved off, bearing away some whose share in this brief companionship will claim many pleasant remembrances. We remained on board, attended a dance, and came off this morning.

The form, for it is nothing more, of examining the luggage occupied a considerable time, and we did not leave the ship until half-past ten o'clock. She gave us a gun as a parting salute, and we left the abode of a pleasant fortnight with some regret, even for the shores of Europe.

I wonder what Yankeedom would say if its water-going journeys were to be performed in a steamer without seat or shelter; yet that was the style of our first travel in the maternal country.

Liverpool is very unlike my preconceived idea of the great commercial city; I had fancied it dirty, dingy, crowded and uninteresting. But my notions have been corrected—no very unusual occurrence. The solid masonry of the long miles of docks is in striking contrast to our dirty piers, and our landing upon the clean pavement of the wharf was as quiet as a walk in a country town.

The Washington is an elegant hotel, just out of St. George's Square. In the broad open place stands a pillar which serves as pedestal to a statue of the Duke of Wellington, and upon one side of the square stands St. George's Hall, considered a very elegant edifice. The smoke reduces all architecture to a common hue, but one is immediately impressed with the solidity of the structures. The street is very clean, but not a vehicle reminds us of its congeners in America. We have had a charming drive to Prince's Park, and a walk in the private gardens, a beautiful extent of ornamental gardening. We have been to St. George's Hall, a fine building, one of whose beauties is the style of column, consisting of a kind of brown variegated marble, finished in tall shafts of exquisite polish, with Corinthian capitals. The concert room is very handsome, but its size struck me as very small for such a purpose, in so large a city.

Aug. 3. I feel how baldly meagre must be any attempt to describe the pleasure of a day at Chester, and yet to pass it over would be to omit a day of sight-seeing than which we can have no other more enjoyable.

We left Liverpool about noon, crossing to Birkenhead, and came by rail to Chester, one hour's distance. Only one hour from this commercial depot of the modern world to the shades of Julius Cæsar!

This ancient city is surrounded by a perfect wall, whose date runs back to its occupation by the Romans, A. D. 61. The top of the wall is flagged and guarded by a battlement of solid masonry, making a beautiful promenade entirely around the old city. It crosses the streets by bridges or archways, called gates, which give names to various streets, such as East Gate Street, Water Gate Street, &c. Flights of steps descend to the footways at each crossing. The whole structure shows great care, both of preservation and restoration.

There are several towers flanking the angles of the wall. From one of these—the Phenix Tower, King Charles the First witnessed the defeat of his army upon Rowton Moor. The upper story of the tower is improved, as the Yankees say, as a museum of antique relics of the city itself, and contains, besides, sundry curiosities from foreign lands. The lower floor, where are vended prints of Chester and its celebrities, was once a Roman council chamber.

Within the castle, now occupied as barracks, is a portion of wall built by Cæsar. At the foot of this wall, and elsewhere throughout the city, have been exhumed innumerable Roman antiquities; and at the present moment an excavation is going on in Bridge Street, where the foundations of an immense temple are exposed, supposed by antiquarians to have been a temple to Diana. The foundations and portions of the massive pillars are plainly visible, at a slight distance below the level of the street.

In a cellar, immediately adjoining, is a Roman bath, in perfect preservation, hewn out of solid rock, and still kept partially filled by some concealed spring or conduit below. Close by is a hypocaust, or large furnace, also hewn in arches from the solid rock, for the purpose of heating a sudatorium or sweating room above.

The wonder is, not so much that these things should have been established upon the island so long ago, but that, through all the upheavals of all the centuries, they should have been permitted to remain, the unquestionable, unchanged tokens of the old Roman inhabitation.

The entire effect of the town is a translation of sympathy and almost of individuality to the remote past, with a sense of the actuality of History, as opposed to the reality of Fiction. The streets themselves close the eyes of one's perceptions to the nineteenth century; and, peering through the mists of the ages, we dimly discern the daily life of the men and women who formed the people, hundreds of years ago. Of those times, History records the public acts of the great lights of the nations; but here we see the very dwellings where burned the rushlights of the multitude—the narrow ways which their feet have trodden—the very altars where they worshipped—the very burial places where they were laid to rest.

Upon one old house—the only one which escaped the plague—is inscribed "God's providence is mine inheritance;" upon another in the same street are quaint carvings representing scripture scenes. Hard by, diving through a narrow entrance to a small square court, we find the Derby House, the palace of the Stanleys. We were shown into the dining hall, now used as the shop of a mechanic, but retaining the same raftered roof and wainscoted wall as when nobility banqueted within its narrow limits. The same iron studded door opened to us that swung upon its hinges to admit the scions of royalty; and little plebeian children played upon the worn oaken staircase which led to the bower of the dames.

Bishop Loyd's palace, belonging to the early part of the seventeenth century, is another curious relic of that which constituted magnificence in the days when the Puritans built their homes in our western forests.

The remarkable feature of the streets is the Rows. The lower stories set directly upon the street, serve as shops, and above, the entire front of the second story is cut away, forming a continuous arcade, within which are arranged the shops of the town. Steps descend to the street at frequent intervals, while the dwellings are still above.

The great points of interest in Chester are two ancient churches — the Cathedral, or the Church of St. Oswald and St. Werburgh, and the Church of St. John the Baptist. The former was erected, mainly, in the fourteenth and fifteenth centuries, upon a site once occupied by a temple of Apollo. The choir is used as a parish church, and cathedral service is performed here twice a day. The cloisters around the quadrangle were to me the most interesting part of the immense edifice, and perhaps the best place to get a definite idea of the great space occupied by the Abbey.

Time is wearing away the massive mullions and stanchions of the arched windows, but the kindly ivy tenderly shadows the unsightly flaws, and converts the jagged outline into a thing of beauty. My fancy went back to the monks who paced these cloisters, four hundred years ago, and were laid, one by one, beneath our feet, and wondered if they found in this green retirement the peace which the human race has since ceased even to desire.

The Church of St. John the Baptist is of still greater antiquity and interest. It was founded in A. D. 689, and the old chancel is still standing in ivy-clad ruin, with great trees thrusting their branches from out the arches of its windows. The carvings and statues of the ancient edifice, though fallen, are still preserved upon the spot, and are gradually incorporated in the renovation of the later church, which is now in progress.

This church, repaired thoroughly in 1581, is of a beautiful style of architecture—Norman rather than Gothic. The part used as a church is simply fitted up, and screened from the open aisles by a partition of rough boards. Upon entering, we found the vicar waiting in the chancel to perform a marriage ceremony. Mr. R. addressed him, and he showed us the utmost courtesy, pointing out many things of interest connected with the ancient church.

The environs of Chester are charming. The great attraction is Eaton Hall, the residence, or rather one of the estates, of the Marquis of Westminster, the largest landed proprietor in England. This estate is twelve miles in length; but miles and statistics can give little idea of such a place. We obtained, in the town, tickets of entrance both to the house and gardens, and rolled away mile after mile, over a perfect road, winding through field and forest and park, all showing the most exquisite culture, and varied with careful attention to effect; and, at length, reached the magnificent lawn in front of the hall, dotted with stately trees, and stretching off in charming perspective to the wooded background in the distance.

The most respectful and respectable of butlers received us in the vestibule, and conducted us "through gallery fair and high arcade" to the show rooms of the mansion. The vestibule is lofty and elegant, and contains several pieces of statuary, and four suits of armor in effigy, belonging to his lordship's ancestors. The dining, breakfast, morning and drawing rooms, the saloon and library, are all en suite, and each impresses one with a sense of magnificence, hitherto beyond my conception. The dining room windows look out upon a wonderful scene of garden beauty, the flowers being not only disposed with great taste in the form of the parterres, but the colors so strikingly arranged as produce the highest effect either of contrast or harmony.

The walls of the saloon and drawing room are frescoed in Spanish scenes, sketched from nature by the Marchioness herself, and painted by Mr. Morris of Chester. There are many valuable paintings in the various rooms—two by Rubens, two by Guercino—besides the family portraits, busts, and other pieces of sculpture that adorn the halls. One long hall is lined with pictures of noted horses that have belonged to the family. To judge from their number and beauty, the race of Le Gros Veneur has not yet lost the ancestral taste.

In a box in a small vestibule is a huge pig of lead, wrought by Roman skill from British mines in the first century. The chapel of the hall is a perfect gem, but the library is the most splendid of all these apartments. It is one hundred and twenty feet long, lofty and elegant, containing, besides the organ and book cases, statues and curiosities too numerous and too interesting to be properly understood in many visits. A faultless Flora, by Wylie, and a bust of the late Marquis, by Chantrey, are the finest pieces of statuary.

Nor does this noble house disdain the work of homelier artists. Among the rare and curious objects in the library stands a table, made with long and patient experiment by a mechanic of Chester, which is ingeniously wrought to show the grain of three hundred blocks of the different kinds of English wood.

The gardens include long ranges of hot-houses, green-houses, graperies, walls of fruit, kitchen gardens, ornamental shrubberies, and artificial lakes, containing plants, trees and shrubs, from all countries and climates. Among the smaller trees, the English and Irish yew were especially attractive.

The view from the east front of the mansion, looking down the broad terraces, filled with exquisite flowers, interspersed with turfy banks and wide avenues, to the inlet of the Dee below; bounded on either side by the graceful sweep of the bosky thicket of trees and shrubbery which shut out the park views beyond, is all enchanting as a dream of fairy land.

Well might a house which can claim this beautiful domain as its ancient heritage be pardoned for the pride of birth. But this is only one of the estates of the Marquis, and he spends but three months of the year in this abode of wealth and art and beauty.

A day at Chester alone, would repay one for crossing the Atlantic, and will enrich the memory with pleasure for a lifetime.

We visited the picturesque cemetery, and walked upon the ancient wall, and traversed the quaint Rows; and found, every where, that strange mingling of the shadows of the dusky Past with the sunshine of the nineteenth century, that constitutes such a charm for the dwellers in a land which has no antiquity beyond the memory of half a dozen generations.

We left Chester with many a lingering look, and travelled through a most picturesque country to Bangor. The tide was down, and, stretching miles away, we saw the sands of Dee; and as we went on, we watched

> "The cruel crawling hungry foam
> Come o'er the sands of Dee,"

where Mary went to

> "Call the cattle home,
> But never home came she."

On this route we made our first acquaintance with castles. The Castle of Grwych rises among the hills of Wales as if it were the legitimate outgrowth of the soil. Conway Castle crowns the summit of a hill under which the railway passes. It is a ruin of great extent. The ivy-covered walls reached along the crest of the hill as far as we could see, on both sides of the railway, and must have enclosed a circuit unusual even in the times of castles.

The scenery of North Wales is surpassingly beautiful. It is a combination of charming fields, bordered every where by green hedgerows, and showing the most careful cultivation, with bold, bare masses of granite, towering high in solitary grandeur, sometimes affording a roothold for a scanty covering of grass, and sometimes lifting their heads in naked majesty to the beating of the eternal storms.

At Bangor we found an inn near the railway station, nestled close at the foot of the hills, quaint in its old fashioned arrangements—the very type of an inn for such a locality, and a delightful summer resort for those who would enjoy mountain excursions.

There, on one of the loveliest days that ever smiled npon the earth, we took a wagonette, a Welsh horse and a Welsh driver, and set out for a drive through a charming variety of scenery for Caernarvon Castle.

The broad road, smooth as a parlor floor, bordered by walls topped with a hawthorn hedge, swept up and down the green waves of the fair country, with the Menai Strait in full view on the one hand, and on the other, the hills rising higher and higher to the lofty range of which great Snowdon is the topmost peak. Bowling swiftly along, with such uninterrupted smoothness of motion, amid such a country, and inhaling the free, bracing mountain air, is in itself an intensity of enjoyment such as is rarely experienced. I never hope for such a day again.

We drove into the little town of Caernarvon upon a holiday. There was a regatta on the strait; Prince

Arthur had visited the castle, and all Welshdom was abroad.

The huge, rude walls of the castle rise from the water side, enclosing a not very extensive court. The walls are sound and massive as when they formed the stronghold of Edward, and the circuit of the court is still solidly complete. Of the several towers, the highest and best preserved is the Eagle Tower, in which Edward the Second was born. The innumerable steps are perfect to the top. Queen Eleanor's chamber is a small, chill, uncouth apartment, with a huge fireplace occupying an entire side, lighted by one loop-hole, and flanked by two ante-rooms for the attendant guards. The poverty of modern womanhood is rare, that would not consider itself unhappily lodged in such quarters, even though they should bear the title of royalty.

One cannot fail to be impressed with the chill discomfort which must have characterized noble life within the heavy walls of those dark, grim, feudal castles. It may have been all very well for knight and squire, but as for the dames, I am glad to have been born in the nineteenth century.

The quaint old town of Caernarvon is utterly unlike any thing to be seen in the New World. One is here every where impressed with the enduring character of all structures. In the most remote of rural dwellings, you feel at once that the solid cottage walls have already sheltered many generations, and will shelter many more.

The Welsh cottages are extremely picturesque, built of stone, neatly whitewashed, and covered with ivy to the eaves. They are surrounded by pretty gardens, gay with flowers, among which the Fuchsia is conspicuous—here a tall, hardy shrub, growing as abundantly as our own lilac, its graceful twigs drooping with a weight of coral drops. The hedges are of hawthorn, and the banks covered with bluebell and a beautiful purple flower which the driver called cleat.

We sped back from Caernarvon, with our wonderful Welsh horse, in the direction of the distant range of mountains, the country growing gradually wilder and higher, until we stopped at an inn on the borders of the beautiful Lake of Llanberis, at the foot of Llanberis Pass. The inn, covered with climbing flowers, bore the pretentious name of Pedarn Villa. Here we exchanged our equipage for another wagonette and a pair of ponies necessary to the ascent of the pass.

Upon the opposite side of the lake are the vast slate quarries of Colonel Pennant, whose residence, Pennryhn Castle, we had passed upon the way from Chester. As the afternoon wore into evening, we saw troops of white-jacketed workmen whirling along the railway upon the bank, returning in hand-cars from their work to the habitable regions below. A little way up the pass stands Pedarn Castle, a picturesque ruin of a single tower, upon a little headland projecting into the lake. Here is another large hotel for the accommodation of tourists.

Still the same smooth, carefully kept road, wound up the mountain way; and, here and there, perched in the almost inaccessible nooks of the crags, were the same neat ivy-clad cottages. The gorge grew narrower, and the cliffs more nearly perpendicular; but every where we could see sheep clinging to the steep sides, and browsing the scanty herbage; tiny rills and larger brooks came brawling over the stony way by the roadside; the bald storm-rent hills grew nearer, and cast their huge fragments at our feet; the defile narrowed, until

> "Suspended cliffs, with hideous sway,
> Seemed nodding o'er the hollow way,
> As if an infant's touch could urge
> Their headlong passage down the verge."

At the distance of five miles we reached the summit of the pass, and looked down the pretty green valley of Gwinnant beyond. About nine miles farther on are Beth Gelert and Cuppel Curigg, but we were too late for a prolonged drive, or for the ascent of Snowdon.

We followed a little girl as guide up the side of the mountain, for a nearer view of the Cambrian monarch, but he had vailed his head in clouds. Mr. R. went on up the sharp ascent until we heard his voice over our heads, but old Snowdon refused to reveal himself, and the lengthening shadows warned us to return.

We came down the pass, and took tea at the inn at the foot. Shades of Llewellyn! what a rapacious crew make merchandise of the grand and the picturesque in this lovely land!

We returned along the shadowy lanes of the silent landscape to Bangor, with a bewildering sense of new enjoyment, and a panorama of wonderful beauty impressed upon the memory for all time.

The appearance of the peasantry of the country through which we passed, was very pleasing. The hardy, smiling, rosy faces, at the doors of the cottages, spoke unmistakably of health and content. A curious feature among them, is the style of begging. Sturdy, well-fed, well-dressed children sped after the carriage, patiently repeating their only English word, "ha' penny;" their rosy, healthy, merry faces, contrasting strangely with their demand. It was of no use to refuse—on they pattered, keeping up bravely with the horse, until a half penny tossed among the group, would institute a scramble which rendered further pursuit useless. I looked with envy upon the brown faces of the little rogues, and could not but admire the philosophy which pitched their demand upon so low a key, that they could not possibly be disappointed in the amount bestowed.

Aug. 5. As we left the pretty, quiet inn, at Bangor, we saw the little Prince Arthur, on his way to lunch at Castle Pennrhyn. He is a nice looking boy of thirteen, very like the pictures of his mother.

We crossed the tubular bridge, vainly endeavoring to realize that it was the wonderful structure of which we have read so much. It is only one among the countless things, whose grandeur we never realize at the moment of contact. Distance seems to be a peremptory element of appreciation, both in the physical and mental world.

We crossed the island of Anglesea, which is much less picturesque than the main land, and took the steamer at Holyhead for Kingstown. The passage was rather rough, but accomplished in four hours. We had a live marchioness on board, with her son and attendants. The harbor at Kingstown is very fine, and the coast much bolder than I had supposed. The ride to Dublin, by rail, was less than half an hour, and, before dark, we found ourselves installed in pleasant rooms at Morrison's Hotel. We have a suite upon the ground floor, opposite Trinity College Gardens.

I must not omit to speak of the perfection of travelling arrangements, so far as we have proceeded. The quiet, security, certainty and speed of the railways, the comfort of the carriages, and the assured conviction that everything is coming out right, in regard to yourself and your luggage, constitute the perfection of travel. The railways cross the public roads, almost invariably, either by tunnel below, or by bridge above; and when obliged to make the crossing at the same grade, stout gates of timber secure the track from the highway until the train has passed. Officials are, every where, conspicuously marked, and their quiet, respectful demeanor, as well as that of servants universally, constitutes a respectability of rank, worthy of imitation by their counterparts on this side the water. One yields an immediate respect to the scrupulous maintenance of position, as well in the lower orders of society as in the higher, which is never rendered to the universal assumption of equality, whatever may be one's theory upon the subject.

The quiet of the railways contrasts strongly with our own. The ringings and snortings are all lacking; the notice to the engineer is a small whistle worn upon the neck of the conductor; there are no platforms to tempt careless passengers, and you are securely locked into the carriages between the stations. The guard unlocks the door at each station where there is sufficient pause, and relocks it before starting. The charges, both of travel and service, are enormous, but, taking them for granted once for all, nothing can be more comfortable than the whole system. The cars are divided into three compartments, each containing two rows of seats placed vis-a-vis. The first class carriages are arranged with three arm chairs, luxuriously cushioned from top to bottom. The second class have undivided seats, cushioned with hair, with a narrow cushion for the shoulders, while the third class seats are simple benches. The difference in price is very considerable.

Aug. 6. The change from an English terminus to an Irish one is striking. Instead of the sleek horses, and the precise liveried coachmen, awaiting your orders in respectful silence, or in the well-bred undertone which characterizes English servants, we found a tangled crowd of ragged drivers, tugging at their lean horses, and vociferating at the top of their voices; a tattered coat seeming to form no bar to respectability. And then the vehicles! It is worth while to ride once, and only once, in a jaunting car. In appearance it bears a strong resemblance to a resuscitated fossil of the age when the bird began to struggle with the reptilian quadruped, the Pterodactyl, for instance. It is a two-wheeled vehicle for one horse; the body formed of a long narrow box, covered with a cushion and running longitudinally. On each side of this spine runs a narrow seat, for two or more persons, sitting back to back; and from the seat depends a step by a hinge, precisely like the open cover of a box. These, when unoccupied, are turned back over the seat. If there be but one passenger, the driver sits upon the opposite side, to trim the craft; but if it be properly balanced, he occupies a high seat in front. The whole affair has a most ludicrous, disreputable effect; and to see these machines scouring the country, filled with men, women, and children, looks, to the unpractised eye, as if the world were holding high carnival, and every body were out on a masquerade. The sitter is exposed to the mud, to contact, and to the elements; and if one is not fortunate enough to be supplied with shawl or blanket for the feet, the position is eminently favorable to the display of crinoline. The carriage affords an excellent view of the country, but the lateral, insecure motion is very fatiguing.

We have been exploring this handsome town. Except that it is not rectangular, it has much the effect of Philadelphia, although more elegant. We have been to some of the gay shops, have visited St. Patrick's Cathedral, and the Castle, and have driven about Phenix Park, and the principal streets. The moist climate has shed its dewy blessings upon us, in every form, up to a pouring rain; and we have performed our explorations, like our neighbors, in a jaunting car—amusing ourselves with speculations as to the probable effect of such an apparition in the Central Park or in Delaware Avenue.

St. Patrick's, the church of Dean Swift, is a fine old cathedral, now undergoing the process of repair, through the liberality of a wealthy brewer, of Dublin, named Guinness, who devoted forty thousand pounds to the work. We saw the Dean's old pulpit, and his tomb, and that also of Stella—"only a woman's" grave. A ragged jacket seems to be the most readily recognized coat of arms in this shiftless land. The intelligent guide, who accompanied us through the cathedral, and translated Latin inscriptions, was ragged; and the crowd of ragged beggars, men, women, and children, that throng the public entrances and thoroughfares, was painful to American eyes.

The chapel in Dublin Castle, the residence of the Lord Lieutenant, is very fine. It is adorned with the armorial bearings of the Lords Lieutenant, from the eleventh century, carved in Irish oak. Nothing can be more beautiful of its kind. The chapel is very ancient, and a part of the original window still remains, much more beautiful than its modern supplement. The present vicegerent, Lord Carlisle, in renovating the chapel, has, with an unaccountable taste, sustituted a handsome white stone pulpit for the old dark oaken one. It contrasts harshly with the rich, dark uniformity of the rest of the building. The State apartments of the Castle are not at all magnificent, but the private rooms wear a cosy, habitable air, and look out upon pleasant gardens.

Phenix Park is a handsome drive, and contains, among other things, a noticeable monument to the Duke of Wellington. Sackville Street, adorned with a statue of Nelson, is a splendid street. The city abounds in handsome buildings. The river, which bears the pretty name of Anna Liffey, runs through the middle of the city, bordered by walls and crossed by bridges of superb masonry.

This masonry of the Old World is, to me, a source of continual admiration. From the structure of a palace to the wall by the roadside in some far away rural nook, each is perfect of its kind, and evidently built to last. The impression which every thing leaves upon the mind is that of enduring, or rather perduring stability. A transcript, perhaps, of the noble constitution, which, out of all the changes and chances of ages, has sifted the elements of stability, and can afford to await the slow growth of perfection — that plant of no mushroom birth — which must develop, like the acorn, by slow and patient growth, into the fulness of its grandeur.

Aug. 8. At Belfast, the Yankeedom of Ireland, By way of keeping a prudent resolution, formed before leaving home, to husband my exertions for extraordinary occasions, I have seen nothing of Belfast, except the pretty green gardens directly before the windows of our pleasant rooms. I propose to content myself with my present knowledge of manufactures and busy streets, and reserve my limited strength for that which belongs distinctively to the Old World. I should judge that this part of Ireland possesses more Scotch than Irish features, especially as regards its industrial characteristics.

Returned to Belfast, after a visit to the Giant's Causeway. The railway passes, by way of Antrim and Coleraine, to Port Rush, through a trim, thrifty looking country; the fields carefully kept, and the cottages neat and precisely thatched. I confess that the air of tidiness which pervaded the whole region surprised me. I could fancy that the cottages were more picturesque as objects of the landscape, than comfortable as habitations; but they had decidedly an advantage in appearance over any other Irish abodes, of the same class, that one sees at home. I had occasion to enter one of the neat, white, stone cottages near the Causeway, and the utter destitution of all that belongs to our idea of comfort, was depressing; the geological specimens which I was taken to inspect, being almost the only moveables in the cabin.

At Port Rush, a small trading town upon the northern coast, we took a jaunting car for a drive of eight or nine miles, to the Causeway. The country is wild in the extreme. Bold, black headlands jut out into the broad ocean, and underneath them the waves have worn great caverns and arches. On one of the most projecting of these promontories, stand the ruins of Dunluce Castle, occupied as late as the sixteenth century. The Castle is upon an island, close to the main land, with which it is connected by a bridge, still standing.

The road wound along the immediate coast, with a grand ocean view for about half the distance to the Causeway; then struck off across the country, to a small thriving village, called Bush Mills, where commences the ascent to the great headland. Here began a line of guides, beggars, and peddlers of curiosities, marvellous to behold. They lay in wait under the hedge, they lurked in the lanes; the most innocent pedestrian became suddenly transformed, at your approach, into a merchant of canes, stones, or plumes; or, more frequently, into a guide, possessed of invaluable information, and of recommendations from innumerable travellers. It frets one into a fever, that we cannot surrender ourselves for a moment to the influence of scenes which are the realization of lifelong dreams, without being dragged down by pitiful, perpetual mendicity. And, to one accustomed to see men and women earning their living by the sweat of their brow, it is unspeakably disgusting to see shoals of broad-shouldered, strong-armed people, hanging upon the steps of travellers, for the mere chance of a stray sixpence; and, at every new beauty in the wonders of creation, to be met by a demand for a shilling. The rapacity of guides, drivers, and boatmen, is a matter of established prestige, and unavoidable; but that is the utmost limit of American patience, and it is intensely provoking to find daguerreotyped into such a scene as the Giant's Causeway, the unfailing beggar. The termination of the land route, is a hotel at the summit of the Causeway, whence a steep footpath leads down to the sea; for it is only by rowing out to a considerable distance into the ocean, that we can obtain a view of this wonder of Nature.

Here we embarked, with a guide, in a boat manned by five oarsmen. The first visit was to the caves, for which the day was unusually propitious. A fresh, strong breeze came in from the broad ocean, and helped to fan the enthusiasm with which we rode out upon the great waves into the grandeur of this storm-worn coast.

We entered first the smaller cavern of Port Coon; no soft limestone cave, worn out by the incessant "war of wave and rock," but a solid vault, arched by the upheaval of the foundations of the everlasting hills. The fine, clean, compact grain of the primitive rock, brings up with it from the fiery bowels of the earth an indubitable record of its origin. And what imagination can picture the convulsion which shot upward these molten masses to harden in black caverns and majestic hills. The depth of this cave, if I rightly remember, is three hundred feet — the height of the arch about sixty; and the clear, glittering water disclosed, at the depth of sixteen feet, innumerable blocks of the same smooth black mass as walled the sides.

The mighty surge, that forever sweeps these depths, leaves neither weed nor leaf upon these sharp crags, save where, here and there, high up in the vault, a solitary fern waves defiance to the longing eye.

The grand cavern of Dunkerry defies description. It stretches away six hundred feet into the face of the rock. On one side jut out the square, sharp masses of trapdyke, and on the other rise the grand basaltic columns of the Causeway, blending in grotesque fusion, at an immense height, in the vault above. Here is still the same strangely clear, glittering depth of water, paved underneath with huge fragments of the combined formation above; and a shout rings back from the cavernous deep, with a boom that makes one long to hear the roar when a tempest lashes the ocean into these subterranean recesses. We rode out again with a fresh sense of awe, into the sunlight, over the glorious waves, to the front of the headland, where stand the stately wonderful columns, which the pictures call the Giant's Causeway.

The formation is triple — trap, red sandstone, and basalt; the columnar structure is usually vertical, but sometimes horizontal. It is necessarily viewed at a great distance, and it must require long practice to appreciate the real height. Different spots upon the cliffs are variously named, from real or fancied resemblances; such as The Devil's Organ, The Chimney, The Pulpit, The Devil's Thumb, The Unshaved Jew, &c. Off what is called the Spanish headland, was wrecked the flag-ship of the Spanish Armada, having mistaken that point for the Castle of Dunluce. A wild, inhospitable shore, indeed, must this prove to the hapless vessel, driven before a northern gale.

But grand as is the aspect of the columnar headland, the Causeway itself, over which, even not being giants, we may walk, is the object of more curious remark. Here stand the huge up-forced masses, closely fitted to each other, yet perfectly distinct, of various shapes, square, rhomboidal, pentagonal, hexagonal; each side sharp and clear as if hewn and polished by human hands. Not in solid column, but in joints of various lengths; always fitting upon each other with a convex and a concave surface, easily detached by the blow of a hammer. And as we tread the majestic mosaic, the same thought is ever present; what mighty throes must have torn the bowels of the ancient earth, to have forced these fiery streams to the upper air. Nor can we fail to read here the record inscribed by the finger of the eternal God, of the unity of His laws, which govern alike the spheres and the dew drop.

The path of our return lay sharply up the breezy verge of the cliff, swept by the strong, inspiriting breath of the ocean; the steep wayside plentifully sprinkled with purple gorse, and bluebells, and — beggars.

After sundry sound and salutary admonitions from one of my indignant companions to the greedy, but good-natured crew, we set out upon our homeward way, in a drizzling rain, and reached Port Rush too late and too tired for a return to Belfast. The little town commands a beautiful view of the wide sweep of the bay, bounded by the Causeway, whose prominent features are distinctly visible, frowning in solemn grandeur upon the storm-beaten coast. We took up comfortable quarters at the wild little port. I have no where felt such a reality of remoteness from the Western World, as in this distant outlook towards the icy seas, from the extremity of Northern Ireland.

CHAPTER III.

SCOTLAND.

Glasgow — The Clyde — Loch Long — Loch Lomond — Ben Lomond — Loch Katrine — Loch Achray — Stirling — Edinburgh — Abbottsford — Melrose— Dryburgh.

GLASGOW, in bed. An inglorious termination to so much bewildering enjoyment. The climb at the Causeway, and a slight fall received while embarking on board the steamer from Belfast to Glasgow, have combined to remind me of my physical disabilities, and I am doing penance, in consequence. I take for granted, on the authority of my friends, that Glasgow is a beautiful city, containing a fine cathedral, the only one spared by the Reformation. The stately arches, once resonant with ave and pater noster, now ring to the music of the precentor, and the prayers of the Kirk.

I have been also obliged to deny myself the pleasure which my friends are enjoying, of a trip to Ayr, the birth-place of Burns, and to summon all my strength for that El Dorado of my lifelong romance, Loch Katrine and the Trosachs.

Aug. 11. Since writing the above, have grown better, and by way of amusement, have taken an open carriage and driven about this beautiful city, up and down its steep streets, through the delightful Park; and have visited the cathedral. I think I have never seen so beautiful a city. The more elegant residences are upon a high elevation above the old city, with gardens in front which we should call small parks. The various rows are called Crescents, although to many of them the crescent shape is lacking. The West End Park is a very fine one, the very ideal of an available park for such a town. Its natural position admits of great variety of hill, valley, plain and stream, and art has improved it to the utmost.

I have heard of moss grown streets, but I never saw them before. Up some of these steep streets the moss covers the entire pavement, and some of the terraces are reached by flights of stone steps. The streets are scrupulously clean, beautifully paved, and abound in statues. A tall column, with a statue of Sir Walter Scott, stands in a small park, in front of our hotel, another to Sir John Moore, and a third to Watt. An equestrian statue of Queen Victoria, and one of the Duke of Wellington, embellish the neighboring square.

Glasgow abounds in handsome churches, among which the cathedral is, of course, the most worthy of notice. It is, indeed, of remarkable beauty. The Choir, with the Lady Chapel, and Chapter House, dates back to A. D. 1170; the nave is later. The crypts are the most noticeable part of the edifice, and are said to be the finest in Europe. Crypts usually suggest the idea of cellar, or place of provisions; these, on the contrary, are nearly level with the ground, and are finished with the care and ornamentation of a church. One of them in particular, dating, I think, from 1480, by Archbishop Blackader, is more beautiful than most of our churches. These crypts have all been undoubtedly used as places of worship. They are now filled with memorial tablets, some of very recent date, although interments in the vaults have ceased. Among the monuments, one very beautiful bronze erection is to an officer, who fell in the recent difficulties with China, and another marks the resting place of Edward Irving. The stained windows are all memorial. Near the centre of the crypts, under the present pulpit, is a small elaborate chapel, which, until recently, contained the shrine of St. Mungo, an ancient patron saint of the cathedral. Near by, are two sarcophagi, containing the remains of some forgotten dignitaries, who need not to have taken such pains with a resting-place, which should long outlast the memory of its occupants. The whole edifice is in perfect preservation, as if it were but a quarter of a century old, and bids fair to last a thousand years longer.

The grounds around the cathedral are filled with monumental slabs, and immediately beyond lies the Necropolis, upon a high hill overlooking the city; a cemetery surpassing any thing of the kind within my knowledge. A colossal statue of the great Scottish reformer, John Knox, crowns the eminence, standing upon a tall pillar, which serves as pedestal. His face and attitude, as he looks down upon the busy city, could never be mistaken by one who had either seen his pictures, or learned his history.

Aug 12. In leaving Glasgow for the Highlands, we eschewed railways, and sailed down the busy Clyde, lined, for long miles, with marine fabrications in various stages of progress; constructions both for peace and war, and suggestive in the present position of affairs, of sundry possibilities as to the whereabouts of their debut into active service. The advertisement of a Clyde-built ship, will have a new set of associations for me in future. About ten miles from Glasgow we passed a beautiful estate, the seat of Lord Blantyre. Dumbarton Castle, the scene of much romantic interest and historic note, the great Scottish stronghold, and the place where Wallace was betrayed to the English, stands in ruins upon a bold, bare promontory; the ivied walls so mingling with the native rock, that they are not every where easy to distinguish. A modern building at the base of the old fortification, still serves as a fort for a garrison. The commandant chanced to come on board the steamer, and gave us, very courteously, much information in regard to the interesting localities of the shore. Within the space enclosed by the old ramparts, stands a tall monument to the memory of Henry Bell, master of the first steamer on the Clyde. The pillar and its position were suggestive. Here stand the decaying mementoes of mighty works, which were the exponent of force; which represent no element of the human character, save valorous attack and stubborn resistance. And, little by little, even their memory fades into the dim distance, fanned into occasional freshness by the pen of the poet, or the brush of the painter. And long ere these remaining walls shall have crumbled into dust, little trace of the histories which made them famous will remain, save in the lore of the antiquary or the poet. But upon, and far above the type of mere domination, rises a memorial of the renovated humanity, which seeks, as the end of its art, the benefit of the universal race; which binds in one common interest the whole brotherhood of man. No crumbling monument can bear away with it into oblivion the memory of such an invention, for it has taken the wings of the morning, and dwells in the uttermost parts of the sea.

Another picturesque ruin stands upon the same side of the Clyde, Dumbuck Castle, and, as a fitting contrast, upon the opposite side beyond, are the beautiful grounds of Lord Glasgow. There are many charming places upon the Clyde, villas and villages, places of summer resort for the inhabitants of Glasgow. Out of the Clyde, we turned into Loch Long, aptly named, a long reach of water, running many miles into the country, and almost meeting Loch Lomond. A small offshoot of its waters opens out to the westward, named Loch Goil, upon which, at a little distance from the entrance, stand the ruins of Ullin's Castle, remembered now only as the home of Lord Ullin's Daughter.

The country grew wilder, and the mountains more bare, as we advanced. One of the highest peaks, Ben Arthur, upon the seaward side of Loch Long, is named the Cobbler. Upon the summit crouches a figure in precisely the attitude of a cobbler, at his bench. Opposite the votary of St. Crispin, and in vast disproportion, sits his wife, represented by a gigantic head covered with a hood. It is more than possible that the poor fellow may have been dwarfed by his vocation; but what he lacks in size is amply compensated by his conspicuous position. In all the windings of all the lochs, the Cobbler is sure to present himself in the most obtrusive manner.

At the head of the loch, lies Arrochar, the landing for Loch Lomond; and thence we drove by coach a few miles over a sweet, lone, bowery road, to Tarbet, near the head of Loch Lomond. Like all the landings on the lakes, it is beautiful; but its beauty has more the charm of cultivation than the native picturesqueness of its opposite neighbors.

The places upon the lake of which I speak, are represented by one dwelling, the hotel. Whether the name applies to the house only, I do not know; perhaps other dwellings, concealed by the woods, may go to make up a proper village.

We took for granted the hole in the rock, down which Rob Roy is said to have let his unlucky prisoners, while he made advantageous terms for himself; and steamed down to the eastern shore, to one of the sweetest nooks to be found by tourist in any land, Rowardennan. The hotel lies at the foot of Ben Lomond ; a neat, quiet house, kept by a canny Scot named Andrew Blair, a shrewd, good old man, whose locks had whitened in this tranquil home; but who had learned the language of one distant land, even the Eternal City, towards which he is travelling. His stalwart son seemed ready to take up the same restful life. And, indeed, it did not seem difficult to lay down the fever of life at the foot of that solemn mountain, by the calm waters of that tranquil lake. We were too late to obtain ponies for the ascent of the mountain, so the young gentlemen temporarily attached to our party, went up on foot, and we of the elders strolled about among the heathery hillocks, and betook ourselves to an early rest, for the early waking on the morrow.

Aug. 13. The morning dawned upon the loveliest day I ever knew. We were wakened at four o'clock, and at five were in the saddle. We had three stout Highland ponies, and a guide.

The grand old mountain looked brown and bare, but very smooth and accessible; and was far from appearing at the distance of nearly six miles, which is his reputed distance by the pathway. He is three thousand one hundred and ninety feet above the level of the sea.

The atmosphere was pure ether, a bespoken day,

sweet, and mild, and still; and "right up Ben Lomond" did we press for a mile or two, before the sun burst over the hills, and completed the glory of the day. Not a breath of mist clung to the mountain, nor dimmed the charming views, gradually disclosed as we ascended. The path grew steeper and more stony, and the smooth face of the mountain opened in craggy furrows; and still each new turn of the winding way brought to light some new scene of grandeur or beauty. But there came a point of climbing which left little leisure for gazing. There was nothing for it, but to take the mountain by storm, and at a sharper angle than I had ever seen accomplished by quadruped before.

One of my companions becoming much exhausted by the continuous fatigue of the ascent, the party lingered behind to rest, and I rode on, a mile or two in advance, exercising great faith in the path and the pony; when, as we struggled up the last straight acclivity, the pony, evidently trained to the spot, rounded the shoulder of the mountain, and stood still, upon a verge that chilled my blood, and hushed my breath.

Just at my feet, struck down a sheer depth of at least three hundred fathoms. In the valley at the bottom, lay the Forth, twined like a silver band among the emerald meadows and the purple moors. Beyond the nearer peaks, as it seemed but a stone's throw, slept Loch Ard; and among the countless hills, shone little lakes, like crystal pools. On the other side, I seemed to overhang the little green spot of Rowardennan, and as for my companions, the path was far too precipitous to catch even a glimpse of them. I never felt before the deadly awe of utter solitude. The lonely grandeur of the scene grew too oppressive, and I gazed up the slender line which marked the path to the solitary summit, with a nervous shiver which I strove in vain to quell. I could see plainly that there was not a foot of danger upon the way, but reason was not, just then, in the ascendant; and the welcome sight of horse and horseman appearing above the rocky shelf, sent the blood to my heart, with a revulsion which nearly deprived me of the little strength which the terror of that scene of awe had left me.

However, we reached the summit in safety. Indeed, there is no part of the ascent at all perilous; it is only toilsome; and even in that respect, I presume, it compares favorably with most other mountain excursions. For a good pedestrian, walking is easier than riding. The bridle path is narrow, stony and tortuous, as if it followed the bed which wintry torrents have worn deep below the surrounding surface.

The top of the mountain is a bare, wind-swept plateau of a few yards in extent, but it is the point of vision for such an amphitheatre as I have no power to describe. The vast peaks crowded each other, far and near; their huge sides unshadowed by tree or shrub; Pelion upon Ossa; the brain ached with the mighty thought of Creation. At the foot, slept the purple bosom of Loch Lomond, studded with myriad islands, and fringed with woody headlands. Here and there, between the bristling peaks, glittered bright lochs; Edinburgh lay in the distance, and the Clyde spread its broad waters to the sun. The silver mists of morning rolled up the sides of the distant hills, giving a softened charm to the landscape, but not a shade dimmed the near vision. Language may recall, but can never express the emotions of that morning.

The descent, after the first ruggedness was past, was far easier than the climb. The eye rested, without effort, upon the constantly varying scene, and pictured it to the memory forever. And, as I rode down into the sheltered valley, where the heather was glowing in the soft light of an October sun, and the Loch lay like a breathless mirror, reflecting the feathery banks and the mighty hills, and the solemn mountain lifted its bald head to the blue heaven, the intense beauty of the earth fell like a hush upon my heart, and Nature seemed to have gathered all the weary children of care to her quiet bosom, and to have soothed them to the rest of peace and love.

The excitement of the morning was too great for any indoor rest, and we strayed along the quiet paths at the foot of the mountain, and sat upon the sheltered banks, and listened to the whisper of the ripples upon the white pebbles of the beach, and drank in the reality of our enjoyment, until the arrival of the little steamer, which was to take us to Inversnaid, a bewitching spot, five miles farther up the lake. Here, a wild mountain cataract comes foaming and brawling down to the lake.

At Inversnaid we mounted a vehicle which has the effect of being a coach, all top. The seats are open — so high that a ladder is necessary to reach them, the luggage being bestowed in a cavernous recess beneath. It is an admirable contrivance where the great object to be gained is a good outlook. We wound up the steep, but smooth and shady road, and rolled swiftly through a beautiful glen, beside a pretty lake, both glen and lake being named Arklee. Upon the left we passed a low stone dwelling, which is remarkable as the birth-place of Helen McGregor. The drive was short, and we presently descended to Loch Katrine, the fairy cup that holds a magic draught of inspiration. Even as I write, I can scarcely convince myself that I have realized my lifelong romance, and that Loch Katrine has left its abode in my imagination for one in my memory.

It is a small, but exquisite lake; the steamer makes its entire circuit, and lands at the foot of the Trosachs. No prose description, even though it were a surveyor's chart, can give a more accurate picture of the scenery, than does the poem. I was surprised and charmed to find the familiar epithets not only beautiful, but scrupulously true. Benvenue, Ben A'an, Ben Ledi, all the points of which we read, are portrayed with such fidelity to Nature, that the eye catches them in a moment, and recognizes them as old acquaintances.

We passed Ellen's Isle, landed, and drove through the Trosachs to a beautiful hotel on the margin of Loch Achray. This hotel bears the euphonious title of Ardcheanochrochan. We were shown to dinner in a rustic hall, covered with "withered heath and rushes dry,"

> "While all around, the walls to grace,
> Hung trophies of the fight or chase."

After dinner, we drove back, and took a small boat and oarsman; visited Ellen's Isle; saw Coir-nan-uriskin, the pass of Beal'nambo, the pass of the battle of Beal an' Duine, Roderic's Watch Tower, and many a spot, already familiar as household words. We lingered while

> "Eve, with western shadows long,
> Floated on Katrine, bright and strong;"

stumbled up the clambering road, among the tangled trees and shrubs, which led to the spot on the tiny islet where once stood a lodge, fashioned after the description of the poet. The rustic edifice was destroyed by the carelessness of some visitor, who threw a lighted cigar among the brushy thicket. In describing the Goblin's Cave, our rower said he believed there were some of the Goblins still remaining there, and, putting his hands to his mouth, he shouted until the echoes verified their goblin origin. The man was a McGregor, who not only knew the

Lady of the Lake by heart, but felt all its witchery. "The shades of eve came slowly down," as we retraced our steps, almost giddy with pleasure.

Loch Achray, "so lone a lake, so sweet a strand," lies before the door of the hotel, and winding paths invite to hidden beauties. The foxglove, the harebell, the heath, the broom, are all here, and all classic. It has been the day of days.

Aug. 14. We strolled about the mountain paths until noon, then took a carriage for Callender. We passed the bridge of Turk; along the lovely lake of Vennachar, to Coilantogle ford; by Bochastle heath; along the Teith; past the ruins of the bannered towers of Doune; near the ruined Cathedral, which marks the spot where Jessie, the flower of Dumblane, once blossomed; and followed the path of King James straight to Stirling. Dumferline looked strange upon a guide-board, but there it was.

Stirling was a place of intense interest. We drove at once to the Castle, and the same flinty street echoed to the clatter of the toiling hoofs, as when

> "Slowly down the deep descent,
> Fair Scotland's King and nobles went,"

in days whose every interest is fast passing into oblivion. The ancient Castle had its origin in times whereto the memory of man runneth not. Its towers echoed the sports, and witnessed the vows of the long line of Stuarts, that ill-fated, misguided, fascinating race. Here is the room in which a

Douglass met his death by the hand of his sovereign. Here is the palace built by James the Fifth, and thronged with "noble dame and damsel bright," when the Scottish court was in its prime. Here is the turret and the Franciscan steeple, which the poet has linked with Malcolm Græme.

We were shown a long, solid, subterranean vault, in which were kept the lions for the royal sports, and the area into which they were let loose, beneath the balcony of the royal spectators.

The Castle is occupied by the troops of the garrison, and the long hall where King James held his court is not open to inspection.

It is with the exterior of the Castle, however, that the most historic interest is interwoven. The view from the ramparts not only sweeps a valley of surpassing beauty, but takes in the mighty Bens in the far distance, and the inferior, but still lofty ranges of hills that lie between. The memory is bewildered with the wealth of association crowded into the scenes beneath the eye, as one stands at the Lady's Lookout, a small opening in the northern wall. Besides the varied charms of natural scenery, he looks down from that castle wall upon the battle fields of Bannockburn, Stirling, Pentland Hills, and to the hills which overlook the field of Sheriff Muir. Below, is the Abbey Crag, upon which is now rising a monument to Wallace, the hero of the battle of Stirling. There are seen, also, the ruins of Cambuskenneth's Abbey, and the bloody Heading hill.

Under the wall, winds the road called the Ballangeich, by which the pleasure-loving King, James the First, was wont to make his unperceived exit, when it suited his humor to put off the circumstance of royalty, that he might watch over insulted laws, "and learn to right the injured cause"— and, perchance, to pursue less exalted aims, if all tales be true. The Castle Park spreads out to the south, the scene of sport, both for noble and yeoman; and the churchyard of Greyfriars, hard by, is hallowed by the dust of ancient martyrs, and made picturesque by the hand of modern taste. But it is hopeless to attempt to record all the features of interest pertaining to Stirling Castle.

Not far off is Linlithgow Castle, where Mary of Scots was imprisoned. Within the town are the remains of Mar's Work, a dwelling which Lord Mar built, in part, from the ruins of Cambuskenneth. The failure in its completion is attributed to that sacrilege.

The gray fortress of the North bids fair to outlast the ravages of time for long centuries to come; a key to unlock the sanctuary of enthusiasm, and a shrine of patriotism to the Scottish heart, for which I fervently envy the sturdy, yet romantic race.

Aug. 15. Edinburgh. We are established in a hotel opposite the East Gardens, and Sir Walter's monument; and in full view of the Castle, on one side, and Salisbury Crags on the other. Took a carriage and commissioner, this morning, for a long day of sight-seeing. Drove first to Calton Hill, a high eminence, overlooking the city, whereon is rising a monument to Nelson. An unfinished copy of the Parthenon, intended to commemorate the heroes who fell at Waterloo, stands like a ruin upon the summit, and a Greek monument to Professor Playfair, and another to Dugald Stewart, also occupy the hill, which commands a wide view of Edinburgh and its environs, Leith, North Berwick Law, the Bass Rock, and the broad estuary which widens to the German ocean.

Edinburgh is, without doubt, a splendid city, but one, also, of great contrasts. One sees magnificent edifices, surrounded by spacious grounds; and narrow wynds, from which tower up tall buildings to such a height as to shut out sunlight and cheerfulness from the unenviable alleys. In such a wynd stands the house in which Walter Scott was born.

John Knox's house still stands in the Canongate, and a small window projects above the street, from which he was wont to feed the congregated assembly below with his strong meat. We saw his pulpit, afterwards, in the Museum of the Royal Institute.

The gateway of the Canongate Tolbooth, still yawns upon the street; but the Heart of Mid Lothian is represented only by a large stone heart in the pavement, where frowned the old gateway, battered down to drag forth Porteus to his terrible fate. In the Grass Market, a small marked spot in the paved street denotes the site of the gibbet, from which many a martyred patriot has passed to his rest.

From the noble Hospitals, the fair green gardens, and the stately monuments which adorn the modern city, the traveller must always turn with deepest interest to Holyrood. It matters little whether he be a partisan or a denunciator of the fair, but not perfect Queen, there is the spot of interest in Edinburgh.

We stood within the ruined walls of the beautiful chapel—in partial ruin even when Mary plighted her troth to Darnley, beneath the chapel window. But in her own apartments there is a tangibility, an internal evidence of authenticity, such as does not force itself upon the conviction, with equal effect, within any of those castled walls, where nothing but the bare masonry presents the record of the past.

Here, upon the threshold trodden by her youthful feet, destined to many a flinty path, you pause to note the very state in which the royalty of the sixteenth century was wont to dwell. There is the very pillow, upon which reposed her golden head; the mirror which gave back her lovely face; the implements of handicraft which her fair fingers employed to beguile the weary hours, in that rigid Northern home, a chilly contrast to the gay court of France. There is the very closet where she watched her favorite writhing under the ruffian steel. One can well imagine the loathing with which she turned from the ill-timed caresses of her jealous lord; for if she indeed loved Rizzio, her heart was breaking with anguish; and, if not, it was filled with fierce indignation. Condemn, despise Mary of Scots, as one may—within the time-worn, blood-stained walls of Holyrood, he remembers, with tearful pity only, the beautiful queen, the unhappy woman.

Within the court of the palace, is a beautiful fountain, adorned with exquisite sculptures, representing the various personages and incidents of Mary's time. In the grand old castle, we saw the room in which she gave birth to her degenerate son, and the window through which he was let down by a basket, to Lord Murray. Here was also a portrait of Mary, differing somewhat from the ordinary pictures, but, as I think, more attractive. The ancient Castle stands like a part of the solid rock upon which it frowns, and swarms with soldiers, as it has done for hundreds of years. Customs, and costumes, and weapons, have changed; but, through them all, the garrisoned fortress has come down from the depths of the time immemorial.

We were admitted to the chamber containing the Regalia, the long-lost, long-sought jewels of the Crown. Sir Walter Scott, (with what interest of Scottish history is he not identified?) obtained a commission to search for the missing treasures, and was the fortunate discoverer of their hiding place. They consist of the crown, handed down with various additions, and with all its thorns, from the early sovereigns to the Stuarts; a sword, mace and sceptre; a splendid chain of the Order of the Garter; a signet ruby ring valued at twelve thousand pounds; a jewel representing St. George and the Dragon, set in diamonds, and valued at thirty thousand pounds; and a locket containing a miniature of Anne of Denmark, worth ten thousand.

The Castle wall, the fosse, the drawbridge, the grooves of the ancient portcullis, the outer rampart, were all full of interest. On the rampart stands Mons Meg, a clumsy cannon, fabricated in the fifteenth century, and famous in several battles of later date. Its last exploit was that of bursting, while firing a salute in honor of the Duke of York, in 1682. If it had chanced to carry off His Royal Highness, it might have deserved well at the hands of the country.

We were so fortunate as to witness the daily ceremony of setting the city time, which is performed in this wise. Upon the top of the unfinished Nelson monument on Calton Hill, rests a large ball, which, shortly before one o'clock, begins slowly to ascend. The time is calculated at the Observatory, for Greenwich, and at the point of one, the ball suddenly falls, and by an electric wire fires a cannon upon the Castle rampart.

We concluded our day of exploration with the Queen's drive, a fine sweep around the base of Salisbury Crags and Arthur's Seat; from which we could see the ruins of Anthony's chapel, and the place of Muscat's cairn. I have omitted much that has occurred during the day, but find it impossible to record it all. We made an effort to hear Dr. Boyd preach, but found, on arriving at his church, that he had not yet returned from his summer vacation, and we went to St. James', in York Place. The service was conducted by the curate, Rev. Mr. Montgomery, and the venerable Bishop, Dr. Terrot. Mr. Montgomery is a fine reader and good preacher. The service varied somewhat from our own, the choir leading the responses, and leading, but not performing, the singing. We were not tempted to seek an entrance to Dr. Guthrie's church, as the reports of the crowds, usually in waiting at the doors, were discouraging.

Aug. 17. Abbotsford — what more is needed than the name! We left the railway at Melrose, and drove through a pretty country, rolling from the Tweed up a low range called the Black Hills. We alighted at a close gate, and entered Abbotsford by a winding descent of trim gravel walk, bordered by hawthorn and ivied wall, reaching the side entrance of a small hall upon the ground floor; whence, after recording our names, a little maid led us up a staircase, to Sir Walter's study. It is a small room, surrounded by book-shelves, a light gallery containing books running around the upper part of the room. At a plain desk in the middle of the room stood a chair cushioned with black leather, and we paused before it, as in the presence chamber of inspiration. Here its master toiled to reproduce the conceptions of his rich imagination; and here he faithfully labored, while giving rein to his varied fancy, to be true to nature and to history, and to keep pure the fountains of poesy and fiction, from which he dispensed delight to the world.

In a tiny room opening out of the study, is his bust, cast after his death. This, his room of private conference, he called "speak-a-bit."

The library contains objects of all kinds of interest. A part of the furniture is ebony, from Carlton House, the gift of its royal master. A part, consisting of elaborate Roman work, was a present from the late Pope. Under a glass case, lie treasures of curiosity and antiquity, such as were just fitted to please his delicate antiquarian taste, along with splendid gifts from crowned heads and distinguished men.

I wish I could remember them all, but the attendant, doubtless weary of his continual duty of repetition, was little disposed to suffer us to linger over objects of such interest to us, and I can enumerate but few out of the many curiosities there preserved. There were golden bees from the mantle of Napoleon; a curiously wrought casket which belonged to Mary of Guise; drinking cups, carved out of rare woods; a glass upon which Burns had engraved a verse; a snuff box belonging to Balfour, of Burleigh; Rob Roy's pouch, a Highland dirk, and miniatures of Scott and his wife.

His own genial face looked kindly down upon us,

from the wall, beside the sweet portrait of Lady Scott, and the hush of his presence was upon us, while we moved among the treasures which his hand so delighted to gather, and trod the apartments upon which he lavished such wealth of toil and taste.

We stood where he yielded up his peaceful breath —worn out, not with years, but with cycles of thought; where

> "The weary wheel of life at length stood still."

In the dining room, where he died, are many fine family portraits; one of his son, Walter, particularly beautiful. There are portraits of his parents, and of his great-grandfather, a bearded old cavalier, who forswore shaving until the King should "have his own again," and, in consequence, he wore the manly appendage to his dying day.

The Armory, a room filled with curious and historic weapons, was Sir Walter's own especial delight. Among other things, I remember Rob Roy's gun, a fine modern looking piece of arms; and Claverhouse's pistols, which made one shudder to remember what fiery streams of cruelty have been launched from their polished barrels. There were swords and knives of all descriptions. I remember Mrs. Hemans' exclamation at the sight of this room,

> "'Twere worth ten years of peaceful life,
> One glance at their array."

There was the cuirass of James the Fourth, and relics of I know not how many scions of royalty. But the royalty lay, after all, in the genius of the place. What has been our journey through the charms of Scotland, but a pilgrimage to this shrine! Its master was the priest and prophet of the land.

The hall is the elaborate room of the suite, filled with armor, lined and ceiled with curious carvings, partly from the ancient palace of Dumferline, and adorned with the armorial bearings of the clans to which he has given an undying interest.

We strayed through the gardens which he planned; saw the old Tolbooth door built into the wall of the house; plucked a few flowers from the garden, and looked our last upon the home of genius, consecrated to a more enduring fame than that of the towns and castles which he loved to celebrate.

We drove along the road, remembering that here were his daily walks; through the little village where his face was once familiar as household words; and took our way along the base of the Eildon Hills, cleft in three by the witchcraft of Michael Scott, to Melrose Abbey.

This beautiful ruin is remarkable for the delicacy of its carvings—and for having been transfused into poetry by Scott. Under the chancel, lie the heart of Bruce, the remains of the Black Douglass, of Alexander the Second, and of Michael Scott, the great wizard, whose stone effigy stands over against his grave.

But vainly did the cross-signed stone press upon the ashes of Michael Scott. When the dread secrets of his sepulchre were laid open, at the command of the Lady of the Border, the wizard essence made its escape, and descended upon a second Merlin; who touched with his plumed wand the barren heaths and craggy shelves of Scotland, and they became fairy land. And by the same touch he peopled them with "ærial knights and fairy dames."

The spell of witchery still lies, as of yore, in gramarye; and, once encircled by its potent charm, the students of its mystic symbols throng the hills and moors and shores of the enchanted land, and do tearful homage in the halls of the enchanter, and bend with reverent step above his dust.

The burial place of Walter Scott is a fit resting place for a poet. Dryburgh Abbey lies in solemn quiet among stately trees, far away from the tumult of the busy world. We reached it by crossing the Tweed in a tiny ferry boat, and winding through a long, quiet, shady lane, among green meadows, mellowed by the soft level light of the evening sun.

The Abbey is of great extent, and exceedingly beautiful. It is said that Gothic architecture takes its design from the forest aisles; in this case, the prototype has resumed its sway. As you look up the nave from the main entrance, two rows of noble trees stretch up on either side; their stately stems, and interlacing boughs well supplying the lack of "long drawn aisle and fretted vault;" while every where within the Abbey precincts, stand huge trees which bear unquestionable record to its great antiquity. We were shown a yew near the entrance, said to bear the same date with the Abbey. The family sepulchre of Scott is in a corner of one of the remaining aisles, defended by a railing, and sheltered by one of the few entire arches of the venerable pile. His wife, his eldest son, and his son-in-law, rest beside him. The Abbey once belonged to his ancestors, and one feels a peculiar satisfaction that he had a right to a resting place in such accordance with his own tastes.

We recrossed the Tweed, and left the charming spot with regret.

It is no harsh transition from Abbotsford and Dryburgh, that we are sleeping to-night at Penrith, within the domain of peerless King Arthur, and that to-morrow we mean to evoke the ghosts of the Round Table.

CHAPTER IV.

ENGLAND.

Penrith — Ulswater — Windermere — Grasmere— Rydal —Ambleside — Lancaster — Haworth — York — Chesterfield — Chatsworth — Haddon Hall — Kenilworth — Warwick — Leamington — Stratford-on-Avon.

We cannot discern "many-towered Camelot," but I thought of fair Queen Guenevere as we threaded the queer, quaint, old-world streets of Penrith, to find the Giant's grave; the resting place of what giant is left to conjecture. Two tall stone pillars, tapering upward, from a circumference of eleven feet, mark the extremities of the grave, fifteen feet in length. The ancient Runic inscription is so worn by time as to leave only a fretted surface to the stone. We stood for a few moments to

—"moralize on the decay
Of human strength in later day,"

and returned to the inn, passing by an ancient school-house, founded, as the Latin inscription upon its front asserts, by Queen Elizabeth.

We mounted the top of a stage-coach, which, by the way, is far the most desirable mode of viewing the country, and a very agreeable style of riding, and passed out of Penrith, by the Castle and the Round Table.

Every foot of English soil is the prison house of genii, and every footfall presses some hidden spring that brings the spirits to the upper air. Penrith Castle and the Round Table; within what a charmed circle do these mystical words enclose us! Within it rises the stately figure of the peerless King, the model of knightly prowess, of kingly faith, of Christian honor, of womanly delicacy. To England belongs the honor of the conception of the purest ideal of uninspired perfection. I say honor, for it is of the essence of national character that the ideal national hero is created. Yet is it a proof of our perverse nature, that we turn with more tenderness of interest to Launcelot than to Arthur?

A few miles out of Penrith is a cluster of Druidical stones, called Long Meg and her daughters; but our path lay in the opposite direction.

Just out of our way, led the road to the Vale of St. John and its enchanted castle. I am glad to give local habitation to the scenes of the beautiful legendary lore of the times of Arthur.

The Round Table is a green turf elevation (a complete circle) of about one hundred yards in circumference, in a field by the roadside.

We drove through a beautiful country, with many peaks in the distance, upon which we were glad to recognize, once more, the purple heather, down to the lovely lake of Ulswater, where a little steamer lay ready to ferry us through its beautiful reaches. The lake winds among the hills in such a way, that but one of its sections or reaches can be seen at a time. You seem to be circling round a mountain-hemmed pool, until a hidden outlet opens to view, and you enter another secluded recess of beauty.

Upon the upper shore of the first reach is Lyulph's Tower, in ivy-clad ruins, now partially fitted up as a lodge to a deer park. In a glen behind is seen Gowborough Park; a pretty opening called Glen Coin descends to the lake; and all along the shores are sprinkled villas and cottages, enticing abodes of summer resort.

The hills rise, every where, in brown bare peaks, each with its distinctive appellation, and at the end of a long perspective of sharp hills in the third reach, stands Helvellyn. Skiddaw, we could not, or did not see, the morning being misty.

At Patterdale, the end of the charming water, we lunched, and set out again by carriage for Windermere. Here we found the counterpart of the pretty vehicle which we remember as associated with the pleasures of Welshland; not the only thing in the day that reminded us of Wales. I do not know any seat in any vehicle, to compare, in comfort and pleasure, with the driver's box of that wagonette.

The three horses which formed our turnout were suggestive, and the way answered the suggestion. The valley was, at first, wide and cultivated; in the bottom lay Brotherswater, and one or two other small lakes, or, as they call them, tarns, whose names I forget. As we advanced to the ascent, the valley narrowed to a pass strongly resembling that of Llanberis; but instead of the craggy impending cliffs, the hills sloped upward with a less threatening aspect.

Thousands of sheep browsed upon the steep slopes or clung to the dangerous summits. Small rills came leaping down the rocky declivities in little silver cascades, ever and anon uniting their streams, until, at last, they flowed in a brawling brook, clear and bright, over a stony bed by the roadside.

The road was, as a matter of course, the same smooth causeway that one finds from one end of the kingdom to the other, but the pass was long, and sometimes steep as Ben Lomond; so steep that we were forced to alight, three horses not sufficing to drag more than the light empty vehicle up the straight ascent.

This is called the Kirkstone pass, and at its head stands a stone from which it takes the name.

At the breathing spot on the crest of the mountain is the highest inhabited house in England, being fourteen hundred feet above the sea.

Now began a descent, quite as precipitous, and far more difficult than the toilsome way upward, but the danger of the way was soon forgotten in the unfolding charms of the scene beneath.

Far in the western distance shone the waters of the sea, and, between, peak after peak lifted its brown head to the sky, and bathed its foot in the crystal waters of the lakes. The bare hills receded from the gorge, and soft green swells began to undulate through the valley, and roll up their waves of cultivation to the heathery moor. And a lovelier scene never greeted the eye of tourist in any land, than that which burst upon our view when Lake Windermere opened below, with all its garniture of cloud and cliff, field and wood, knoll and meadow, park, villa and cottage, spread out beneath our feet, in endless variety and matchless beauty. None but those who have threaded the charming maze, can comprehend what it means, to say that our way lay through Rydal, by Rydal water, and Mount, and Hall, to Grasmere; to the quiet churchyard, where lies all that was mortal of Wordsworth, and Southey, and Hartley Coleridge. If I should choose a home out of all the world, it would be in the midst of the combined beauty and cultivation of the Lake country.

We dined at Ambleside, at an inn beside the lake; and eschewing speed and steam in such a world of soft, rich, quiet beauty, we took an oarsman and drifted down the silent water, with the exquisite scenery in our vision, and the reverent memory of genius in our hearts.

Watson, Wilson, Martineau, Arnold, Hemans, Wordsworth, Southey, Coleridge — what a constellation glitters upon the bosom of these lovely waters.

Aug. 19. We slept at night at Lancaster, at an

inn which has been kept as such for two hundred years; filled with antiquarian collections of pictures, china and curiosities. There were portraits of Queen Elizabeth, Milton, Hannah More, a lovely face which Mr. R. thinks one of the Jennings, and an elegant full-length portrait of a nobleman by Godfrey Kneller. The house is full of quaint, carved oaken work, and was really a sight in its way—and so was the bill in the morning.

From the red rose to the white. We came to York by way of Leeds, stopping at Keighly to make a pilgrimage to the home and the grave of Charlotte Bronte. I am glad to have been able to diverge from the beaten track, and to see the new aspect of life, presented by this drive to Haworth. This remote village is built of the stoniest houses, up the steepest, stoniest streets that humanity has often chosen for its habitation, and a more uninteresting class of people in appearance it would be hard to find. Men, women, and children, gaped upon us from the doors of the comfortless looking dwellings, and grinned at us in the streets, as if we were a small menagerie of curious animals. It was impossible to stop on the way, for the necessity of starting anew would have proved too much for the insecure footing of the horses.

The only ornament of the village was its pottery. Whether the place has a monopoly of license for the vending of earthen ware, or whether the pavement is the approved deposit for the display of household stuff, the same array of vessels of honor and dishonor flanked the entrances of all these stony abodes. The district is evidently a manufacturing one, and troops of stolid, heavy-looking women, with woollen shawls over their heads, were streaming down the hill to their afternoon work.

The parsonage, where Miss Bronte passed her chilly life, stands at the summit of the long steep hill; before it stretches the densely populated churchyard, one continuous pavement of memorial slabs; and below is the church, in the chancel of which she lies beside her family. The stone under which she rests is in the aisle, directly in front of the communion table, and a slab in the chancel wall records the deaths of the whole family. We were shown her seat in the rectory pew, and her signature in the marriage register. A more untoward spot than this for the suggestions of fiction could scarcely be imagined; but genius takes of imperfect materials and constructs edifices which challenge the admiration of the most cultivated.

Our journey this afternoon has left the barren peaks and the moorlands far behind, and has led among green fields and ripened grain; a soft, rich, smiling landscape, which speaks of the cultivation of generations, and tells of antiquity as truly as do the ivy-grown abbeys which we have passed, with great boles of trees overtopping the encircling walls.

Aug. 20. It is the week of the races, and we

bade fair to be forced out of this ancient and curious city by the sheer want of a bed. We, the ladies, spent an hour and a half at the station, while the gentlemen went in fruitless quest from hotel to lodging house.

At last, in desperation, they came up to take a moonlight view of the Minster before leaving the city to seek more hospitable reception elsewhere; and by a combination of good fortune and perseverance, found lodgings under the very shadow of the great Minster, which lifts its solemn front as if it were the growth of the ages, and no construction of the puny hand of man. We were wakened many times in the night

"By the mighty Minster's bell,
Tolling with a sullen swell,"

the waves of sound floating out upon the air, just above our heads.

We were out, betimes, pacing the court, to gain some conception of the cathedral's extent and exterior beauty, and were quite ready for the opening of the doors at nine. I cannot attempt any description of York Minster. It is stupendous in its extent, solemn in its grandeur, exquisite in its beauty. It is in wonderfully perfect preservation. It was founded in A. D. 626, and has gathered added beauty and size from succeeding generations. The thirteenth and fourteenth centuries contributed most towards its perfection.

Among the splendid windows, that of the north transept, called the "five sisters," is remarkably beautiful. It is more than fifty feet in height, exquisite in harmony of color and delicacy of design. The great chancel window, seventy-seven feet in height, is considered the finest in the world. It is a specimen of English art, and was finished in less than three years.

It seems strange that with all the modern improvements in science and the arts, these ancient windows defy all attempts to approach them in the combined splendor and softness of their coloring. One discerns the imitation at a glance. It would need a volume to describe the beauties of this mighty structure.

We saw, in the vestry, a most curious relic of antiquity, the drinking cup of Ulpho, the donor of the site of the edifice, by which the chapter holds the fee of the bequest. It is an elephant's tusk, polished with great skill, bound with silver, and inscribed with various designs. Archiepiscopal rings of great value, and a silver crosier, a present from Catharine of Braganza, to her confessor, form a part of the curious possessions of the church.

Monuments of Archbishops, lords and benefactors, are scattered around the edifice, or affixed to the walls. The Chapter house is a gem of beauty; the delicate carvings and rich windows are nearly four hundred years old, perfect in preservation; and the room still serves the purpose for which it was constructed. The choir is screened with elaborately carved oak, but has been twice destroyed by fire; once at least the work of an insane incendiary.

Here we attended morning prayer. As it was my first experience of cathedral service, curiosity mingled with my devotions. But it was an awe-inspiring service, to kneel where prayers went up a thousand years ago to Him in whose sight "a thousand years are but as yesterday when it is past." The service was intoned by one of the minor canons, and the lessons read by another; the president and another canon being present in their robes. Intoned prayer has, to my taste, more the effect of a performance than of devotion, but the music was superb; led by the grand organ, and chanted by a choir, not of boys, but of men, it was satisfying, even under the roof of such a cathedral.

After service, we ascended the lantern, which rises like a square tower from the centre of the cross. It is one hundred and ninety-one feet high, and has at the top an area of sixty-eight feet square; a broad platform from which the view takes in miles on miles of country, with varied field, and waving woods, and distant hills. From it you see also the ruins of the palace of William the Conqueror, the Abbey of St. Mary's, and the wall which partly encircles the city, with its massive bars or gateways. For York is an ancient city, the great Roman capital, dating before the Christian era. Here Constantine the Great was born, and Constantius died; and here in later days has been the seat of royal abode and national consequence. We came to England to see not only things, but people; and by way of accomplishing the latter purpose, we drove out to the races.

I had never imagined myself capable of growing enthusiastic over a race course, but it was even so; it was one of the most exciting and gayest of scenes. The running was beautiful, the lithe steeds seeming scarcely to touch the turf, and to enter with an intelligent interest into the excitement. We saw five races; the two most important were for the York cup, and the great Yorkshire stakes. The winners were Mr. Naylor's Macaroni, and Mr. Savile's Ranger, beautiful horses both. In the Gimcrack stakes, the winner, Coast Guard, was a fine horse, but the second, Syren, was a beautiful creature, that tempted one to covet; a small, dark, delicate-limbed thing, seeming to understand and appreciate the admiration which she received.

The scene in the enclosure beneath the grand stand, upon which we were seated, was a study. The perfect babel of betting, the eager hush of breathless excitement, and the revulsion at the result, were in excessive contrast to the usual notion of British imperturbability. However, every nature must have its outlet, and perhaps betting is the English safety-valve. It is strangely incomprehensible to womankind.

From the races, we came on to Chesterfield by rail; and thence by carriage to the quiet inn at Edensor, where we repose under the shadow of the great Duke of Devonshire, whose beautiful domain of Chatsworth, we visit to-morrow. We have driven through a grazing country, not unlike the hills of New England. The country about Chesterfield is of great beauty, broken into soft irregular swells, and covered with the green and gold of field and harvest. Indeed, beautiful is the only epithet applicable to the landscape of the whole country.

At Chesterfield there is a spire upon an ancient church, which has the appearance of having been twisted and distorted from the perpendicular by a whirlwind. The villagers assured us that it was many feet out of plumb; but we afterwards learned that the effect is produced by the peculiar manner of putting the lead upon the wood of the spire, and that, notwithstanding its apparent inclination, it is perfectly erect.

The inn at Edensor is one of the prettiest, quiet, country places, just at the park gates. From the windows you look out upon the smooth green glades, where a thousand deer troop among the forest aisles, undisturbed by beast or sportsman.

Aug. 21. We drove up the smooth park road to the famed dwelling of the richest Duke in England. Chatsworth is not imposing as a structure, being an extensive, but rather plain, square-looking edifice. It fronts upon a succession of garden terraces, by which is the descent to the Derwent, a sweet, quiet stream. The entrance is by tall gilded gates, at one of the extreme wings. Indeed, one seldom sees here what is apt to monopolize the better part of American dwellings, an entrance upon the main front.

The interior is on a scale of magnificence worthy the establishment of a Duke who has crowned heads among his guests. The spacious extent of grand halls, lofty stair-cases, splendid corridors, and magnificent apartments, is crowded with works of the highest art, and with every appropriate expression of the wealth and taste of the owner.

The apartments overlook not only the distant park, but a wonderful variety of pleasure grounds and gardens, such as belong to no other estate in England.

The most striking beauty of the rooms themselves, independent of the rare and costly articles to be found in them, is the exquisite wood carving which adorns every room, and especially the chapel. It is by Gibbons, and represents flowers with minute delicacy, like the most carefully moulded wax petals. The graceful wreaths that surround the wainscoting, stand out from the heavy wood as if just suspended in natural garlands; and among them nestle birds with plumage just as delicately rendered. In one of the rooms hangs a frame, in which is enclosed Gibbons' masterpiece. It is a small bird, with a bouquet of flowers, and folds of richly wrought lace depend from them. It seems incredible that a material so heavy as wood can be wrought into such a perfect representation of an airy fabric, fine as threads of gossamer.

Among the choice works of art, too numerous to

be mentioned or even noted with more than a passing glance, was a splendid green malachite vase, a present from the Emperor Nicholas, and a still more splendid table of the same magnificent stone, from the Emperor's daughter. Among the Imperial gifts were also busts of the Emperor and Empress. The Czar was guest at Chatsworth during his visit to England.

The great attraction at Chatsworth, in my eyes, was the collection of sculpture. Canova, Chantrey, Powers, and other masters have contributed to this rare embellishment of a private mansion. One large hall is devoted to statuary of the choicest description. It was pleasant to see a fine bust of our own Everett in such companionship. Among the pieces of sculpture which I remember with most pleasure, were a group of Venus with Cupid extracting a thorn from her foot; Mars and Cupid; Endymion and his dog; Madame Letitia and Pauline Buonaparte; and a splendid Hercules.

Two grand lions couchant guard the entrance from the hall of statuary to the orangery; and here begins the wonderful part of Chatsworth.

Sir Joseph Paxton, the architect of the Crystal Palace at Sydenham, was the Duke's gardener, and Chatsworth grounds were the scene of his many years' toil and success. The gardens cover many acres. The conservatory itself has a broad carriage drive through its centre. A light, beautiful glass structure rises, like a gigantic air bubble, from the conservatory, and within are found plants from every corner of the tropics, from fern to palm. One may imagine the height of a building which permits the palm to spread its tall fans beneath its shelter.

Through the midst of the conservatory a stream of water is brought, in a continuous fall, over a succession of rocky terraces, to feed an artificial lake beneath the drawing-room windows.

You presently pass out of the elaborate gardens, filled with exotics and artfully massed shrubs and flowers, into what seems a wilderness of uncultivated wildwood, which is, nevertheless, a work of art, still more elaborate than the former.

Thousands of huge rocks lie scattered in irregular confusion, like the primitive occupants of the soil; and among them grow forest trees and underbrush; heather clings to the stony earth, and ferns and maidenhair spring luxuriantly from the dim crevices. Here and there tall cliffs overhang the solitary way, seeming solid as the everlasting hills; and yet they have been artificially constructed of rocks blasted from their original position in the primeval hills, and carefully replaced here in their native order. Little streams trickle through the clefts in the rocks, where green mosses thrive under their droppings. The path is a woodland way; no mark even of the shears reminds one that he is within bow-shot of royal magnificence. By and by the way leads under a long fissure in the rock, and a mass of stone, of many tons' weight, seems to bar farther progress; but at a touch it turns upon a pivot, and proves to be only a gateway to the egress. Near by is a rocking stone, so nicely poised that the pressure of the finger sets it in vibration.

Then the notice is drawn to a palm-like tree, stiff with bristling points, from every twig of which suddenly bursts a shower, met by tiny leaps from a hidden fountain below. At every little lakelet the attendant disappeared, and presently a feathery fountain shot into the air, and fell in a shower of pearls upon the surface of the pool.

Wealth and art seem to be exhausted in attaining, within this charmed space, all the varieties of nature. Yet all this outlay keeps up, not a home, but a show place, for the Duke is at home upon another of his splendid estates, and Chatsworth delights the eye of the public more than that of its noble master.

On one side of the park, near the house, is the remnant of a tower called Mary's bower, the place of confinement for the Queen of Scots for a time, under the charge of the Earl and Countess of Shrewsbury. I have an impression, but do not know whether it is correct, that this was also the place where Lady Arabella Stuart was confined when she made her unsuccessful attempt to join her husband.

As we drove back through the park, a herd of more than two hundred deer came leaping over the low hills, as unconcerned at the presence of man as if he were no more dangerous enemy than the sheep which were browsing in the quiet pastures.

Haddon Hall is one of the ancient relics of the

grandeur of past generations, as Chatsworth is the representative of modern magnificence.

The walls of the gray old dwelling and fortress are in perfect preservation; the rooms all whole, just the same, with the exception of the furniture, as they were in the days of the Peveril of the Peak. The walls are still hung with Gobelin tapestry, and portraits still adorn the walls. The old door, black with the storms of years, admitted us, through a narrow wicket, to the quadrangle, around which stand the massive walls and ancient towers, and beyond a second court are pretty terraces, with walks of noble trees; and the unfailing ivy clothes both walls and trees with cheerful verdure.

The great banqueting hall resembles, except in its spacious extent, a very old-fashioned kitchen. The floor is of stone; a huge fire-place nearly fills one side, and oaken benches are ranged along the heavy worm-eaten oak tables. Around the upper part of the room runs a gallery, from which perhaps the dames sometimes looked down upon the wassail below.

In one of the chambers still stands Queen Elizabeth's state bed, with all its ancient hangings; and her portrait and that of Leicester hang in the drawing-room.

We explored the chill, stony chambers, and climbed the highest turret to catch the sweet picture spread out beneath the low afternoon sunlight, and went back once more to enjoy the terraces and gardens, crowded with the dim shadows of the long past.

In the extreme tower is shown the door by which one of the damsels of the house, Dorothy Vernon, escaped to join a favored lover, forbidden to press his suit in the approved way, from what cause does not appear in the legend. Perhaps family feud, perhaps prejudice may have influenced the fair one's guardians; it is just possible that a prudent and loving regard for her welfare may have been the spring. Be that as it may, the old, yet ever new tale of love, stronger than law or prudence, still remains—the best remembered, because of its most enduring sympathies, of the legends of the Hall. This Hall, once a present from the Conqueror to his son, is, even by virtue of that same elopement, the property of the Earl of Rutland, and he preserves the possession with that reverent love for the links which bind the present to the hoary past which distinguishes this nation, so rich in the proofs of the prowess, the chivalry, the power and the splendor of the past—so full of magnificence and enterprise in the present.

From Haddon we came to Rowsley, and thence by rail to Rugby, a place than which no shrine of devotion for the scholar and the Christian should be more dear. Here lived and labored the lamented Arnold; and from this quiet home of learning have gone forth streams which shall purify and gladden the earth for long years to come—perhaps I should say forever. We slept at Leamington, a modern town and fashionable watering place, the handsomest of all the smaller towns that we have seen in the country.

Aug. 22. Left Leamington for that charming enjoyment, a long drive through English scenery. One cannot go amiss; the country presents some new beauty at every step, and these counties through which we have just been passing, are one continuous garden. The green hedgerows encircle fields bright with the emerald verdure of lawny grass, or golden with the wealth of ripened grain standing in abundant sheaves, while the busy gleaners gather the stray ears of corn from the stubble—a labor more picturesque to the tourist, I fear, than profitable or pleasing to the poor harvesters, whose scanty store needs the addition of such meagre plenishing.

As we sweep along the quiet country over these perfect roads, we cannot help wondering where are the people who make up the dense population of the island. Our own country roads are not more lone than these. We see abundant traces of the hand of man in the tillage of the soil, but the dwellings are scattered, and the hamlets small. It is eminently suggestive of the probable congestion of population in the larger towns.

The English love to seclude their homes, and a gateway opening through the wall that lines the way, is usually the only indication of your near approach to some abode of beauty or stateliness within. But the simplest names upon the guide-boards are classic with associations which have been familiar to us from childhood.

Our way lay to Kenilworth, the most picturesque

ruin in England. The very name calls up a picture which is as poetic and romantic as it is historic. Robert Dudley, the handsome, fascinating, but not very faithful favorite of the great Queen, is the middle figure in the scene; but a woman's heart aches for the stern lonely fate of the woman whose strong sense of the necessities of her nation taught her to put down her woman's love with a resolute grasp, and embittered, with a thousand pangs, that inner life in which her sex must find its happiness or misery.

One cannot see this stately, ivy-clad ruin, rising upon the landscape, with only the ordinary interest attached to the historic past. The busy fancy builds again the ruined walls, hangs banners upon the perfect towers, peoples lawn and park with prince and noble, knight and squire, and catches a glimpse of the fair face of Amy Robsart at the window of her lonely tower—happier even there, in her innocent love, and her ignorance of her coming doom, than the monarch in her presence chamber. The date of Kenilworth is lost in antiquity, but it was a place of importance in the time of Henry the First. The most ancient and the most perfect of the towers is called Cæsar's Tower. One side of the court contains buildings erected by John of Gaunt; the southern side was built by Dudley; the western was the work of Henry the Eighth, and is entirely gone. It is remarkable that the later edifices are the most perishable, and are crumbling away, while the towers of most remote date are firm and solid, and even the windows are still perfect. The whole ruin shows that it was a palace of great splendor. The feudal times, when the desideratum in a castle was simply its power of resistance, had passed away, and light, and beauty and grace began to be possible in the time of Leicester.

The windows would be handsome and graceful even in these times, and they must have commanded a beautiful scene of lake and wood. The lake is now converted into a meadow, and the great portal which Dudley built, and through which Elizabeth made her splendid entrance, is now a well-kept farm-house for the tenants who take care of the place.

Leicester's bed-room, the State apartments, the dining hall, the drawing-room, are all easily distinguished. Mervyn's Tower contains the room in which Amy was confined during Elizabeth's visit. Lord Clarendon, the fortunate possessor of this most picturesque ruin, spares no pains to keep it in good preservation. I have never seen such luxuriance of ivy. In addition to the ordinary ivy, which we cultivate at home with so much care, and which seems here to be the natural garb of inorganic matter, another species hangs its full leafy garlands upon the walls, with a growth almost like a shrub, making, upon the rough outline of the ruins, a verdant wall of beauty, ever fresh and ever charming. One of the acts of vandalism that disgraced the rule of Cromwell was the giving up of this noble mansion to his soldiery for pillage and destruction. Without some such act of intentional violence, the Castle of Kenilworth might have been standing in perfection, at this very day.

On our way through the country roads from Kenilworth to Warwick, we passed Stoneleigh Abbey, the residence of Lord Leigh; seen only by glimpses, and withdrawn from the public thoroughfare, as English country-seats delight to be, by winding avenues beyond the walls of enclosure. Guy's Cliff, the property of Hon. Bertie Percy, is an exception. It breaks upon the view with a most unexpected pleasure. As the high road passes a small water, you look up the opposite side, through an avenue of noble trees, to the house, standing in a wilderness of flowers.

The story of Guy's Cliff, as the legend runs, is romantic. Guy, the first Earl of Warwick, a renowned giant, went with his peers to the Crusades, leaving the Lady Felicia, or Phyllis, as she was called, at home. Becoming weary of the Crusades, and of public life, he privately returned in the disguise of a palmer, and under the protection of the Lady of Warwick, he hewed himself a dwelling out of the rock, not far from his own home, where he passed the remainder of his life. He met his sorrowing, solitary wife, as her almoner and ghostly adviser; but kept his secret fast locked in his own breast, until the near approach of death loosened the strong grasp of his will, and he sent for his wife, and revealed himself to her. She survived him but a short time, and they both lie in the rocky home which his own hands had fashioned. Alas! poor Lady Phillis!

Warwick Castle is the perfect realization of one's ideal of an English nobleman's home. It is approached by the ancient town of Warwick, where one sees the hospital for old soldiers, founded by Robert Dudley, guarded still by the cloaked veterans, as it was three hundred years ago. But the town gathers around the base of the great castle, as tiny shoots cluster at the foot of a majestic oak. You feel, as you see the gray, massive towers looming against the sky, that you are approaching the abode of royalty; and in good sooth the instinct is a true one, for here dwelt one whom royalty must needs acknowledge as a King maker.

You enter a massive porter's lodge, in which the keeper shows you a room containing many relics of the great Earl Guy aforesaid. He was over eight feet in height, and his armor, and that of his horse, are here entire; with his halberd, his lance, and his porridge pot, the latter capable of containing one hundred and two gallons, made of bell metal, bright as a modern tea-kettle. The portress said she saw it thrice filled with punch on the occasion of the present Earl coming of age. There was the flesh hook with which the giant fished his meat from the caldron. I think Shakspeare may have commemorated this very pot in his Witches' caldron; he was a near neighbor, and must have been familiar with it. There were in the same room some arms taken from the Armada. From the lodge, the way is hewn out of solid rock, higher than a man's head; ivy and shrubs cover the top of the rocks, and overhang their sides.

Over the massive inner gateway still hangs the portcullis, and no touch of time has crumbled the mighty structure of these walls. The wide green court is surrounded by the solid, perfect wall of the ancient castle, flanked by tall towers at each corner of the quadrangle. Here is Cæsar's Tower again, Guy's Tower, bearing date 1394, and the Keep. Under the first mentioned is a strong square dungeon, which, within the present century, has served for the county prison.

The present dwelling forms the south side of the court, and is the home of the Earl, as it was the home of the great King maker whose portrait hangs upon the wall within. It is one great charm of the place, that, with all its stately magnificence, it is still a real home, and I could feel far more pride in the possession of Warwick than of Chatsworth.

The entrance is flanked by two small cannon. The baronial hall into which the vestibule leads, is a splendid room, sixty feet long; its huge fire-place is filled with logs of wood ready for kindling, and chairs are placed ready for guests.

Here are many curiosities; several complete suits of armor; the buff coat worn by Lord Brooke, when he was wounded at Litchfield; a helmet belonging to Cromwell; abundance of arms, horns of deer and elk, elephants' tusks, and Indian curiosities. The ceiling is very elaborate, and adorned with the armorial bearings of the family. From these windows there is a charming view of the park, with a long winding sweep of the Avon, and an artificial waterfall; an exquisite scene of quiet beauty.

The Castle is filled with fine paintings, especially a large collection of Vandykes; paintings by Rubens, Corregio, Da Vinci, Lawrence, Reynolds, Holbein and Teniers; a sweet picture of the Duke of Buckingham (Villiers) and his brother, and many family pictures. The most striking is Vandyke's large picture of Charles the First on horseback, at the bottom of the hall. The rooms exhibited are en suite, forming a vista of three hundred and thirty-three feet. They are truly magnificent, yet not so large as to exclude the idea of habitation.

The dining and ante-dining room, the Red, the Green, the Cedar drawing rooms are all filled with splendid furniture, and adorned with valuable pictures. The most curious thing of all is a sideboard, carved out of an oaken trunk from Kenilworth, a present to the Duke from the county. It represents upon its back the entrance of Queen Elizabeth into Kenilworth, after Scott's rendering, in a kind of alto relievo; at one side is the meeting of Amy with the Queen in the gardens, where the poor girl claims the royal lady's protection, and on the other the interview in which Leicester shrinks from avowing his marriage in the presence of the indignant monarch. At the corners are single carvings of Dudley, Raleigh and others. The famous possession of the house is a table inlaid with precious stones; a wonder of design and of jewels. The State bed-room contains the bed and furniture of Queen Anne, a full length portrait of her Majesty, and a toilet table of Queen Victoria, hung with pink silk, covered with point lace. The room adjoining is the Countess' dressing room, elegant with rich furniture and buhl ornaments.

The gardens are handsome, and the lawns more beautiful than we have seen any where else; and down the long vistas of the park stand cedars of Lebanon, stretching their wide branches over English earth; perhaps brought from Palestine by the great Earl Guy himself. The entire grounds are charming for their homelike seclusion.

In the conservatory stands the great Warwick vase, two thousand years old; dug out of the earth at Tivoli, and bought by the late Earl in 1774. It has a capacity of one hundred and sixty-eight gallons. The sculptured wreaths with which it is adorned, and its exquisite design, are too often reproduced to need description. Of all the "stately homes of England," I like Warwick best.

I thought of the Lady Phyllis as I gazed up at the gray old towers, and pitied the lone woman, who climbed their weary height, day after day, until her eyes grew dim with watching the mysterious East; who, night after night, pressed the sharp pang of defrauded love to her heart, until the aching wound grew too deep for cure; and all this while, her lord was treading the daily paths at her feet, shrouded in a disguise which even love could not penetrate.

We turned from Warwick with reluctant steps, and went on through the same pretty country roads, to Stratford-on-Avon; a name which one never utters without a mental act of reverence. Here in a low cottage, whose stone floor and bare rafters are in striking contrast with the tesselated pavement and magnificent arches which elsewhere encircle his monument, is the chamber in which the immortal Shakspeare first saw the light. The cottage is bare of all furniture, except a table and chairs for the accommodation of visitors. It contains a very fine portrait of the poet, by an unknown artist, and two or three busts. Even the genius loci of Shakspeare's room has not sufficed to restrain the petty vandalism which, in striving to become famous, succeeds only in rendering itself infamous. The walls and low ceiling are black with the meanness of names—as if the name of royalty itself would not pass unnoticed in that august presence.

From the cottage, we proceeded to the Church of the Holy Trinity, where lie the remains of the poet and his wife, with the quaint and most unworthy epitaph of his own selection.

Over against the stone which covers his vault, is a

tablet, with a portrait bust of colored marble, and a Latin inscription. The bust was covered with paint for many years, and has been cleaned and restored in the present century. It represents him in a crimson doublet and a ruff, with a pen between his fingers, and a book in his hand.

The church itself is very ancient, and has much architectural merit, containing also some curious ancient tombs and effigies. The broken font in which Shakspeare is supposed to have been baptized is still preserved.

We crossed the pretty Avon, upon whose border rises the quiet church, the casket which guards more sacred dust than any urn "between the withered hands" of Rome; and took carriage at last for London, scarcely daring to look at the enticing towers of Oxford, which must wait a more convenient season.

Blenheim and Woodstock are in the same category. Our charming English tour is ended; and henceforth our English interest must circle about London and its environs. Coming up to London! Who has not looked upon that dim possibility, as the consummation of earthly desire; and, indeed, one might be well content with what is gathered within its walls. It is the metropolis of the World. I think no one who has ever read English literature would feel as a stranger in the streets of London. You cannot saunter along its ways, without meeting at every corner a familiar name, or striking some chord of association that goes vibrating through all the memories of your lifetime, and ringing changes upon all the great names of the literary world.

We are established upon the Strand, next door to Exeter Hall; not, however, on account of our Exeter Hall proclivities, and are tolerably masters of our position.

CHAPTER V.

ENGLAND.

London — Spurgeon — St. Paul's — Westminster Abbey — Windsor Castle — Tower — British Museum.

Aug. 23. Went in the morning to the Tabernacle, on the Surrey side of the Thames, to hear Spurgeon. The crowd is so great that his own people are admitted by tickets. Strangers assemble in a dense multitude before the closed doors, to await the hour of service. If the rush into the church be any index to the spiritual state of the worshippers, the kingdom of Heaven bids fair to suffer violence.

The building is an immense edifice for a church; it has three galleries, one above the other, around the entire amphitheatre, and altogether seats five thousand people. I saw very few vacant seats on this occasion, and many people stood in the aisles. We obtained seats near the door, and my first thought was of the impossibility of hearing a word at the farther end of such an assemblage. The choir sat in a large enclosure beneath the preacher. Some official conducted him through to his place, which is on a level with the lower gallery. Mr. Spurgeon is a stout, country-looking man, much older in appearance than in years.

The first tone of his voice dispelled my doubts in regard to hearing; it rang clearly and distinctly through the great building, and made every word audible. The service followed the usual extempore order, the reading of Scripture being acccompanied by a running commentary upon the text. There was no organ, but there was something grand in seeing that vast assemblage of worshippers, one mass of living people, stand up to sing the praise of God. Mr. Spurgeon first read the hymn, and then lined it as the people sang. His sermon was without notes, and he stood without desk or pulpit, at a low railing before his seat.

He preached from Isaiah, 62: 12. "Sought out;" the analysis running thus: The expression "sought" proves the natural state of the thing sought, to be lost, or "the condition of man by nature." Secondly, the manner of seeking especially noted. God's people are not only sought, but sought out, effectually, divinely. It needs divine omniscience to discern, divine omnipotence to secure, divine love to persevere in rescuing the lost, who neither hope, nor desire, nor intend to be found. Thence was deduced the duty of individual Christians to make it their especial business to seek out the lost among their fellow men. He dwelt upon the necessity of carrying the gospel to those who will not come to listen to it; or, as he said, to be "grandly impertinent" in winning souls to Christ. His discourse was eminently orthodox, and deeply imbued with a zealous, affectionate earnestness; pure in diction, fluent in utterance, and persuasive in tenderness and practical application. There was no mannerism about him, no self-consciousness, but an evident earnestness in the Master's work.

In the afternoon we went to St. Paul's, and heard a choral service. "Heard" applies to the grand music; the great organ thundered through the arched roof with such Glorias as I had dreamed of, but never heard, and the chanting was magnificent; but prayers and sermon were alike inaudible. It is no great wonder, for speaking in St. Paul's must be very like speaking under the open heavens; and prayers chanted in the dreary monotone of the choral, lose all individuality of utterance. It is a most undevout style of prayer, at least to an untutored perception. But the choirs are beyond all description. From the full deep bass, through the rich tenor, up to the sweet, well-trained treble of the younger voices, all was pure, satisfying harmony; and the anthems, a part of the service unlike our own, were inexpressibly thrilling. I have heard no hymns nor metrical psalms.

Aug. 24. Our way to-day has been through the Strand; under Temple Bar, where the heads of traitors used to be exposed; through Fleet Street; up Ludgate Hill, past many a familiar corner; through St. Paul's churchyard, which means the circular street that encloses the Cathedral, into Cheapside; all ways which our imagination has trodden years ago. Our only sight-seeing has been the Cathedral, quite enough for one day. We went through it, from turret to foundation. The edifice itself, built by Sir Christopher Wren, after the great fire of 1666, does not compare, in splendor of architecture, with the great Minster, but it is imposing in its vastness. It is five hundred feet long, one hundred wide, and four hundred and four in height. It contains many monuments, among which are those to Howard, Dr. Johnson, Sir Joshua Reynolds, Bishop Heber, Nelson, Cornwallis, Sir John Moore. The choir contains some of Gibbons' beautiful wood carvings. The windows are nearly all plain; but some of the arches are gilded, as are the galleries around the top and bottom of the dome. Upon the great dome are frescoes by Sir James Thornhill, representing eight scenes in the life of St. Paul, viz.: His conversion, Paul and Barnabas at Lystra, St. Paul and the sorcerer, St. Paul and Silas in prison, St. Paul after the shipwreck at Malta, St. Paul before Agrippa, St. Paul on Mars' Hill, and the burning of the sorcerer's books at Ephesus. The ascent to the top of St. Paul's is a matter of some note, and we have qualified ourselves to speak of it.

The early part of the ascent is quite easy, so far as the whispering gallery, which encircles the inner base of the huge dome. Here you may look down into the space below, and gain some idea of the height from the diminished size of the people upon the pavement. The guide places you against the wall, while he goes to the opposite side of the gallery, whence his whisper is instantly and audibly transmitted to you.

Corresponding to this gallery is an outer one, of stone, from which you obtain a view of the city, which would be very satisfactory but for the haziness of the atmosphere. But this is not all of the ascent; three hundred and fifty-six steps more are necessary to bring you to the desired point of vision. Visiting the clock and bell rooms, by the way, you see a great bell, which tolls only for the death of the royal family, the Bishop of London, the Dean of St. Paul's, and the existing Lord Mayor. The last time it sounded, its knell fell upon the great city in the dead of night, announcing the death of the lamented Prince Consort.

The Golden Gallery is around the exterior summit of the dome, whence you take in the great panorama of London, with tower and spire, park and palace, street and river, at a glance.

But there is a higher attainable point, and it is not in Yankee nature to stop short of the possible, so we climb on up the steep stairs of the lantern; the stairs become ladders before we reach the top, where, between the pillars which support the gilded ball, we gain a still loftier glimpse of London. This seems fairly the extent of any faculties less agile than those of a monkey, but the attendant, who seems rather proud of our enterprise, calls out from below, "higher," and small brass rods at last reveal themselves in the ornaments, which become stepping-stones to our ambitious footsteps. Masculine feet find it no very hard matter to mount them, and by the careful assistance and direction of the guide, I find myself also in the close little ball, the very top-most step of the lofty Cathedral. I feel rather proud of the exploit, and shall content myself with this feat in the way of climbing.

"Facilis descensus" was a misnomer upon this occasion, for as the operation is to be performed by the feet, while the head is still in cloudland, a misstep is possible, and would prove more than awkward.

But, by the same kind assistance, my blind feet were safely planted upon the lantern, and then the descent was only steep. The fee which my kind friend bestowed upon the helpful guide, unlocked his heart, and with it a generally forbidden door, which led to the inner Golden Gallery, from which immense height we looked down, not only upon the pavement and the pigmies below, but upon the dome itself. This is the point for seeing the frescoes of the dome, and for getting a realizing sense of the great height of the building.

Our next visit was to the crypts, in which are entombed the remains of Reynolds, Lawrence, Fuseli, Turner, West, Wren, and Rennie. There lies Nelson, in his granite sarcophagus, and, last and greatest, the Iron Duke himself, the great Wellington. His monument is of porphyry, and inscribed with the list of his victories. Behind it stands the imposing funeral car upon which his coffin was drawn to the tomb. It is cast from the cannon captured in his successful battles, and is of many tons' weight. Upon it are wrought the cap, the sword and Marshal's baton. It is covered with a heavy pall, and surmounted by costly ostrich plumes. It was drawn by twelve horses, which are here represented by basket work, covered with black palls. The strong foundations of such a cathedral make a fitting resting-place for the dust of such heroes.

London and the play are as characteristically interwoven as London and its cathedrals, so in the evening we went to the nearest theatre, the Adelphi, and saw some very good playing in a new comedy, "The Hen and Chickens."

Aug. 25. Have been to Westminster Abbey—through its crumbling cloisters; through its many chapels, overlaid with tombs and effigies, and enshrining the noble dust of ages. King and Queen, noble and priest, warrior and statesman, philosopher, courtier and poet make these dumb walls eloquent. Here lie most of the royal dead of England, from Edward the Confessor to George the Second. Here, from Edward to Victoria, have the sovereigns been crowned. The chair used for coronation, from the time of James the First, is a heavy, plain oaken chair, destitute of any ornament. It is impossible even to mention the tombs of interest, or to enumerate the tablets of the Poet's Corner—that shrine for the pilgrimage of the world. The tablets of Shakspeare and Handel pleased me most. Handel's finger points to the music of his great anthem, "I know that my Redeemer liveth." Shakspeare bears a scroll, upon which is inscribed his own lines, "The cloud-capt towers, the gorgeous palaces," &c. Campbell also wears his finest lines as his own inscription, "This spirit shall return to Him," &c. The numerous chapels contain the ancient treasures of the Abbey; the royal monuments are all in them. Even Mary of Scots rests near her illustrious cousin, and the remains of the little smothered princes are gathered in an urn among their kindred. I should need to copy the guide-book to enumerate all the tombs that interested me. Among the tablets, one to Aymer de Valence struck me with many romantic associations.

One scarcely thinks of looking at the Abbey itself, there is so much more in it than of it; although if one had not seen York Minster, it would seem more imposing for its own sake. I have unconsciously taken that grand and beautiful structure as the standard of cathedrals, and must needs find more satisfaction in the associations than in the architecture of Westminster. It is extremely unadorned, except by the memorials of the illustrious dead. The arches of the cloister windows, as restored, are beautiful, but the ancient material of the edifice shows painfully the ravages of time, and seems in some places to be completely disintegrated, a mere dust.

The playground of the great Westminster school seemed to me peculiarly unattractive. The heavy stone pavements beneath these low arches seemed as little as possible like a place for schoolboy amusements. It possesses one desideratum for tutors, there is nothing by which boys could possibly get into mischief.

We went to the Queen's stables, Pimlico; saw Her Majesty's horses and carriages, and the state carriage for the royal progress upon state occasions. It is one hundred and four years old, is ornamented with painted panels and gold, and weighs four tons. It is drawn by eight cream-colored stallions, which stand in luxurious idleness meanwhile.

The horses and equipments of the Master of the Horse are also exhibited. They are black, with splendidly mounted black harness; that of the state horses is scarlet and gilt; altogether, the cavalcade must have a dazzling effect when in full train.

Visited the state apartments at Windsor Castle, for which an order is necessary, which can be obtained free upon application to certain specific places in the city.

The very name of Windsor Castle calls up the spectres of almost a thousand years. It was begun by the Conqueror, and has received additions from almost all his successors. It is a right royal home for the royal lady who inhabits it. The state apartments are stately, but not elaborate. Some of them are adorned with Gibbons' carvings, but I think them not so fine here as at Chatsworth. There are many splendid paintings by Vandyke, Lely and Lawrence; and two rooms are hung with Gobelin tapestry, representing scenes from the book of Esther.

There is one room devoted to armor, curious weapons and Indian trophies. The private apartments are in another part of the Castle, which seems, in extent, more like a town than a dwelling. I do not know how large acircuit it encloses, but it must be many acres.

The famous Windsor Terrace is a broad walk, with a heavy stone balustrade overlooking the Terrace gardens at a great height above them. The descent immediately below is a great depth, and, I fancy, drops into the ancient moat. The wealth of greenness in tree, and shrub, and vine, which mantles the depth, is perfectly charming. The view takes in Eton College, at no great distance. Here it is, or was, the custom for the royal family to walk on Sunday afternoons in the sight of the multitudes which then frequent the gardens.

We were so fortunate as to be in time for service in St. George's Chapel, a beautiful church. The service was choral, as usual, the music charming. After service, we had a little time for exploring the chapel. The upper part of the screen is filled with effigies of Knights of the Bath; a smooth slab in the centre of the choir covers the remains of Henry the Eighth; and all the sovereigns since George the Second have been interred in the chancel vault. There is a very elegant little chapel containing a monument to the Princess Charlotte. It represents the Princess in a careless, reclining attitude, enveloped in drapery, which, however, reveals entirely the outline of the figure. At each corner of the couch kneels a figure in the attitude of woe, also completely shrouded in drapery, which is a triumph of art over stubborn marble. Behind the couch is a sculpture representing the Princess ascending, attended by two angels, one of whom bears her infant in his arms. We went also through the cloisters.

This is a part of an ecclesiastical edifice which touches me with a more powerful charm than even the stately aisles and the lofty arches. The green seclusion speaks of peace and rest; while the busy fancy readily frames pictures of the past, peopled with the long succession of worthies who, though monks and friars, were human still, wrestling with human passions, and sorrows, and temptations, as they paced these quiet precincts, and gazed from these windows, now shadowed by the tenderness of the mantling ivy; while they wove in the loom of Time the web whose ravelled threads we here gather up with reverent care, and guard from contact with the tangled skein of the present.

The Home Park is very open; the trees are all great oaks, planted either in long noble avenues, or in simple clumps, and are the grandest specimens of trees that I have ever seen. The wide open expanse is dotted with sheep. We have learned to look for this unfailing feature of park and field — England is one great sheep pasture.

The view of Windsor from the direction of London is very impressive. The Castle stands high and displays, with very imposing effect, its massive walls and stately towers, from which fly the royal banners, while the masses of verdure that gather around its base, and the river which encircles it, add to it the charm of cultivation and beauty. It seemed to me that if I had been suddenly awakened from a dream upon the other side of the Atlantic, to the view of this kingly abode, I should not have failed to recognize it as English and royal.

Windsor and Westminster! we have known them long as the abode of sovereigns; the home of the living and the resting-place of the dead. They have lost nothing of their ideal grandeur—the reality exceeds the pictures of the fancy.

Aug. 26. We intended to have visited the parks and Kew gardens, but the weather proving unpropitious, we went, instead, to the Tower and the British Museum.

It seemed as if wild beasts were the necessary addenda to one's idea of the Tower, and, although they have been long removed, the Warden told us that people were every year made fools on the first of April, by being sent to the Tower to see the lions washed. The attendant warden was in the uniform of Henry the Eighth; a tunic of blue cloth edged with scarlet, fastening upon the shoulder, and wrought in front with a scarlet crown. The hat had at the base of its large crown, a wreath of red and blue knots, like rosettes. We saw many soldiers here, wearing medals in token of prowess in engagement.

An East Indian regiment which had been fighting the Sikhs, was on duty.

The Armory is very interesting. Effigies clad in the suits of armor actually worn by the sovereigns and nobles of England, are mounted upon mail-clad horses, and men-at-arms and squires stand, with lance or halberd in hand, as if ready for the tilt. Some of the armor and arms are exquisitely wrought and inlaid. There are also weapons from every scene of conflict in which England has borne a part.

A large part of the old Tower, including the room in which Lady Jane Grey was imprisoned, has been consumed by fire and rebuilt, but the tower still remains in which Anne Boleyn was confined; the one in which the little princes were murdered, and the narrow, dark prison in which Sir Walter Raleigh spent twelve years of his life, and where he wrote the History of the World.

The state prison is in the Beauchamp Tower; its walls are covered with quaint devices, the amusement of many a weary hour. Among them is some of the work of Lord Dudley, and the name of Jane carved by his own hand.

Within the Tower yard is the spot, and within the Tower is the block, upon which were beheaded Catharine Howard, Anne Boleyn, Lady Jane Grey, and the Earl of Essex; the last being the only man beheaded within the walls. The heading hill is just without the Tower precincts, and peacefnl green trees grow upon the soil watered by such torrents of noble blood. Opposite the great entrance, the Traitor's Gate opens to the river; by which the condemned were re-admitted to the Tower. To such a man as Sir Thomas More, was not the pang of entering his prison under the obloquy of traitor, sharper than the headsman's sword?

The Crown jewels are among the sights of the Tower. The magnificent crown made for the present Queen, has upon the top a Greek cross, composed entirely of diamonds, having a very large one in the centre; a large ruby, said to have been worn by the Black Prince, and an enormous sapphire glitter beneath it; the cap is of crimson velvet, and the band is studded with jewels. The ancient crown, with which the Queens-Consort are crowned, is preserved here, with a diadem made for the second Queen of James the Second; and the crown of the Prince of Wales, of plain gold without jewels.

There are sceptres; the royal sceptre, surmounted by a cross; St. Edward's staff, upon which is an orb; the sceptre of equity, supporting a dove; the Queen's sceptre; one of ivory, belonging to the Queen of James the Second, and another, made for Mary of Modena. Then there are swords, temporal and spiritual, and the sword of Mercy, without an edge. There are many vessels of pure gold, among which are the anointing cup and spoon, a baptismal font, a wine cooler, a salt-cellar in the form of a tall castle; if I remember rightly, this article was a present from the city of Bristol. A sacramental service, used at the coronations, and thrice a year besides, and several other articles of the same precious metal, complete the state treasures. A model of the great diamond, the Koh-i-noor, is kept here, but not the jewel itself. The value of the whole display is reckoned at four million pounds sterling.

The best exterior view of the Tower is from the river, and the structure seems necessary to the identity of London, it is so interwoven with its history.

The British Museum is a bewildering labyrinth of all the wonders of nature, in flora, fauna, rock, precious stone and fossil; and of art in various specimens of work from every age and every clime. From the skeleton of the mighty mastodon of our own western wilds, down to the minute specs of shelly life, every gradation of existence seems to be represented. A gigantic ichthyosaurus made me inwardly thankful that my lot was not cast in the reptilian age; it measured eight of my utmost steps. A splendid mass of selenite, from Germany, presented by Prince Albert, is conspicuous among the minerals.

The libraries of the Museum contain every choice and valuable work to be found. It has been enriched by the gift of several valuable libraries, since the founder, Hans Sloane, designed the beginning. The reading room is a circular room, beneath a fine dome one hundred and forty-two feet in diameter, surrounded by book-shelves, to which two gilded galleries give access. And here, without fee or reward, the people may come, upon proper introduction, and read and write, or study the vast accumulation of knowledge here stored up by national and individual munificence. It is a noble institution, and does for the literary world what no amount of private wealth and research could ever do.

Being foreigners, we were kindly given an order of admission to this speechless room; ladies, however, being permitted to advance only to the bar just within the entrance; a significant utterance of the reputation of the sisterhood on the score of silence. I thought it would have been a pretty device to have carved a rose in the apex of the dome. I was more interested in the autographs of the Museum than in all its other curiosities.

The letters and various writings of authors, statesmen, warriors and sovereigns, are here carefully preserved. Some beautiful penmanship of Queen Elizabeth, of Edward the Sixth, of Lady Jane Grey, are in the shape of books of prayer. Here is the original Magna Charta, much defaced by fire. There are autograph letters from the distinguished men of several generations, Americans among the rest; Nelson's last letter unfinished; and there are the manuscript copies of the works of great authors. But under a glass, apart from all the rest, stands a frame covered with a silk curtain, carefully preserved—and for what? It is only a deed of a house, but one little scrawl in the corner is the signature of "Will Shakspeare." In the Museum there are many new discoveries of statuary and sarcophagi, especially from Egypt; and here are the Elgin marbles, but it needs more cultivation than I possess to appreciate them, and one wonders how Lord Elgin should have despoiled Greece of her marble treasures, with any more propriety than Napoleon, who appropriated the works of art from the scenes of his conquests.

We strolled out for an hour, the last delightful day of our stay in London, and saw many places well known to us by book and picture. We passed Trafalgar Square, where was once the village of Charing Cross; the open space contains several monuments, the principal one to Nelson, one to Napier, and also one to one of the Georges. We saw Northumberland House, the Royal Academy and National Gallery, and walked down Pall Mall to see the rows of club houses. We passed through a bazaar, crowded with every purchasable commodity one could think of, and some that would never have entered my untutored brain. There we saw, too, the far-famed Punch and Judy—the automatic delight of childhood from time immemorial.

The rest of London we put aside reluctantly, until we shall re-visit the great city. I doubt if we shall find any foreign sights that will eclipse the interest of English splendor and English associations.

In leaving England I would record an unqualified dissent from a commonly received notion that we must find the English brusque and ungracious. The unfailing well-bred courtesy of equals, and the unfailing respectful civility of inferiors have, so far as our experience has gone, given a daily refutation of that error, and goes to establish that which I like to believe true, that good breeding is a cosmopolitan virtue, and however its expression may differ in small matters of national custom, yet it recognizes its shibboleth in the glance of the eye and the tone of the voice, and gives a ready response to the claim upon its sympathies. But it is no new thing to find the prejudices of the multitude exalt a mistake into a proverb, and because it is a proverb, the better informed accept it as a truth.

CHAPTER VI.

BELGIUM.

Ostend — Brussels — Waterloo — Antwerp — Malines — Cologne.

Aug. 28. Left England with regret, even for the continent. The ride through the Kentish country is decidedly rural. It is a farming region, planted with hops, corn and potatoes, and villages appear only at long intervals.

The chalky hills of Dover soon greeted our eyes, and the new sea washing their base. I thought of Aunt Betsey Trotwood as we looked back from the harbor upon the cottages along the downs. The place has a foreign air, not even English, as it seemed to me. I suppose it is of necessity that the ports on both sides the channel should have something of a hybrid effect. We embarked in a little steamer for Ostend. It was a beautiful day, and there seemed no earthly reason why the little vessel should perform such very complicated movements; a corresponding movement soon took place among the passengers, and I among them was obliged to betake myself to a state of prostration in the cabin, until the sea grew smoother. It was both ludicrous and vexatious, to be forced to submit to the tortures of sea-sickness without any apparent reason. But the roughness was of short duration, the entire passage occupying only five hours—and the North Sea smooth as a lake. We had the Prince and Princess de Joinville and their children on board, and saw their reception by the Duke of Brabant, at Ostend. We wended our way to the Custom House, where the officials performed a cursory examination of the luggage. No sights can ever impress one with the sense of being in a foreign land, like the unfamiliar sounds; for it is a very different thing to catch the confused jargon of tongues in a mixed multitude, from comprehending sentences addressed to one's self.

We fell in with pleasant English people in the railway carriage; came on to Brussels through Bruges and Ghent. In the latter city some dwellings were pointed out to us as Spanish buildings of the time of the Duke of Alva.

Aug. 29. Went to Waterloo over a heavily paved road, through a flat but rather pretty country, as unlike England as possible. The wide fields, planted with vegetables and grain, are without fences, and the roads, elevated above the fields, are marked by long, straight rows of stiff trees, carefully trimmed of all the lower branches, which gives them the look of palms. We were attended with more than Irish assiduity by rows of little beggars, who ran persistently beside the carriage, varying their applications by turning a somersault, or by making cartwheels of themselves in the most extraordinary manner, girls and boys alike. The bestowal of alms silenced them only until the quarrel which it occasioned was adjusted, and then they overtook us with astounding celerity.

We passed a beautiful wood, called the forest of Soigne. It is very closely planted, and the large trees grow tall and straight, with a remarkable equality of height; the turf beneath is like a lawn, free from shrub or underbrush. A beautiful avenue opens through it, by which the English army marched away from the field of Waterloo.

In the village of Waterloo there is a little church, filled with memorial tablets to those who fell upon the field, and there is a good bust of Wellington. Beyond the village of Waterloo is the little hamlet of Mont St. Jean, and still a mile beyond this is the broad field itself, upon which the fate of Europe was decided. The various points of interest remain much the same as at the battle. The headquarters of both generals are preserved, the farm house where Napoleon spent the night preceding the battle, and the points of the extreme wings of both armies.

At the central point of the English line a huge mound of earth has been thrown up, of a conical form, sixteen hundred and eighty feet in circumference, and three hundred feet in height, including the lion, which stands on a high table at the summit, with his paw upon a globe, and his face set defiantly towards France. The lordly emblem was surreptitiously deprived of his tail during the sojourn of some French troops in the neighborhood, but their commanding officer compelled its restoration. We climbed the steep mound, which afforded us an extended view of all the localities connected with the battle, but the wind was too high to allow us, the ladies, to scale the ladder to the pavilion on the back of the lion. Indeed the feat proved too much for the nerves of the English gentleman of the party. We visited the farm of the Chateau d'Hougoumont, the point of most fierce attack and repulse; the house and the garden wall are still riddled with the marks of the cannon balls. The little chapel of the old chateau contains an image of the Virgin, which is supposed to have protected it; a spent ball having just reached her feet, whence it fell harmless to the ground.

The guide described the battle and its position well. One could almost see the terrible conflict, the anxious suspense, and the overwhelming despair of the brilliant warrior, as he fled from his last field, crushed beyond the peradventure of escape.

One's faith is continually put to the test by the production of relics purporting to have been taken from the field, and as each individual case is possibly authentic, it is just as well, and a great deal less trouble, to take their genuineness for granted; but credulity scarcely extends to the making one's self master of such dubious possessions.

We returned to Brussels in time for dinner, which

is an ,event in the Flemish day. The elaborate courses, and the delicate variety of cookery, are something new and tempting; and notwithstanding the apparent incongruity of some of the concoctions, they form altogether the most savory viands that we have found abroad. Each article is served in a separate course, with a change of plates. One could imagine a thirteenth labor of Hercules to get up and clear away the accumulations; and there are two such dinners in the day.

Aug. 30. The Sunday morning was charming, and we went to the Cathedral, heard splendid music, and, on my own part, saw Romish service for the first time. The church was beautiful, the priests gorgeously attired in robes heavy with gold, and all the paraphernalia of worship was magnificent; but the puerility of the service was disappointing and offensive.

This cathedral has, among its ornaments, a pulpit of remarkable wood carving, of considerable antiquity. It is a gorgeous edifice, but hidden away at the top of the narrowest of streets, and no stranger would ever light upon it by accident.

We came home through streets thronged with people in holiday attire, and gay with beautiful shops, with their various merchandises displayed in tempting array; there being evidently no distinction between Sunday and other days, except in the increased gaiety. In the afternoon we took a walk upon the boulevards and in the park, where we found a fine band playing classic music, and all the world was abroad, as at a fete. This is a really beautiful city, the streets are clean and well built, and the display of warehouses elegant. There are dignitaries at our hotel. The Count de Bodensky and the Prince Von Altenberg.

The hotel surrounds a large, shaded, paved court, which our windows overlook, where people may sit at table, and enjoy the air without going abroad. It is entered through the house by a porte cochere, and gives a pleasant retirement in the midst of a city. We begin to feel like foreigners, where no English meets our ears, except from a chance traveller. The German and French are strangely conglomerated in a mixture called the Flemish. The medium language, however, is French; waiters and officials all speak it, and some are sufficiently versed in English to understand usual orders.

Aug. 31. Malines, formerly Mechlin. A most charming day. Weather has smiled upon us from the day of our embarkation, and, on the continent we have found the summer which we missed in England.

We left Brussels for Antwerp, a fair type of an ancient Flemish city. There we saw the far-famed dykes for the first time. Our first visit was to the Church of St. Jacques. It is most attractive in the beauty of its sculptured marbles. The screen of one of the altars is carved entire from one piece of marble, with exquisite delicacy; representing cherubs, flowers, fruit and corn; one figure of a child is remarkably beautiful. It is by Van Bruggen. The pillars which support the entablature above two of the altars, are adorned with similar sculpture, and many tablets of alto relievo, in the chapels, are perfect gems. One chapel in particular, contains scenes of the crucifixion, which for delicacy and purity are wonderful.

The great feature of the church is the sepulchre of Rubens, in a chapel devoted to his family. Above his tomb hangs one of his own paintings; pictures of himself, his two wives, his children, his father, and cousin. On either side of the same chapel is a fine piece of statuary representing two reclining female figures, also belonging to Rubens' family. The windows of the church are very beautiful, and the whole building is so crowded with choice works of art, that one could find food for a month's study within its walls.

We did not attempt to visit the multitude of churches, in each of which is stored up some choice work, but went only to the cathedral, beautiful in its decorations and its famous tower.

The wealth and the genius of centuries have been lavished upon these vast edifices, and they bewilder one with the multitude of beauties. Here were costly shrines, wonderful carvings in wood, fine paintings, and — Rubens' Descent from the Cross. I can describe it only by its name. To one who has seen it, that is sufficient, and to one who has not, any description is inadequate. Artists were busy at their easels, copying the splendid painting, but the master's strokes set their power at defiance. The painful and the sublime in such subjects are separated by a very narrow boundary; the students were upon one side, and the master immeasurably upon the other. Over the High Altar is Rubens' Assumption, and opposite to the Descent is its companion picture, the Elevation. The latter is a great picture, but so much surpassed by the Descent, that it should always be shown first, in order to receive any just appreciation. In one of the chapels is a Crucifixion, by Vandyke, which seems to me inferior only to the Descent.

We made the long ascent of the beautiful tower, by six hundred and twenty-two steps, and were amply repaid for the toil, by the fine view, not only of the city with its quaint buildings and narrow streets, but of the surrounding country far and wide, the windings of the Scheldt, and the distant sea. As we re-entered the church, the devout had come in to pray. A sort of halberdier, wearing insignia enough to be mistaken for a knight of all the orders of the continent, was stationed, weapon in hand, to enforce proper spirituality; and by way of accomplishing that excellent purpose, he notified my friend that she was not permitted to lean upon her husband's arm during the hour of prayer. After having swallowed the camel, Holy Church has no longer capacity for such a gnat.

After leaving the cathedral we drove about the

city, saw a statue of Rubens, and the house in which he lived. The front having been destroyed by fire, it was replaced by a tasteful building, adorned with sculpture, and surmounted by a bust of the great painter.

Our pleasant drive ended with a circuit of the beautiful public gardens. One cannot too much admire the beneficence which, upon these eastern shores, opens such fair green resorts for high and low, and scatters such wealth of art with a liberal hand for the refreshing and cultivation of the public taste. I loved to see the Flemish woman sitting with her knitting in these lovely gardens, with the works of the great sculptors before her eyes, educating her unconsciously into the love of the beautiful, and the appreciation of art.

The al fresco life here is very picturesque; people take their lunch at little tables upon the sidewalks, or in the pretty courts around which the houses are built, and undoubtedly enjoy both pleasures more for their combination.

We are staying this beautiful night at Malines, and have been enjoying the glorious moonlight in a balcony overhanging numberless groups of merry people seated at the little tables below. This is the point of convergence for the northern railways.

We have just missed a spectacle which was concluded here yesterday, having lasted a week, which accounts for the companies of queer looking priests upon the railway. It is an ecclesiastical fete, which takes place here once in twenty-five years. The whole city turns out daily in grand cavalcade, each profession and class appearing in all the splendor at its command; the ladies of the city in full dress, blazing with jewels, while the treasures of the churches are borne by the priests in full canonicals. From the descriptions we have heard, it must have been a gorgeous pageant.

Sept. 1. From Malines to Cologne, by Liege, Verviers, and Aix-la-Chapelle, the railway lies through vast, flat, highly cultivated plains. As it approaches Liege, the country begins to roll back upon hills, and, after crossing the Meuse, becomes more and more uneven, until the plain is exchanged for a picturesque combination of pretty wooded valleys, with cottages, gardens, and country seats, and steep, shaggy cliffs, where broom and heather re-appear, welcome as old friends.

The wildness of the country, watered by numerous streams, and reclaimed by cultivation at every available point, is very charming.

The railway, which, by the way, seems in Europe to find no especial obstacle in a mountain, is cut through many tunnels, and carried over many viaducts. As it approaches Liege, the descent is so sharp that the locomotive is detached, and the train let down by cables attached to an ascending engine.

From Horrem to Cologne the way is by the Konigsdorf tunnel, right through a mountain, a mile and a quarter in length; cutting from the country drained by the Meuse, into the valley of the Rhine. There are many pretty towns and villages dotting the country, and occasionally a castle, the rude remains of feudal life, but none are especially picturesque. Cologne has the narrow, heavily-paved streets of the other towns of the country, but we did not find it so odorously distinguished from the rest as we had been led to expect. The luggage passes the Prussian examination here, although the frontier is as far back as Hebesthal. Our effects being evidently those of travellers only, were not touched. Indeed, this irksome duty is every where performed with as little annoyance as possible.

We spent this afternoon in the famed Cathedral, a grand, unfinished structure, very beautiful in its style of architecture, and especially splendid in its stained windows. Those of the choir are indescribably beautiful; so is also a row high above the inner roof now in process of construction, which will unfortunately exclude them from view. This church will be a model of perfection should it ever be finished. Workmen are busy upon it at present, and the great organ is in progress of repair, to my great chagrin; the hearing of this organ was one of my pleasures of anticipation in Europe. The absence of paintings and other decorations is owing to the disordered state of the building. Large contributions have been lately made towards its completion, and the King gives annually thirty thousand thalers for the purpose.

We ascended the tower, and had a fine view of the city and the far-famed Rhine. The ascent to these cathedral towers is always, for a part of the way, by outer galleries, which enable one to examine the architecture in all its noble combinations of turret, battlement, flying buttress and decorations, and you get a much more vivid conception of their height and vastness, than by simply taking a bird's eye view, at the top of the steeple.

The unfinished tower, moss-grown with age, has still the crane by which the massive stones were carried, but we did not venture out upon the dizzy, unprotected verge.

I cannot connect the idea of construction with such an edifice as this. It seems to me to belong to the primeval creation as much as a mountain, and quiets the busy streets like a superior presence; wearing the records of the forgotten ages with a calm, still grandeur that rebukes the pettiness of the stream of daily life flowing beneath its shadow.

We took a delightful drive through the city and the park beyond its limits, following the bank of the river, the Rhine itself. We saw the house in which Rubens was born, and one in which lived Mary of Medicis. In passing a handsome house, the commissioner pointed out two white wooden horses projecting from an upper story window, serving to mark the place where, hundreds of years ago, lived a lady, who, having suddenly died, was interred in a tomb. Some one, coveting a ring upon her finger, entered the shrine, and using force to remove the ring from her finger, she revived. On returning to her house, the terrified servant who met her at the door, hastened to acquaint the husband with the astounding intelligence of his wife's return. The Baron immediately replied that he would quite as readily believe his horses to be in the upper story; whereupon, as the legend ran, according to the commissioner, the horses were found looking out at the upper window. The miracle overcame the Baron's incredulity, and he accepted both the fact and his wife; and there these commemorative horses have remained for six hundred years.

The official aforesaid, by way of vindicating his claim to the knowledge of French, German and English, threw the vocabularies of the three languages into pi, and left each native to select the words which he best understood. The result was an occasional bit of information, extracted like a tooth.

The space near our pleasant hotel is filled with women and girls, sitting beside their baskets of fruit; a grateful sight, and very suggestive to palates deprived of the usual summer luxuries of American abundance.

Sept. 2. We went to visit the Church of St. Peter for the sake of seeing Rubens' picture of the Crucifixion of St. Peter. On our way we passed through the Church of St. Mary, situated where the capitol of the Romans once stood.

It has no feature of interest, except its great antiquity, having been built in the eleventh century. The Church of St. Gereon bears date 1066. We were invited to examine the relics of eleven thousand virgins, in the convent of St. Ursula, but took them for granted, as not being among the specific objects of our trip.

At St. Peter's, instead of the pleasure of seeing the desired picture, which was presented by Rubens, in consideration of his having been baptized in the church, we came upon a service of high mass; and, after consuming a precious hour in waiting for the cessation of the censer-swinging and genuflections, we were forced to come away unsatisfied. It was curious to see oleanders and other shrubs in large boxes, standing about the pavement of the church, making a verdant bower of the aisles. While the priests went through their elaborate offices at the altar, I was much interested in watching the common people, as they dropped in, with their market baskets in their hands, and with all the tokens of their ordinary avocations about them. They crossed themselves at the benetier, fell upon their knees, repeated their prayers, and went on their way. Whatever the creed, there is something very touching in this unaffected mingling of religious service with the homely duties of life, far more than in the gorgeous service which was going on in the other end of the church. The music was very fine, and the harmonies that swelled up through the roof, from organ and choir, were like those with which we have been long familiar in the grand old German tunes at home.

We grew weary of the protracted service, and went away to the Walraff Richartz Museum, a noble building, filled with choice pictures of all the German schools. One of the great beauties of the exhibition is the exquisite painting upon glass. Scenes of exceeding delicacy, both sacred and secular, are delineated with a softness and richness of coloring, not to be equalled upon an opaque surface. Among the most charming were, the Adoration of the Magi; a Madonna and child; a Boat Scene, very lovely; three children drifting down a stream, having lost an oar, which the boy is vainly endeavoring to regain; one little one has sunk down in helpless grief; the other encourages her brother, while they are all unaware of the near approach of safety in the person of the father, whose vigorous strokes have brought him within an oar's-length of the little mariners. Peter Walking upon the Sea, is very beautiful; and there is a simple, lovely, suggestive picture of a weary maiden standing in the heat of the sun upon the threshold of a convent, while in the cool shadow within the door, stands a sister, bidding her welcome.

We saw also pictures by Vandyke, Teniers, Holbein, Rubens, and others of their several schools. Pre-eminent among them is Rubens' Prometheus. The straining muscles, the agonized countenance, the writhing form of the sufferer, and the eager, fluttering ravenous clutch of the vulture, are intensely real.

In the same room is a modern painting of great dignity, by Leinwand; Galileo in Prison. The philosopher stands at his full, stately height, his inward eyes looking far beyond his narrow cell, while yet his patient brow bears the marks of his long confinement. His window is darkened by a group of idle starers from without, of whom he is either unconscious or disdainful.

Another picture in the same room is charming; "By the Ruins of Babylon;" there is also a very forcible picture of Cromwell beside his dying daughter. Another striking picture is one of a sinking French ship at the battle of Trafalgar. The eagerness with which the sailors watch the tide of battle, as they cling to the masts and rigging, shows that the intense interest of the fight, and the fierceness of the shame and disappointment of defeat have swallowed the thought of their own danger.

There are very ancient pictures in the collection, and, to my untutored eyes, the only merit of many of them lies in their antiquity. It is strange to me, that with nature ever before the eye, the artists of long ago should so often produce distorted and unnatural imitations of her works. The coloring of these pictures is wonderfully fresh, but the conceptions of the present age, are certainly more true to nature, than the ideal of six hundred years ago. A painting of the Last Judgment has a novelty of conception which succeeds in arriving at the comic, even in the face of solemnity. The devils hold a firm grasp upon sundry dignitaries and respectable sinners; cardinal and monk struggle in sometimes dubious strife with their adversaries; the painter must have incurred the risk of an auto da fe for his profane suggestions. The miser finds retribution in gold thrust down his throat, while the hypocrite goes reluctantly downward, still wearing his sanctimonious aspect, and clasping his missal to his breast. On the other hand, a troop of the blessed (suggestively feminine) enter a door guarded by St. Peter with his keys. There are scores of Madonnas and impossible angels, but, ancient as they may be, one of the sweet glass paintings is worth them all.

On our way home we made some purchases of fruit, consciously at incredible disadvantage, in consequence of that ancient disturbance at the tower of Babel. Nothing was spoken or understood except German, and the names of the coins and the numerals in practical Dutch were very different from those of the guide books. It was excessively ridiculous to stand silently by, and see ourselves imposed upon by the demure women, who had little idea that we were impotently aware of their dishonorable tendencies. It was very homelike to see peaches again, even under the shadow of Dutch cupidity.

CHAPTER VII.

GERMANY.

Konigswenter — Drachenfels — The Rhine — Mayence — Weisbaden — Frankfort — Baden Baden — Strasbourg — Basle.

LEFT Cologne by steamer for the passage up the Rhine. A handsome pontoon bridge crosses the river just above the landing. There is little of interest upon the flat banks between Cologne and Bonn. The grandeur of the Cathedral dawns upon one more distinctly in receding from the city; long after the town has sunk to a mere inequality upon the horizon, the great edifice stands up looming against the sky. Above Bonn, the border of the river becomes broken, and the seven mountains stretch across the view. They come thronging to the river, the Oalberg, the Wolkenberg, the Lowenberg, the Nonen-Stromburg, the Drachenfels, and the Hemmerich.

The afternoon was charming, and there was abundant time to ascend the Drachenfels, and watch the sunset, and the shadows deepening in the defile through which the river cuts its way. We landed at Konigswenter, where one of the Cæsars was imprisoned by the winter snows, and proceeded to make the ascent of the mountain; my friends on foot, myself upon a donkey. The creature being purposely trained to obey neither voice, bit, nor whip, required a leader, and a guide attended to make "explications;" an imposition which one, in due time, learns to avoid.

The ascent is by a good road to the very summit, and might easily be driven in a carriage. Here we saw the first vineyards. The vines are trained upon short poles, like beans, and at a little distance, present the appearance of corn in its early growth.

There is a fine succession of views at the various turns of the road; the country is very pretty, and the whole course of the winding river is visible for many miles. Far in the distant horizon looms up the grand cathedral, keeping watch over the now invisible city beneath. In the other direction are the pretty island of Nonnenworth and the castle of Rolandseck.

The views from this summit are very extensive, but do not compare in majesty with the wonderful sights from Ben Lomond. The castle of Drachenfels is a complete ruin, picturesque in the distance, but clumsy upon near approach. A monument stands on the brow of the mountain, commemorating the passage of the Rhine in 1814. I climbed a steep cliff below the ruin, while awaiting the arrival of the pedestrians, and caught glimpses of a lone, sweet path, leading among the clustered hills, and the long dim line which marked the way to the chapel on the

Petersberg. We sat at the foot of the ruined walls, and watched the twilight gathering upon the river and its pretty banks, while we were still in the full rays of the level light, until the sunset warned us to return.

I unluckily asked the donkey leader for a bit of our old friend, the heather, which was blooming in a cleft of the rocks; whereupon, inferring my general fondness for vegetation, he deserted his charge for every blossoming weed that sprang up by the way, and presented me, at the foot of the hill, with a bundle of the green things of the earth, wondrous to behold. Meanwhile, the wretched little brute, taking dishonorable advantage of his master's gallantry, made sudden incursions into the wayside vineyards after clusters of green grapes; or, watching his opportunity, he set off down the steep hill at a pace that threatened to make a projectile of his rider. The one advantage of donkey riding, is the ease with which one can disengage himself from the precarious seat, and step to the ground, when the creature's antics become intolerable.

About half way down the mountain, is a secluded dwelling of considerable pretensions, belonging to a gentleman who has made a fortune in America, and has returned to enjoy it in his own land of legend and song.

We supped in a vine-embowered piazza, overhanging the Rhine, with only German voices in our ears, and foreign sights for our eyes; and, as I am going to bed, those for whom I write are sitting down to dinner; not, I venture to say, without some kindly thoughts for the absent, whose nightly benediction goes forth upon the western sky.

Sept. 3. We rose early, to leave Konigswenter by the first boat, but, to our chagrin, she was so far in advance of her regular time, that we were left behind, to the serious derangement of the programme of the day. We found sufficient amusement, however, in watching the troops of women and maidens in snowy caps and aprons, coming up from the market boats, with laden baskets upon their heads, and ranging themselves upon the stones of the small square court behind the hotel. There was a shrine and a fountain for their comfort, but neither seat nor shelter. The women took their stand beside their baskets, their fingers busy with their knitting, while they awaited their customers.

We replenished our fruit basket with better success than at Cologne, either on account of our own improved quickness of comprehension, or from the superior honesty of the merchants, and were ready for the boat at nine.

We had purposed leaving the river, and crossing some of the bordering hills, to vary the scenery, but were deterred by the assurance of experienced travellers that we could enjoy the Rhine region no where so well as by remaining on the river.

And a beautiful river it is; sometimes bordered by vine-clad hills, sometimes by rocky cliffs; sometimes the country sinks into plain and valley, always picturesque, and always possessing the interest of ancient association and ruins of legendary attraction.

It is wonderful to see with what minute and patient toil the rocky face of the mountain is made productive, where seems scarcely roothold for a lichen. The acclivity is terraced, and the narrow beds covered with soil, often transported thither for the purpose; and the vine is planted where the clinging tendrils may find support from the very ruggedness of the cliff. When there is not even a practicable spot for a plantation, baskets filled with earth are suspended from the rocks, and from them the plants twine upward. Nevertheless, the vineyards of the Rhine are not in themselves picturesque; they are pruned too closely to retain their proper grace, and look stiff and stunted.

The banks of the river do not need them for beauty, being so diversified in natural features as to present some new attraction at every turn. Nevertheless, I am undeniably disappointed in the Rhine. The fault is evidently in my own misconception, and not in the scenery. I had supposed it to be even more grand than the Highlands of the Hudson; and, except in the length of the Highlands, and in the ancient ruins that crown their summits, it is inferior to our own river. It lacks the majesty of the mighty mountains that bathe their feet deep in the magnificent river, and lift their solemn heads with imperial grandeur to the clouds.

The Rhineland is, instead, exceedingly beautiful. The river, after a most unusual fashion, widens as it nears its source. The lovely islands that dot its bosom have each their own legend, and the ruined castles that crown every promontory speak forcibly of the importance attached to this frontier ages ago.

It was, even then, evidently a populous country, and the grape hung its fair clusters over these rocky terraces before the iron heel of Rome was planted in their borders.

The points of the route which had the most interest for us, were the ruin of Rolandseck and the adjacent island of Nonnenworth; the frowning fortifications on the rocky eminence of Ehrenbreitstein, opposite Coblenz; the black perpendicular rock of Lorelei; the castle of Stolzenfels, the possession of the crown Princess of Prussia; and, the most exquisite spot of the whole river, Rheinstein. This has been fitted up for the summer residence of the King of Prussia, and is the most charming of green nests, perched upon the crest of the rock, and adorned with all the rustic beauty that wealth and taste could bestow upon a position of great natural advantages.

Hatto's Tower still stands as a warning to those who would oppress the poor, although I believe plain truth exonerates the prelate from the odium of the legend. But what respectability can cope with a popular legend? The "pale waves of Nahe" empty into the Rhine just below "dear Bingen," and the blue Moselle debouches at Coblenz. Beyond Bingen, the abundant rain and the dimness of early evening prevented our seeing any thing except the quite uninteresting villages that cluster upon the banks.

We found Mayence a very German city; what motive, even in the rudest times, could have induced such narrow, tortuous lanes to erect themselves into streets, it would be difficult to conceive.

We went to the Museum and the Dom Kirche, or Cathedral. The former contains an extensive collection of Roman altars and other curious antiquities found in the neighborhood of Mayence; a large number of pictures, some very good; an astronomical clock; a model of the stone bridge which Napoleon projected for the Rhine, and an unusually extensive collection of zoological specimens. The Cathedral differs from any other that we have seen. It has two choirs and two cupolas. The eastern choir dates back as far as 900 A. D.; the other, of the twelfth century, looks as fresh as if just completed. Its windows are very beautiful. The old choir contains, among several ancient tombs, the sepulchre of Fastrada, the wife of Charlemagne. The Dom has a fine exterior effect, and crowns the city with a somewhat imposing magnificence.

The garrisons of the Austrian and the Prussian powers seem to be the most important considerations of the city. Ten thousand troops are quartered here, and overshadow the common citizens, forming one fifth of the entire population, and proving an institution far from peaceful.

In crossing the river to Castel, we observed, as we had done at several places farther down, a row of boats, anchored without any apparent purpose in the middle of the stream. We found them to be mills for grain, the wheels turned by the current alone.

Sept. 4. From Mayence we went to Wiesbaden, the beautiful watering place and resort for both foreigners and natives. It is a lovely place, and every appliance is added to render it inviting. The gardens and public walks are delightfully laid out, and the Kursaal, the great point of attraction, is a splendid place.

It is a succession of elegant halls and saloons; some intended for music, some for reading, some for lounging and conversation, but most of all for the great business of the place, the gaming tables. It was a deplorable sight to watch these tables, filled with men — to the honor of the sex, there were few women — deliberately casting wealth and honor on the chances of a ball. I could only think of the anxious hearts hidden beneath the well-tutored countenances. The polite officials of the police were every where at hand, to check any external demonstration, but they could not subdue all the expressions of feverish interest at the turn of the wheel. I breathed more freely in the open air. The gardens of the Kursaal are elegant and spacious, and the adjoining colonnades are filled with displays of all tempting merchandise.

The hot spring boils up from a fountain near the

baths. Its temperature is 160° Fahrenheit, and it tastes like weak chicken broth. After proving its properties, we drove through wide smooth avenues to the Greek chapel, which commands a view of Wiesbaden. It is a monument chapel to the first wife of the Duke of Nassau, and contains her tomb, with a beautiful portrait effigy of the Dutchess in Carrara marble, by Hofgard of Biberich.

The royal lady was a niece of the present Czar, being the daughter of the Grand Duke Michael. She died at the age of nineteen. The chapel is a perfect gem, filled with small exquisite paintings by Nef, of St. Petersburgh. The dome is in gilded frescoes, and the reading desk is overlaid with enamels, representing scenes in the life of our Saviour. The chapel is very small, but perfect of its kind, and its gilded domes form a conspicuous object from a distance. From Wiesbaden we came to Frankfort, just too late to assist at the congress of crowned heads. I trust they did not suffer seriously from our absence.

Sept. 5. Frankfort. We first visited the Cathedral, which, however, offers little of interest beyond having been the scene of the coronation of the German emperors. We ascended the tower, which we reached by three hundred and eighteen steps; and at the top, what was our surprise to find the dome inhabited by a family of six persons. The effect of finding household avocations going on in such an eyrie was ludicrous. The appearance of the family, however, was not that of people lifted above the cares of common life; and the master repudiated the suggestion of my friend that he must be nearer Heaven than his neighbors. He is the fireman, and is stationed here, ready for alarm.

I looked over the battlement as he spoke of his little children, and thought, with a shudder, of the celerity with which my Young Americans would be sure to make the descent if they were denizens of this airy abode. The tower commands a fine view of the Maine, and the villages and mountains in the distance.

We drove through the principal streets of the city, and our coachman, although unable to speak any thing except German, was very intelligent, and moreover, much interested in doing the honors of his city. All sorts of traffic seems to be carried on in the streets, and it was a mystery how the driver managed to thread the narrow ways among the throngs of brittle wares upon the pavement, without causing extensive destruction.

It is pleasant to meet the kindly looks and friendly greetings which you are sure to receive from the people here. In the Ross Market, an open space near our hotel, is a group of statuary, representing the three great prophets of printing, Faust, Gutenberg, and Schöffer. A fine statue of Göethe stands in another square, and at its foot lay a fresh garland, and another hung over the door of his own house. The seeming incongruity of the German in the abstract, and the German as individual, is a continual puzzle to me; the one full of poetry, music, and the spiritual; the other of beer, smoke, and the physical. Imagine garlands at the foot of a statue in an American city, or their remaining unmolested if placed there—like Mrs. Glass' hare, it is necessary first to imagine the statue.

We drove through the Jews' quarter, within which that unhappy race was once severely restricted; even locked in at eight in the evening; saw the birth-place of the Rothschilds there, and, in quite another atmosphere, their bank and house. The mansion of the great ruler of empires wears no unusual pretension, and the bank looks very little like an institution for the control of Europe. I do not believe that the suburbs of Frankfort are surpassed in any city in the world. The environs are a succession of elegant edifices, surrounded by extensive and tasteful gardens, all giving evidence of great wealth and high cultivation. Rothschild's gardens are open to respectable applicants, but the recent rain prevented our taking advantage of the privilege. The city seems quite surrounded by a park, or circle of public gardens, and long avenues of trees form a continuous arbor through some of the streets. It was a great surprise to me to find so much that was beautiful at Frankfort.

We visited the Roemer, where is the Kaiseraal, the place in which the emperors were elected. Here was a banquet hall, whose walls were covered with fine pictures of all the emperors, each with his Latin motto. Some of these mottoes were very striking; I should like to know whether they have been bestowed in modern times as characteristic, or whether the emperors were gifted with such mental insight as to select always a sentiment significant of their character and fortune. A banquet was held in this room during the late royal congress.

We visited Bethmann's Museum, a private gallery, open at certain hours to the public, to see a fine statue of Ariadne, by Donneker. It is a great work of art. Afterwards we went to the Stadel Museum, more especially to see Lessing's splendid picture of Huss' Defence, which seemed to me faultless. It is much more of a study than the Martyrdom of Huss. The figure of the pleader, and the countenances and attitude of his tribunal, are in themselves a history; and there is visible in the whole picture the rare art of portraying the expression of mixed motives and emotions, which shows the artist to have been a profound student of human nature. The coloring is in itself a fascination. There were many fine pictures here, which tempted us to linger beyond the limits possible to our visit; two in particular, the Wise and Foolish Virgins, and a country scene, in which a peasant has evidently been killed by falling from a tree, and his family and neighbors are grouped around him. This is of the Dusseldorf school, and very expressive. Visiting one of these continental picture galleries is like entering an enchanted palace; a spell is upon you, and it needs some external necessity to force you away.

Sept. 6. We came on to Heidelberg through a hilly, sometimes mountainous wine country. The hills are terraced, with a wonderful amount of labor, for the roothold of the vine. A part of the way from Frankfort, the interval grows very wide, and here re-appears the Holland gardening, such as we saw in Belgium. Many ruins crown the peaks of the hills. The population seems not to be spread over the country, but always gathered into villages, after the fashion of the times when it was necessary to seek the protection of walled towns at night. Labor seems to be mainly performed by hand. Sometimes one sees a team, consisting of a pair of cows, curiously fastened by their horns, and harnessed to a plough or cart; and occasionally a horse team appears.

Heidelberg is nestled in one of the most attractive spots in this mountain region. The Neckar, a pretty but shallow stream, winds among the hills on its way to the Rhine, whose course we trace in the distance by the range of mountains that skirt the western horizon. The scenery around the town is charming, but the ruins and park of the castle of Heidelberg, throw all other points of interest in the shade.

The castle itself, a ducal possession of 1522, is of ornate architecture. The façade of the three fronts still standing, exhibits elaborate carving, and numberless sculptures still remain in perfection. It was evidently an abode of royal magnificence, far exceeding even the grand ruins of England. It is only a hundred years since it was struck by lightning and partially consumed. A part of the towers were blown up during an attack by the French, I do not know at what particular time.

The material of the beautiful building is a soft red sandstone, permitting much elaboration of architecture. The broad terrace which still remains with its entire balustrade, commands a lovely view of hill and vale, river, plain, aud distant mountains. The ivy mantles the walls with a luxuriance such as we have seen no where else, and hangs in graceful festoons and long streamers of tender green from every shattered tower, and crumbling parapet.

But the vast extent of the castle park and gardens affords as much interest as the ruins themselves. Broad avenues, winding shady paths, turfy banks, tangled glades, craggy descents, tinkling fountains, still dark pools, smooth green lawns, and stately trees which have withstood the storms of three hundred winters, are among the elements which make up the beauty of this royal domain.

The old moat is a perfect bower. Tall trees have grown up within it; its walls are hung with tapestry of ivy; mosses spread their carpet beneath the thicket, and long ferns wave their plumy foliage beside the fountains that still well up from hidden springs, and waste their bright waters in these lonely recesses. I envy the inhabitants of Heidelberg, who may explore at will the beauties of this magnificent estate; and I think, were I the princess of the land,

I would make the castle of Heidelberg once more the envy of crowned heads.

We attended the English chapel here, and were glad to hear the familiar service in a familiar tongue. This evening, have taken a walk along the shaded avenues of public promenade, and looked at the University. The town looks very German, and sounds more so, but I could imagine a residence here to be a very pleasant condition of life.

Sept. 7. We rose at half-past five, to ensure a long day at Baden Baden, where we hoped to meet a friend. Arrived there at half-past ten, and found all the world assembled for the great continental races. We made our way through the broad, winding street to the Conversation House, and breakfasted at the elegant restaurant attached to the establishment. The whole affair, besides being the resort of invalids and fashionables, is the great gaming house of Europe. The Conversation House is another edition of the Kursaal in Wiesbaden. The Drink Hall is a splendid building, into which the water is conducted from the spring for the accommodation of visitors. There is a magnificent colonnade adorned with frescoes along its front, which is ascended by a broad flight of steps running along its entire length.

Baden is a charming nook, fit for the resort of Dryads and Oreads, embosomed in a tiny green valley, which is completely encircled by high and picturesque mountains.

The pretty stream of the Oos runs through its midst, guarded by ivied walls, along which are seen pretty lawns and flower gardens. The public promenades are beautiful, and to-day were crowded with people in elaborate costume. Indeed, the place is more rigid than a court in the exactions of fashion.

The Grand Duke has his summer residence here, in what is called the New Palace, in distinction from the old castle, which is now visited as noticeable ruins. They looked very high from our position at the foot of the hills, and we declined the ascent, the more readily that we perceived donkey riding to be the approved fashion of accomplishing it. We were also rather disappointed at not finding it practicable to ascend the Staufenberg, or Mount Mercury, from which may be had a fine view of the valley; but it looked even higher than the castle, so we concluded to go to the races instead. But upon making inquiry in regard to a conveyance to the course, we found the price beyond the most imaginative conception; and having nothing at stake, and our York admirations not being entered, we remained in the charming little town, and strolled about the paths, and watched the display of dress and equipage. Of the latter there was every description, from the splendid coach and four, with two postillions, to a machine like a hayrack, filled with chairs; all equally bound to the races.

We made an ineffectual search for our friend; it was no time to enquire for any one, and the police, who could probably have satisfied us, were guarding the public peace at the course, and the bureau was deserted. It was a great disappointment. We had been looking forward to this meeting with the interest of real friendship, and were completely baffled. We came reluctantly to the conclusion that our friend had already returned to his distant home towards the Pacific; and wended our way to the station. On the way we encountered another party of friends of Great Eastern memory, and left them with regret, on their way to Heidelberg.

We came again into the beautiful valley of the Rhine, and crossed the river into La Belle France, from Kehl to Strasbourg. We have enjoyed our glimpse of Germany, but cannot regret it, with Switzerland before us.

Sept. 8. We visited Strasbourg Cathedral this morning, and ascended the spire as far as the first platform, half-way to the top, and two hundred and forty-five feet from the ground. There we found an esplanade of considerable extent, with a dwelling, containing several rooms, upon it; the unoccupied space is surrounded by a high parapet, and has stone seats and tables, for the convenience of those who sometimes make parties of pleasure here. At one end of this space is a circular tower, enclosing a room of perhaps twenty feet in diameter; and just outside this tower, rises the tall, slender, open spire, which seems almost to vibrate in the strong breeze.

A curious fancy it seems to live in a steeple, but

tastes are not to be gainsayed; and the view of the Rhine, the city, and the surrounding country as far as the Vosges mountains, is splendid. At this point we discovered that in order to finish the ascent of the spire, it was necessary to have applied to the Mayor and presented our passports. It was difficult to see of what possible interest it could be to the city dignitaries, whether one should go up two hundred and forty-five, or four hundred and ninety feet into the air, but a second climb was not to be thought of, and we consoled ourselves with the reflection that the difference in the extent of view could not be worth the additional fatigue. Nevertheless, we had conceived a fancy for making the ascent of the highest construction in the world; but I have since learned that the open ranges of stairs against the pierced spire, are considered dangerous.

The Cathedral is magnificent; the windows among the most gorgeous of all specimens of stained glass. There are some fine monuments in the choir, but the great curiosity of the church is the famous clock, an astronomical construction showing the relative position and magnitude of the heavenly bodies, the sun and moon, the real and apparent time, the ecclesiastical calendar, the zodiac and its signs, and has upon its top, among other devices, the figure of Christ, and below it one of Death. A dense crowd was assembled to see it strike twelve. At noon a tiny figure glided from a recess, and struck the four quarters with a little hammer upon a bell. Then Death struck twelve with his dart upon a shield; the twelve apostles passed before the Saviour, with a reverence which he acknowledged by a gesture of benediction towards all except Judas; and a large cock, perched upon a pillar at the side, flapped his wings, swelled his feathered throat and crowed three times. At the conclusion of the last crow, all present must leave the church, and the doors are closed.

From Strasbourg to Basle the country is very beautiful. The broad Rhine valley is always picturesque, fertile in vineyards, and encircled by grand hills, upon whose peaks continually appear either ruined castles or stately chateaux, with their villages at their foot. The river is wider here than farther down the valley, and, taking the whole length from Basle to Cologne, waters a country of wonderful beauty. At Basle it is a broad, rapid stream, and the city is beautifully situated on both banks, which are connected by a fine bridge.

We have taken a walk this evening along the quiet promenade by the river bank, and tried to realize the journey by which we have come to the heart of the Rhine land; the country of legend and song; the great highway of Roman and Teuton, of Crusader, Knight and King; the disputed possession of all the later agitated centuries down to the days of the great Napoleon; still wearing the footprints of the Roman tread and the tokens of feudal force; still pouring wine from her sunny hills, and harvests from her smiling lap; and, amid all the changes of political life, still guarding with quiet conservatism, in her quaint cities and her peculiar peasant life, the habits and fashions of centuries ago.

CHAPTER VIII.

SWITZERLAND.

Basle — Lake of the Four Cantons — Rigi — Sarnen — Brunig Pass — Meiringen — Rosenlaui — Brienz — Interlachen — Lauterbrunnen — The Staubbach — Thun — Berne — Lake Leman — Geneva.

SEPT. 10. Yesterday we left Basle and the lovely Rhine. We took an early walk across the river, which is here a broad rushing stream, spanned by a fine stone bridge, and sweeps in a large crescent through the town. We paused to admire the consideration for rest and enjoyment, which has placed seats in recesses retiring from the footwalk of the bridge, where one may sit and enjoy the charming scene from its best point of view.

Nothing gives such fine effect to a city as a broad river in its midst. It is the only way to get a proper distance for its important buildings. The great chasm of the Norloch, between the two cities at Edinburgh, performs the same office there. You feel that you comprehend a town when you have attained such a point of view.

The streets of Basle are narrow, winding, steep and densely built, and afford little of attraction to the stranger's eye; but we found our inn a very peaceful and comfortable caravanserai, nothwithstanding its ferocious appellation of Black Bear, which looks still more carnivorous in German.

Nothing can be more unlike our idea of a hotel than such as this; stone halls, stone staircases, bare floors, single beds with a feather bed for a counterpane; and, withal, an artistic cookery and nicety of detail not always to be found in our very pretentious establishments. We have been much pleased with the hotels of Europe; in all the essentials of comfort they are carried to a point of great perfection.

The railway to Luzern passes through a most charming country, fertile and cultivated in the plains, the undulating hills clad with vines, and the distant mountains foreshadowing the glory of the coming Alps. The Vosges is no mean range in itself, and makes a distinguished background for the rich variety of the scenery below.

We passed from the Rhine valley to the basin of the lake by long tunnels, of the same massive masonry that we have found to admire from Wales to Switzerland. Long before we reached the lake, the majestic summit of Pilate towered up to the heavens, and the Rigi lifted its stately Kulm in the summer sky. With what language shall I describe the unfolding of that leaf in my memory upon which is written —The Alps.

The lovely Lake of Lucerne lies embosomed in an irregular valley, encircled by vast ranges of mountains, whose countless, sharp, jagged peaks rise from the very margin of its blue waters, and glitter in the sunlight far up in the dome of heaven, or veil themselves in clouds.

Mont Pilate, the tremendous peak that rises directly above Lucerne, is a mountain of most irregular outline, far surpassing any other within range of the eye, being six thousand eight hundred and forty-one feet in utmost height, and the lower peaks scarcely less.

On leaving Lucerne, the lake makes a long reach to the left, at the head of which lie the small towns of Sempach and Kusnacht. Passing this seeming outlet, and rounding one of the mighty columns of the mountain, we reach Weggis, a small village at the foot of the Rigi.

Here we landed, and took horse for the top of the grand mountain which seemed to overhang us, while its long ranges of bare precipice terraced the green slopes which lost themselves in the upper distance, and seemed to the inexperienced eye to form the desired summit. We learned the mistake in due time.

The path up the mountain is a very good one, and might, for a part of the route, be scaled by wheels. The ascent wound through every variety of way; first by the cultivated fields under embowering trees; then through the mowed land and pasturage; sometimes on the verge of a wooded upland, sprinkled with wild flowers, and strewn with huge masses of the conglomerate rock of which the mountain is built. And every where we turned to gaze upon some new charm in the bewildering scene.

At first, as we ascended, the beautiful lake opened to view, with the great mountain promontories jutting into its waters, but as we rose higher and higher, the lake lost its attractiveness in the mighty vision that began to be unfolded.

Peak after peak shot up behind the nearer summits that shut in the lake, until the vast distance was peopled with the countless throng, some sombre with their garb of pines, some clad in eternal snow. Then the eye grew accustomed to the higher level, and took in a new horizon at every step. I cannot imagine any thing more grand than the continual revelation of that majestic scene.

By the time we had gained half the ascent, we had ceased to be charmed with the verdure of the nearer hills, and the pretty habitations that nestled under the shadow of the rocks, "where scarce was footing for a goat," and were wrapt in the solemn grandeur of the sea of mountains that crowded the whole amphitheatre of the horizon. It is worse than useless to attempt to describe it.

When we had scaled the face of the precipice which concealed the summit from the foot of the mountain, we found that we had accomplished one half the ascent.

The rock formation here is very singular, being conglomerate, not too densely massed, and lying heaped in huge fragments of fantastic form. In one place the path led through a natural arch, formed by the piling together of these fragments of the mountain; some of them I think not less than a hundred and fifty feet high.

For the last third of the way, the trees mostly disappear, but the vegetation remains a green close turf to the very top, which is over five thousand five hundred feet high.

The latter part of the way lies along the verge of the precipitous descent to Lake Zug. Turning the back upon the vast forest of the Alps, one looks down upon the exquisite beauty of the valley; at that height it seems a miniature picture of landscape. Midway between Kusnacht and Immensée is a conspicuously white spot, which proves to be the chapel of William Tell; for this is the Lake of the Four Cantons; and Lucerne, Uri, Schwitz, and Underwald, are classic ground for the hero or patriot.

The way was enlivened by many groups of travellers, riders and pedestrians, both ascending and descending; and swarmed with peasants, mostly girls, carrying heavy burdens of supplies for the summit, in baskets upon their backs; all quick with the courteous greeting and smiling aspect which belongs to this part of the world; and, lest we should forget that "peculiar institutions" exist in some form every where, the unfailing mendicant was stationed at every resting-place.

Girls with smiling pertinacity offered fruits and drinks, and troops of return horses, with guides, and empty chaises-a-porter, met us at every winding of the path.

As we climbed the last third of the way, the sultry day was exchanged for a chill, cloudy evening, and the wind swept across the narrow neck which we were pursuing, with a wintry blast. It was evident that the angry clouds would swallow up the desired sunset. Nevertheless, it was a glorious scene. On one side the mighty Kulm fell down to Lake Zug, with such sharpness of descent that one might almost drop a pebble into its waters. Lower mountains masked the view of Lake Zurich, except for occasional glimpses among the hills. On the other side ran the long green passes between the several peaks of the Rigi, and lines of travellers dotted the threads of path from Arth and Goldau. Far to the south, lay a thousand peaks, slowly veiling their lofty heads in the mists of evening.

And here, at this apparently inaccessible height, are three large hotels. Sitting at a luxurious dinner in the handsome saloon, surrounded by all the appliances of advanced civilization, piano and all, it was difficult to believe that nine long miles lay between us and the level of every day life; and that all the luxuries and comforts of such an establishment, had been brought to this remote spot by the toilsome steps of patient peasants.

No nationality seemed unrepresented in the assemblage of the dining room; and one caught a very good idea of what Babel might have been.

We went to bed, prepared to make an early sortie to behold the majesty of the rising sun; but that dignitary refused to be made, any longer, a spectacle, and we beheld, instead, the rain—unwelcome sight—shutting out all view of hill and valley, and making chillier even the chilliness of early morning.

If there were Babel over night, what should be styled the confusion of tongues at the moment of departure; landlord, waiters, porters, guides, travellers, all speaking in unknown tongues, with none to interpret; each guest anathematizing his bill after the peculiar fashion of his own country. We had the assurance of the guides that we should find better weather farther down; so we set forth upon the toilsome descent. Some courageous pedestrians followed; among them two ladies, who arrived before us, worse for mud and rain. Meanwhile, it rained, at first gently, then pouringly; we halted for a time under the friendly shelter of a chapel roof—one of the countless shrines of this land, but it presented no attraction as a permanent abode, and the weather gave no token of amicable purpose, so we emerged once more into the deluge, and trooped downward. The path along the direct face of the precipice, which is accomplished by striking it obliquely, is steep but good, and it seemed incredible, on looking back at the mighty barrier, that we had scaled it without wings.

All things have an end, and so had the descent; we arrived at Weggis, little the worse for wear, and quite ready for breakfast. About eleven, the clouds having discharged their contents and departed, we embarked for a tour of the lake; and such a tour I do not believe can be made upon any other lake in the world.

We were borne along at the foot of the mighty ranges, each turn of the meandering lake revealing new grandeur in the upper world, and new beauties in the soft green slopes below.

Some of the mountains are dark with pines to the water's edge, while some are dotted with chalets, and green with pasturage to the very top. Several villages skirt the lake. Among the largest are Gersau, Brunnen and Fluelen.

The first mentioned is an unusually pretty village, embowered in fruit trees and chestnuts. It is somewhat remarkable, even among Swiss villages. For four hundred years this tiny corner of the world existed as an independent government, until 1798, when the rapacious hand of France, for which nothing was too great to assail, nothing too small to grasp, swept it into the vortex of the political gulf, and it is at present like the rest of Switzerland, under the confederate government.

Among its other curious customs of many years' existence, is a beggars' fete; when for three days in the year all the beggars from the country round are gathered to a feast by the firesides of their more fortunate neighbors.

At Brunnen, the extreme end of Lake Lucerne, upon a house beside the water, are painted figures of the three patriots, Werner Stauffacher, Arnold Melctal and Walter Furst; and also two figures engaged in mortal combat, with the inscription, "Schwitzer est vainqueur de Swen et fonde Schwytz."

From Brunnen the lake thrusts out an arm called the Lake of Uri, and becomes still more remarkable for the beauty of the waters, and the majesty of the mountains.

The defile which encloses the lake is narrower, and the peaks higher. At a great elevation to the right is Rutli, where stands a chapel, marking the spot where the three patriots met, in the solemnity of the early morning, to swear the oaths of liberty; and from that spot are said to have welled up three springs, to which pilgrimage is still made by the believing.

On the water's edge at the left of the lake, is a chapel ornamented with various commemorative designs, marking the place where Tell sprang to the shore, and sped the fatal arrow to the heart of the tyrant Gesler.

The waters of the lake are here eight hundred feet in depth, and wear the peculiar green which I have noticed below the Falls of Niagara.

Busy workmen are engaged in hewing a grand road out of the face of the rock, hundreds of feet from the water, and have already constructed tunnels through several projecting points. It will lead by St. Gotthard into Italy.

The end of the navigation is Fluelen, whence one can look down the lake still further to the narrow pass which closes the view. It is the present way to St. Gotthard by Altorf.

On the opposite side of the lake the mountains rise to the greatest height — Uri Rothstock being over nine thousand feet high, and upon its distant brow we could discern a shining glacier. The whole sweep of the range upon that side of the lake is very high, and scarcely broken by a descent, as is frequently the case upon the other side. The return to Lucerne by the same route only deepened the awe which the Alps inspired on the first view.

Upon reaching Lucerne, we took another boat for Alpnacht, en route to Meiringen and the glacier of Rosenlaui. We came on to Sarnen for the night, but alas! the sound of the renewed rain augurs ill for a mountain pass, unless the clouds should be exhausted by morning.

Sept. 15. We were wakened early by the tidings, that, as the upper mountains were covered with snow, there was promise of a pleasant day; the giant peaks serving as a barometer for the commonalty. So we put ourselves in trim for the day's travel, and left Sarnen by carriage.

The two pretty and intelligent daughters of our host, who were also the servants of the inn, were among the best specimens of native women that we have seen. They spoke French and German equally well, and English tolerably, and were as modest as they were intelligent.

The dress of the women in this region is peculiar.

The mode of dressing the hair in Underwald, is by braiding it with thick white ribbon or cotton; it is worn at full length, or wound around the head and fastened by a pin nearly a foot long, with a flat head about two inches square, set with glass or stones. They wear what we call Swiss waists, with snowy underdress, and short stiffly starched white sleeves, with closely fitting black velvet sleeves, reaching from the elbow to the wrist. The back of the waist is finished with a broad square collar, ornamented at the corners with silver; and from a hook in the collar depends, upon each side, a silver chain which fastens another hook in the side of the bodice. The head is bare, or covered only with a handkerchief tied under the chin. The broad-brimmed straw hat began to appear below Lake Brienz. But this costume is far more picturesque upon a pretty American girl than upon these sun-tanned, weather-beaten women, who bear heavy burdens upon the back, and dig, and mow, and rake in the fields, and draw heavy carts, like oxen. We rarely see a man in the fields; they are acting as guides, porters, drivers and waiters; but it makes one melancholy to see the complication of labors laid upon womanhood here. I have not seen a single peasant woman with even the remains of attractiveness or femininity about her. They look harder and coarser than the men, and their unceasing industry becomes almost painful; the babies and the knitting are ever at hand to fill up the intervals of harder labor.

Our road to Meiringen was through the valley of Sarnen, and over the Brunig Pass, a grand gorge through the mountains. On the right are the lakes of Sarnen and Lungern, and in the distance the Lake of Brienz. A superb carriage road winds up the long pass, on one hand skirting closely the shaggy sides of the mountains, and on the other, overhanging the green meadows and scattered cottages of the valley. How green such a valley can be, is known only to one who has seen the Alps. The short thick turf is perfect emerald, and has a look of velvet smoothness which no carefully kept lawn that I ever saw could attain. No fences break the long swell of the meadow, watered by clear rushing streams from the mountain springs.

The cottages, precisely like the fancy cottages of the toy shops, are built of wood, fancifully carved; the roofs are of wood, crossed by long strips of board, held down by stones. There is usually a carved balcony running along the second story, covered with flowers, ivy, or dried corn, and on the Geneva side with grapes. Altogether they have the most temporary, unsubstantial effect, and seem little adapted to the long cold winters of Switzerland. Indian corn began to appear in these valleys. The mountain formation is very remarkable. On the upper side of Lake Lucerne it is a mass of conglomerate, easily disintegrated, although I have been told that at the very summit of the peaks the metamorphic rock peeps out.

On Lake Uri the bald face of the rock is gnarled and twisted into every variety of gneisitic contortion, intermingled with the later stratifications; and here, in the Brunig Pass, we found the same thing, the outcrop striking at every conceivable angle, and the rock a fine, compact, igneous stone.

So far as I have observed, the same formation prevails throughout the range, with sometimes a mixture of slate, sometimes of clayey strata, and very seldom a slight appearance of quartz; on the Wetterhorn the hornblende is streaked with distinct veins of smooth white quartz.

As we toiled up the long high Pass, we found a varying scene of wild grandeur and romantic beauty. The last hour of the ascent is up the Kaiserstuhl, a sharp climb to the south, overtopped by the three great snowy peaks of the Wetterhorn, which looked down upon us from above the clouds. As the heavy sky which had overhung us all the morning began to break, we looked up, hoping to catch once more the clear blue of heaven, and where we expected to find it, loomed out great masses of rock and snow, almost in the very zenith; and still farther on appeared the Wellhorn. These immense mountains are on the left of the valley of Meiringen, and are the chamois mountains of the Bernese Alps.

After reaching the summit of the Pass, we took the mountain on our right, the scarped, rugged rock rising perpendicularly above our heads, in some places a thousand feet, and gradually impending over the road, until at one angle the huge mass had been tunneled, and the road passed directly under it, while the enormous boulder far overhung the valley beyond.

On the left, the mountain fell precipitately to the valley; indeed the whole splendid road is carved upon the very face of the mountain with incredible labor and expense.

On the opposite side of the valley, through which the milk-white torrent of the Arve rushes foaming to the Rhine, rise the majestic heights of many solemn peaks, few of whose names I find it possible to retain.

The Engelhorn is directly opposite, and here and there, at each change of direction, appeared the summit of a new wonder. Beautiful cascades leap down from the long curtain of mountain which faces the valley; among them is the Oltschibach, and, finest of all, the Reichenbach.

The descent to Meiringen is sharper and shorter than the ascent from Lungern, and we found ourselves about two o'clock at the hotel of the Wilder Mann, arranging ourselves for a trip to the glacier of Rosenlaui.

It rained a little, but we were assured that the road was perfectly good, "a little steep, perhaps," which was true without the perhaps. A worse road I never saw, not indeed, quite perpendicular, piled compactly with large, closely massed trap rocks, set mostly on edge, with an occasional boulder, of a height to make even the trained animals pause to consider the mode of ascent, and their riders to cogitate the probabilities of the return.

After gaining, in this way, a considerable elevation, the way ran along the verge of the gorge of the Reichenbach, a deep torrent which roars against vast accumulations of boulders and fragments that obstruct its course. At about half the distance up, the beautiful fall of the Seilerbach projects itself in two chutes a distance of a thousand feet, into the Reichenbach. At a short distance above this fall we came upon a veritable Alp, that is, a wide, green pasturage, high up on the table of the hills.

Large herds of the peculiar cattle of Switzerland were feeding here, with flocks of goats, and the unfailing chalet perched itself in the nooks of the rocks. It is astonishing to see upon what a height these summer resorts are built. Scrutinize what mountain you will, and, at any distance below perpetual snow, there will be sure to peep out the tokens of a human dwelling. In these airy nooks the Swiss watch their herds and make their cheese, and on the approach of winter they drive the milky mothers down to the cottages of the valleys.

The cows are handsome; their hair has the fineness of a fur; they are of a light dun color, and, as a distinctive peculiarity, their long projecting ears are filled with long white hairs. Their hoofs are uneven in length, and are twisted crosswise at the division, from the constant necessity of keeping footing upon a sharp acclivity. They are the riches of the Alps, and show the care with which they are tended. The horses, on the contrary, are lean, coarse animals, and far from fleet. It was curious to watch the feeding of the horses on the way to Brienz. At Tracht out came a man, armed with a huge loaf of bread, which he cut into bits alternately, for the horses, whose avidity for the morsels showed their appreciation of the civilization of cookery.

To return to Rosenlaui; the rain deepened to a pour, with an interlude of hail, from which the dark mossy pines only partially sheltered us. But it seemed befitting the sombre cleft of the wild mountains, whose savage fastnesses we were penetrating, and it had nearly ceased when we crossed the Reichenbach and dismounted. Here were the ever present guides, with the very uninviting chaise-a-porter. It seems to be the impression of the natives that foreigners lack the ordinary use of their faculties while upon a journey, and though the object of your trip may lie within your reach, you are supposed to need a guide for "explications," and the intensity of your enjoyment of Nature is often sorely marred by the irritation. At the present time we declined the privilege of being borne upon the shoulders of officious attendants, and climbed the stony paths, which were now only the bed of trickling streams. One pertinacious guide followed, awaiting some opportune disaster which should render his presence desirable.

As we crossed the deep chasm of the Weissbach, a boy stood with heavy stones poised upon the slender rail of the bridge, ready to launch them into the abyss at our approach. The silence which awaited the sullen thud of their arrival at the bottom, showed an immensity of depth, and the eye sought in vain any glance of water in the darkness below.

We scrambled on up the wet, slippery paths, stumbling among the gnarled roots of projecting trees, to a second gorge of the same stream, crossed by a frail little bridge, suspended between the smooth perpendicular sides of a very suggestive chasm. The approach to it was by a short ladder, and up the narrow ascent on the other side in the same way. The plank was narrow, covered with sleet, and defended by a single rail. However, it was the only approach to actual insecurity that I have found in Switzerland, where I had dreaded so much. We crossed in safety, notwithstanding, and before us hung the glacier, white as a drift of newly fallen snow. Its upper part was shrouded in clouds, so that we could get no proper idea of its height, which is twelve hundred feet. We ascended by steps cut in the ice to a crevasse, which has been artificially enlarged into a passage about thirty yards long. Its extremity is hollowed into a circular chamber, whence one can watch the effect of the light upon the crystal mass. It becomes a deep blue wherever the light penetrates the cracks, and the entire arch of the cavern was of the color of a twilight sky. This glacier is remarkable among its fellows for its unvarying purity, the flinty formation of the adjacent mountains sending down no discolored debris. We emerged with a shiver, to be greeted by a considerable fall of snow, and having refreshed ourselves at the little cabin near the glacier, we commenced the return. That we were hopelessly wet spared us the trouble of any attempt to care for our garments, and we launched ourselves down the steep at full speed. That wet could become wetter I learned by measuring my length in one of the temporary brooks. After crossing the Wiessbach, I turned aside to explore the banks of the profound depth, but was warned to retreat by the ice which encased every blade of grass. How the dwellers upon these dangerous heights escape disaster and destruction I cannot well comprehend, yet little children play upon the verge of the precipices and torrents, apparently without any especial protection. The chalets often rest upon slopes, where it would seem that an unguarded step must prove the step between us and death.

The shadows of the mountains were grown very sombre, and the two grand peaks of the Engelhorn and the Wellborn, between which lies the glacier, frowned heavily upon the way, while the Wetterhorn and the Faulhorn kept guard upon their sides. Nevertheless the shadowy ride down that long romantic pass beside the foaming torrent, sprinkled by the spray of the silver cascade, and shut in by those tremendous mountains, was delightful, even though the streams from our garments dripped from the stirrups.

By the time we had reached the steep rocky descent it was nearly dark, and the path, bad enough by daylight, was not to be thought of on horseback, so we dismounted, and the horses went on, sliding and jumping down the way, as we trudged carefully downward, sometimes varying the craggy path by an excursion to the mud of the adjoining meadow. We had a mile or two of riding after reaching the foot, and were glad to find dinner and fire awaiting our arrival, with which, being refreshed, we spent the evening in pleasant chat in the travellers' room, examined the treasures of wood carvings, and went to sleep to the roar of the Reichenbach.

The following morning was beautiful, and we came on by carriage through Brienz to Interlachen. As we left Meiringen, the great glacier overtopped the mountain, glistening in immaculate whiteness in the morning sun.

The road along the lake was charming, with meadows even greener than any we have yet seen, and the fall of the Giessbach here shot into the lake with a distant roar, which seemed unaccounted for by the size of the fall. We left the carriage at Tracht, and walked on beside the sweet lake, to linger upon the fair picture of creation spread before us.

The rugged mountain curtain, studded with peaks, still guarded the valley, but receded to a little wider interval from the turbid Aar, leaving a smiling valley, sloping to the southern sun, and rich in all the charms of Alpine beauty.

At Interlachen the great monarch of the Bernese hills, the Jung Frau, rose white with eternal snow, and the Silberhorn spread a snowy shroud upon its upturned face, like the still covering of some gigantic dead.

The immense height of this range renders its distance inappreciable, and it seems within a pistol shot while at a direct distance of eighteen miles. I longed to put away the curtain of the dark, pine-covered mountains in front, and look upon the King in his majesty.

The village of Interlachen is one of those spots, rare as they are charming, in which exquisite beauty is combined with grandeur and solemnity, and it is the one centre from which radiate the most desirable Swiss excursions.

We drove to Lauterbrunnen to see the Staubbach fall, and to get nearer to the Jung Frau, as we could not go to Grindelwald. The mountain seemed still farther off than at Interlachen. The Staubbach is pretty, hanging like a misty veil from the crest of the mountain; the water, falling from such an immense height, becomes dissipated into vapor, and seems scarcely to possess a substance; but the very respectable brook which it forms, proves it to be a real stream.

One of the most noticeable features of the trip to the Staubbach was the ingenuity with which the demand was continually made upon the purse. One went at each step prepared to spring a mine. No face of cabin was so innocent that it did not fly open at our approach, and disclose the peculiar wares of the country; ingenious carvings in wood, bone and ivory, tempting displays, both for beauty and utility. Then there were prints of the surrounding views; children followed us with a bench for our repose, or croaked a jodel for our edification, while others, without pretext, demanded tribute. It was ludicrous to see the anxious speed with which every individual within the range of vision hurried to make merchandise of the unwary traveller. As we approached the corner of the lane leading to the fall, a boy hastened to place the long Alpine horn by the wayside, and brought echoes from the hills which might have seemed the voices of the wood-nymphs, reverberating in musical notes, again and again, from the narrow strait.

We had twelve applications during the ten minutes' walk between Lauterbrunnen and the Staubbach, and at the stopping place there were nine guides, all desirous of pointing out the fall, which was meanwhile directly before our eyes.

We spent the Sunday at Interlachen, and each hour added to our admiration of the spot. I could fancy no more delightful place for a summer abode. One may make the wildest excursions into the heart of the Bernese Oberland, and return to enjoy the sweetness of plain, stream, and valleys, and all the appliances of luxury and repose.

We followed the crooked, winding street through

the village to the bridge across the Aar, whence there is a comprehensive view of all that is grand and beautiful in scenery; from the snowy summit of the majestic Jung Frau and the darker mountains of the nearer range, to the sweeping river, with its verdant banks and picturesque mills, and the pretty dwellings dotting the valley.

The drive to Thun is only another edition of these sweet valleys; and the sail down the lake was very delightful. Conspicuous above the other mountains of the region, the gigantic pyramid of the Niesen overhangs the lake; the banks are cultivated, and tasteful dwellings appear frequently.

Thun itself is very beautiful. The steamer passes a narrow entrance between an elegant villa on the left, and on the right, a hill slope, covered with fine buildings, and crowned by a chateau and a handsome chapel. The narrow inlet is, I believe, still the Aar, and the steamer enters beyond the power of turning. Here we landed from the crowded little boat; not even the Rigi afforded a more complex nationality than the deck of that little steamer. English, American, French and German tourists, peasants and Swiss soldiery all hurried off to the station; among them our unlucky selves, supposing the aforesaid place of departure to be in immediate proximity to the pier, when it proved to be a mile away.

We came by rail to Berne, where we spent the night, but did not remain to explore the city of Bears.

From Berne again by rail, through an increasingly picturesque country, to the beautiful town of Lausanne, where we embarked for Geneva. I can do no justice to a sail down Lake Leman, its blue waters guarded by the Alps on the south, and the long chain of the Jura on the north. A fertile, highly cultivated country alternates with handsome towns and stately chateaux upon its banks. Coppet, the residence of Madame de Stäel, is on the northern bank; also the chateau of Prangins, once the possession of Joseph Buonaparte, now of the Prince Napoleon.

Just before we reached Geneva, a distant, snow-capped chain of peaks began to dawn upon the eye —and there was Mont Blanc.

At a distance of more than fifty miles, it seemed little farther off than did the Jung Frau at Interlachen. Nothing else could engross the sight afterwards; the eye was ever seeking that mighty domain of ice and silence.

The view of Mont Blanc from Geneva is very good. Here the Rhone, which enters the lake below Villeneuve, rushes out again in a deep blue rapid stream, very different from the green depth of the Rhine.

I think Geneva must prove a charming residence, uniting the climate of the mountain country to the pleasures of cultivation, and directness of access to the great world every where.

We drove out to Ferney, the residence of Voltaire. It is a most favorable exhibition of French gardening, and one cannot but wish that he had confined his genius to horticulture, and had not touched the profound depths of the spiritual life with an unhallowed hand. We were shown his bedroom and saloon, in the same state as when he occupied them. In a stone urn in the saloon is preserved his heart, according to his own direction.

A fine full length portrait of Catharine of Russia, a present from the Empress herself, hangs over his bed. The garden is still preserved in his own design. An arbor, several hundred feet in length, beautifully trained in beech, and a tall hedge enclosing the grounds trimmed in the same arbor-esque fashion, are kept as they were in the days of the noted owner.

The environs of Geneva are pretty, but seem tame after the grandeur of the past week, but we are looking forward to Chamouni and Mont Blanc.

CHAPTER IX.

SWITZERLAND.

Chamouni — La Flégère — Sources of the Arveiron — Tête Noire — Martigny — Pierre à voir — Brieg — Simplon — Domo d'Ossola — Lake Maggiore — Arona.

THERE is little to say of the way from Geneva to Chamouni, although it is a most interesting route to remember. We made the journey by diligence, the day hot, and the way dusty. The road leads from Geneva, at first up a steep ascent, through a well cultivated country, and fields blushing with the colchicum; then it becomes gradually wilder and steeper; winding up sharp passages above deep gorges, through which flows the white torrent of the Arve. One soon learns to distinguish the glacier rivers by this peculiar whiteness, owing, perhaps, to the impalpable dust of the rocks, ground to powder in the attrition of the glacier. In eating the clear glacier ice, I sometimes found the sand remaining abundantly in the mouth.

One never ceases to wonder, upon this route, at the thought of the mighty convulsions whose traces are scattered so thickly along the course, in the huge fragments of every form which have been detached from the impending mountains. The whole valley below is evidently at times overflowed by the stream, for all along its now confined bed lie vast accumulations such as are heaped up only by the progress of mountain torrents. The scene in the spring when the icy fetters of the waters are first loosened, must be worth seeing.

Just before reaching the village of Sallenches, we exchanged the heavy but comfortable diligence for light carriages, as the journey is too difficult to be performed farther by large vehicles; and even these carriages we were forced to abandon at some of the precipitous ascents.

A bridge over the Arve, built upon a double set of arches, is one of the finest specimens of masonry I ever saw.

The same features of scenery continue; the vast mountains grow higher, their rocky faces more precipitous; the gorges narrower; the hum of conversation grows hushed, and the awe of the savage solitude gathers over us beneath the darkening sky; the stream roars more madly over its obstructions, and finally, in the vista of the narrow defile, rises the pure white summit of the "sole sovereign of the vale." Mont Blanc, like Niagara, needs time to allow one's mind to grow up to the recognition of his mighty proportions. I think these are more truly appreciated at the distance of Lake Leman than on a nearer approach. But his height is best apprehended by being viewed from some great, though inferior elevation in his neighborhood. In truth, the first view of the great mountain from his foot is disappointing, especially after having been imbued with the poetic descriptions, which lead one to seek its summit almost in the heavens. The air is so clear, and the mountain so enormous in its proportions, that it seems neither so very high, nor at any very impracticable distance.

Then one's own stand-point in the Valley of Chamouni is six or seven times higher than the Palisades on the Hudson, and the mind fails to add the height of an entire day's journey upwards to the remainder of the mighty mass.

Sept. 18. We spent the night at a hotel in full view of the mountain, and it seemed higher in the morning. There are many excursions to be made in the neighborhood; the usual one, unless the stay be protracted, is to the Mer de Glace, by way of the Montanvert, across the glacier, and a return by the Mauvais Pas and the Chapeau. There were two objections to this excursion in my mind. Upon the Mer de Glace there is no view of Mont Blanc itself, and the return is by a difficult and fatiguing walk along a path which must be rugged and dangerous indeed, to deserve, in these regions, the name of Mauvais Pas.

So by way of combining a coup d' oeil of the mountain with a visit to the great glacier, I chose the ascent of La Flégère, and a return by the sources of the Arveiron. La Flégère is upon the opposite side of the valley from Mont Blanc, five thousand eight hundred feet high, and intensely steep. The narrow path is forced to double continually upon itself, making at each detour a small angle by which the mountain is finally scaled.

For the first hour we oscillated upon the face of a bare hill, apparently not more than half a mile in length, mounting, by slow gradations of the flinty path, at right angles to the general direction of the mountain. We then made a sudden turn to the right and plunged into a wood, which shut out the surrounding views, while it afforded a grateful shelter from the hot morning sun. There was still the same slow alternation of advance and retrograde; the path from being only stony, became rocky and difficult. At one point it crossed a pretty mountain stream, where there is a rustic bench for the rest of the wearied wayfarer.

About half the way up is a pavilion perched upon a projecting knoll on the side of the mountain, where the views of the valley begin to assume appreciable proportions. I think the height of a mountain is best comprehended at such a stopping place. You take in the distance already attained, and that still before you, at the same glance; while at the foot or the summit, the great distance obliterates the detail by which you measure. The path attains a still more direct steepness after leaving the pavilion, and clambers among the rocks and bared roots with an irregularity and difficulty which demands continual attention to the proprieties of horsemanship, and made even the mules give signs of a determination to retreat. We had a model of a guide; careful, attentive, genial and polite. Henri altogether surpassed any attendant that we have ever had, and seemed, besides, altogether innocent of the rapacity of his class; receiving gratuity or refreshment with a well-bred modesty rare to behold in these regions.

The view, when the top of La Flégère is once attained, is worth any fatigue. The vast body of Mont Blanc is spread out like a picture, with the long parallel ranges of mountains that form its sides filled with enormous glaciers, from which flow the various tributaries which finally pour their waters through the Arve to the Rhone.

The great Needles point skyward as if they would pierce the heavens. Above all, farther off, and higher than when seen at its foot, rises the serene, immaculate front of the "great Hierarch," pure as if newly dropped from the skies, and seeming to bid defiance to all stain of human approach, as indeed he does—for although the rashness of adventurous spirit sometimes plants a footstep in these sublime solitudes, the lone monarch hastens to obliterate its traces with his icy breath, and suffers no human power to fix landmark or pathway in his solemn abode.

The height of La Flégère reveals an immense expanse, entirely hidden from the village by the intervening peak, which seems to be filled with pure crystal ice; the blaze of the sun showed its transparency even at that distance. This is what is called the Grand Plateau; it had something appalling to me, so calm and cold in its defiance of human skill and research. In full view from our point of vision were the glaciers of des Bossons, d'Argentière, du Tour, and the mighty Mer de Glace, which at its lower extremity takes the name of du Bois.

The Mer de Glace presents a slope of several miles, filled with tall pyramids and blue crevasses, then grows apparently smoother up to the point of divergence between the branch which turns to the right, toward the Col de Geant and that which leads to the Jardin. The latter is a spot of green turf, surrounded by eternal snow, at a distance from the valley of nearly nine hours. The guides assert the length of this glacier to be, in all, eighteen leagues, but eighteen miles seem more credible.

We were unfortunate in not being aware of an ascent of Mont Blanc while we were at La Flégère, as from its summit the party may be watched with glasses. Just as we reached the valley on our return, a cannon announced the arrival at the Grand Mûlets, the cabin where the first night is passed by the aspiring traveller. The next morning the terrible journey is made over the icy way to the summit, and the descent accomplished to the same point, where the second night is usually passed, although some energetic travellers return to Chamouni the second day.

The danger of concealed crevasses, the intense cold, the toilsome way, the painful respiration, and the oppressive sense of hunger, all combine to render this one of the most dreadful excursions ever undertaken, under the pretext either of pleasure or advantage. And when to this is added the fact that the view, under the most favorable circumstances, is limited to the sight of the most elevated mountains, and that the length of stay at the summit can be prolonged to little over a quarter of an hour, it would seem that "the game would not pay for the candle." Two guides, at least, are necessary to the ascent, (the first attempt was made with seventeen,) and porters are needed to carry food, fuel, wine, and garments for the night; the cost is not less than a hundred dollars for the guides alone, and varies for the entire trip from three to five hundred.

Meanwhile we are resting at the top of La Flégère. The descent of a steep mountain, upon horseback, with a side-saddle, is extremely fatiguing, and having found a mule a very different affair from a horse, I inferred the propriety of making a part, at least, of the downward journey on foot; so leaving guide, mule and companion behind, I set forth.

The footpath may be made a little shorter than the bridle road, but the great steepness renders it impracticable to diverge much from the beaten track; a slight misstep in traversing the short cuts between the zigzags generally sufficing to bring down upon one an avalanche of rocks which have a precarious hold upon the side of the mountain, and crinoline is eminently adapted to secure all the chances of such mishaps. Then, too, a very promising divergence is not unlikely to end in a thoroughly impracticable precipice, and the steep way is to be retraced.

The exhilaration of that free mountain air renders walking a perfect pleasure, and I had no mind to exchange it for the mule, so kept on to the valley, stopping to chat by the way with the sprightly mistress of the pavilion, whom I encountered at the pretty resting place where the stream overflowed the road. I rested at the bottom, and watched the caravan of mules and footmen trailing its slow length along the tortuous descent; then remounting, we took our way across the valley to the foot of the great glacier. A ride of about an hour brought us to perhaps the most beautiful sight of the whole region. The Arveiron gushes in a foaming torrent from a vast arch in the clear solid ice, brawling over the great rocks dropped from it, in its slow but steady onward march. It is an enjoyment of which I should be never weary, to watch the outpouring of that tide from the heart of that frozen sea; ever and anon whirling down a huge fragment of ice, or booming with the plunge of some loosened boulder from the arch above; then rushing away down the valley with the joy of sunlight upon its bosom, to mingle its white waters with the whiter Arve.

There is something appalling in the desolation of the moraine at the foot of the glacier. The plain is encumbered for many rods with enormous masses of rocks, immense boulders, and vast heaps of sand, ground to powder by the fearful attrition; while far up lie the same huge debris, brought by the great silent river from the rocky fastnesses above. A forest of pyramids clusters in the distance, and occasionally a tall needle topples over in sudden but noiseless prostration.

The glacier has retired many rods within the memory of living inhabitants, furnishing an illustration of the theory that glaciers are steadily retreating, leaving their terminal moraines as foundations for the inhabitation which is gradually pursuing them to their citadel in the savage heart of the mountains.

We scrambled across the lateral barrier, and made our way with difficulty along a rough surface very little like ice, except where we paused to brush away the sand, or to dislodge a stone from its bed to assure ourselves of the presence of the crystal beneath. It was very toilsome, and the tall pyramids were a long way off, and I satisfied my curiosity with gazing upon them at a distance, while my companion, a young English lady, went on with the careful guide, and looked into the dark blue crevasses, and explored the glacier to her satisfaction.

I sat, meanwhile, wrapt in the hurrying river, the shadowy cleft of the lower valley, and the spotless peaks whose afternoon splendor was yielding to the soft glow of sunset.

We entered a grotto in the foot of the glacier, which differed from that at Rosenlaui in its utter darkness, due, I suppose, to the accumulations of sand above. It was lighted by lanterns, which sent a starry reflection from the dripping walls. The whole excursion occupied seven hours.

We have had delightfully clear weather at Chamouni; not a cloud dimmed the rosy light of sunset upon Mont Blanc, and his snowy summit cut a clear outline against the depths of the early sky as I looked out to catch a glimpse of the first dawn upon his "bald awful head."

Sept. 19. A memorable day was the one on which we made the passage of the Tête Noire. The distance is twenty-four miles, and we sent forward the mules to Argentière, and took carriage to that last station for wheels. The morning was cold, and it was long before the sun of the upper world visited our path. But we fortified ourselves with a meagre breakfast, and mounted. I have been assured by eastern travellers that the motion of a mule is worse than that of a camel, and I can readily believe it. Fortunately they only walk, however level the road; but the most complicated problem in my mind at present, is this: Given, a mule and a mountain; required, the amount of possible dislocation.

The road across the Tête Noire is a very good one; for the most of the way to Trient practicable for wheels, except for the narrowness of the road. So far as the Tête Noire rock the way is wonderfully wild, hemmed in by dark, rocky mountains; one of these is the abode of innumerable eagles, which keep the inhabitants of the neighboring village in continual terror, as they have been known to pounce upon little children and bear them away to their inaccessible eyrie.

The path becomes narrow, rocky and steep as it leads up to the height of Les Montêts, the dividing point of the tributaries of the Arve and Rhone. From this summit the road leads along the Eau Noire, a dark, clear, deep stream, into a defile continually narrowing and deepening. At a sudden turn in the way Henri faced the mules about and exclaimed, "Adieu! Mont Blanc!" There indeed, in the sharp close of the vista formed by the long ranges of mountains on either hand, rose, fair and solitary, the immaculate crown of the mighty mount, grander and more beautiful by being deprived of the accessories which served to diminish his height as seen from the foot.

We turned ever, with lingering gaze, so long as any part of the spotless outline was visible against the clear blue sky, and then plunged into the recesses of the savage defile. The path cut the edge of a gorge, whose depth was measured by endless tiers of tall pines, and at the bottom roared the foaming stream, fretted into a thousand falls by the opposing rocks, the mighty droppings of the overhanging mountains. I do not know whether it may be the effect of excitement, or that one learns implicit faith in guide and mule, but the sense of danger seems dormant while one gazes down from the unguarded edge of a path, where you may drop a pebble, almost from your stirrup, a thousand feet into the depths below. A slight rail served to give an appearance of security to the path at an angle of the mountain where it projected far over the precipice, then by a sharp turn we passed under the arch of a tunnel, hollowed through the solid battlement of rock; here rose the tall, black, dripping face of the Tête Noire rock, on which the sun never shines.

This was the culminating point of the wild grandeur of the pass; that, for which, if for nothing else, the passage should be made. A few minutes brought us to the hotel of the Cascade, situated upon a point of rock which commands, at one glance, the wildness and grandeur of the pass from which we had just emerged, and the beauty of the leaping cascades upon the other side of the chasm.

Here the mules were to rest for an hour and a half, and having taken a lunch, we walked on through the magnificent fir forest of Trient, where continual streams came trickling down the mountain side, and mosses, ferns and flowers bordered the way. Even here we found the heather.

As we turned, at last, the base of the Tête Noire, the valley opened from the forest along the banks of the now quiet river, into fields of some cultivation; where, as usual, we saw only women toiling at the hoe and scythe, and bearing home upon the back, in heavy burdens, the product of their labor.

We walked on through the sheltered valley to Trient, where, as the way seemed to lead up a considerable ascent, we sat down to await the arrival of the mules.

We had passed the Tête Noire, and, in our happy ignorance, fancied that the remainder of the way was descent; what was our consternation, when having attained what seemed to be the top of a long slope, we found it only the first reach of one of those detestable zigzags, by which it seems possible to scale the face of any hill, not absolutely perpendicular. Far above us showed row after row of the same pathway; on we went, right up the mountain, each turn seeming still more astounding than the last, until we reached the Col de la Forclaz, fifteen hundred feet above the top of Ben Lomond.

But in this world, the penalty of elevation is descent; and, having got up the mountain, the next thing was to go down. At the bottom, as it seemed but a bow-shot, lay Martigny, in the broad valley of the Rhone, which spread out like a map beneath our feet; but there were, nevertheless, eight mortal miles of zigzag between.

The road, despite the tiresome twists, was beautiful, but the wood soon excluded the pretty view of the valley. As we trooped along, in such meditative mood as may consist with a precarious seat upon the neck of a mule, a shout from the rear faced us about to a tableau at once terrifying and ludicrous; the respected head of our party, dismounted beside his prostrate beast. The terror lay in the possibility of serious harm to the rider; the ludicrous in the placid air of the animal, who wore the serenity of one who has made up his mind. I had remarked his cogitative manner of stopping to survey certain difficult passages of La Flégère the day before, and had been amused at the variety of changes rung upon "Allez! en avant! marchez! en route!" with which each tug at his bridle was enforced; but to-day, albeit not a ruminating animal, he had evidently jumped to a conclusion, and hence his attitude of repose. Fortunately, he had couched himself with such deliberation that the rider was able to extricate himself from the saddle in time to escape injury. Sundry cogent arguments from the baton of the guide brought mulêt to his feet, if not to his reason, and we again slowly wended our way downward.

As for myself, the point of endurance was passed, and I deserted my four-footed friend for my own independent locomotion. One plunge across the steep interval between the paths put me beyond the reach of my lawful guardians, and they shouted after me a commission to order the dinner at Martigny, while I addressed myself to the downward way. A line of flinty pebbles presented itself, crossing the successive meanderings of the route, wearing the doubtful aspect of either pathway or water-course. A countryman assured me that it was a veritable path, leading to Martigny, but added with hesitation that it was "un peu rapide," which meant, not quite perpendicular. I, however, pursued the unpromising way—it might sometimes more properly be said to have pursued me, inasmuch as that which is true of a part is true of the whole — and after a mile or two of sharp exertion, I arrived at tokens of human habitation. The descent afterward, although intensely steep, was delightful. It was a charming afternoon; the free inspiriting mountain air breathed like the elixir of life. I deserted the flinty causeway, now for a pretty green orchard, now for a velvet meadow; stopping here and there, to rest beside a stream, or to exchange greetings with the peasant girls at work in the fields. Now and then I encountered the friendly face of a specimen of the unmistakable genus, tourist. As the shaggy mountain descended into cultivation, it became possible to look back upon the heights which we had been traversing, and to catch distant glimpses of the trains of riders and pedestrians upon the galleries above. On the opposite side of a ravine which seemed also to descend from the mountain, came winding down a similar caravan from the pass of the great St. Bernard.

I lingered with reluctant steps, even upon the fatigue of that long walk, for it led away from Switzerland and the Alps; and in that solitary way, I realized the intensity and actuality of my enjoyment, as one can scarcely do when his perceptions are busy with scenery, and his sensations with a mule.

Presently a village hum floated upward upon the breeze; the whirr of a mill, the creaking of wheels, the evening sound of herds, and the voices of homeward bound laborers; a cheerful, welcome contrast to the solemnity of the lonely mountains.

The village of Martigny is a little, crooked, uncouth hamlet, with almost city pretensions, in its paved streets and close rows of dwellings. Passing through the village, the way to the city stretched out indefinitely. I inquired the distance, and was answered by the usual formula, "ten minutes;" which is, as I believe, to the mind of a continental, the only distance less than an hour.

It was a pretty walk — long trains of low carts, piled with grapes, came trailing along the broad shaded road, and troops of harvesters, laden with their implements of husbandry, paced beside, merry with song, and ready with a courteous greeting. Yet the lack of intelligence and the distortion of figure often visible, is very painful — for the Valais is the especial haunt of crêtenism, and goitre displays itself as almost the normal condition of the inhabitants.

A fine bridge crosses the swift Dranse at the entrance of the city, which is unlike any other cities which I have seen, in its almost rural aspect. The Hotel de la Poste, the proposed bound of my walk, proved, of course, to be at the further extremity of the city, but I arrived at last, half an hour in advance of the zigzagging beasts and their weary riders. How weary were all, and how lame were some of us, one should cross the Tête Noire to know.

We found Martigny a very pleasant stopping place. The inn had the appearance of having served in some of the past ages as an ecclesiastical dwelling. It was certainly very unlike an inn in its long vaulted passages and ivied cloisters. The table was better than at any other place, city or country, that we have found upon our journey. Here, by way of game, we had the chamois, not the goats' flesh which has done duty in so many places for its wilder brother.

There was a most enticing peak stretching up into the air above Martigny, called Pierre á voir, commanding, it is said, the whole view from Mont Blanc to the Jung Frau; reached by five hours of mule — ay, there's the rub. The descent is made to Martigny le bourg in three, by means of sleds, drawn by men; a great economy of time and fatigue, but, doubtless, subject to excitement in view of the possible contingency of a failure in the locomotive power, similar to that which attends the railway descent at the foot of Niagara. However, we did not attempt Pierre á voir, but came on to Sion by rail, and thence, by a most fatiguing journey in the interior of a diligence to Brieg, the sleeping place upon the Simplon route.

In the morning, in lieu of the diligence at five o'clock, with the possibility of a place in a lumbering omnibus instead, we made a party with a young British officer, fresh from the tigers of India, who bore still some traces of their familiar acquaintance, and took a carriage and four for the pass, leaving Brieg at eight o'clock. After six hours of hard climbing we still overhung Brieg at the same angle, and had not yet turned the flank of the great Glisshone, which stared us in the face in the morning.

The pass of the Simplon is a miracle of engineering skill. The route was projected by the great Napoleon after the battle of Marengo, and commenced in 1800. It was completed in six years, at a cost of more than eighteen million francs. It is a magnificent road, from twenty-five to thirty feet in width, cut like a thread upon the precipitous sides of the mountains; supported by superb masonry, and overhanging depths which disclose at every turn scenes of the grand and beautiful below; while above, the horizon is bounded by the snow-capped peaks of the Bernese Alps on the one hand, and the rocky fortresses of the Savoy summits on the other. The long upward route follows the indentations of the mountains, until that becomes no longer possible, and then, by a grand curve, it spans the chasm, down which the Wiessbach rushes, roaring and foaming to the Rhone, and begins the difficult dangerous ascent on the other side. This part of the road, up to the very summit, is swept by avalanches, that continually destroy the fortifications, which are as continually renewed. The direct curve, by which the road almost returns upon itself after crossing the Wiessbach, gives one the whole view of the pass at a glance.

Along the more exposed portions of the route, the road passes beneath immense galleries, constructed in heavy arches, opening towards the valley, which guard the road from obstructions caused by the falling rocks; and where the face of the mountain becomes absolutely inaccessible, the way is hewn through the solid rock. Every where, in mid air, rise alternately peaks and glaciers; the streams from the latter, shooting, ever and anon, from beneath the road, and leaping to join the torrent below.

One grand cascade from the enormous Kaltwasser glacier, is carried directly over the gallery, and one sees it through the open arches, falling in a glittering sweep above his head.

Within the space of one league upon this dizzy crest, are six houses of refuge, some of them rendered useless from their exposure.

One often hears of a bird's-eye view. I know nothing that so nearly approaches the reality, as the vision that lies beneath the eye of one clinging to the steep sides of these stupendous mountains. After passing the Kaltwasser glacier, the distant view passes the great glacier of Aletsch, and reaches the spotless peaks of the Bernese Alps. Below lies the profound depth of the valley of the Rhone, with the ubiquitous Brieg still in full view. On the right, tower up the mighty slopes of ice plains, which you approach so nearly as to appreciate their immense extent, and to have also a shuddering sense of the dangers which their steady march hurls upon the exposed expanse below.

The summit of the Simplon is a sterile, broken amphitheatre, between four and five thousand feet in height, bounded by dark, rocky pinnacles, and vast glaciers, whose near approach is appreciable in the frosty air. Here is a hospice, for the accommodation of poor travellers, designed by Napoleon, but completed only so late as 1825.

We stopped for an hour at the desolate village, so far removed from all that makes life enjoyable, and despoiled the inn of all the supplies of its larder.

From the summit one passes through the valley of Algabi to the valley of the Gondo, in which lies after all, the wonder of the Simplon pass. Here all the elements of savage grandeur seem to be gathered in the wildest, vastest, sublimest combination. Here are still long galleries forced through the stubborn rock; and stupendous masses of black, fissured, jagged cliff overhang the road, sometimes at the height of two thousand feet. The gorge grows narrower, darker, more appalling at every step, and casts all previous experience of mountain passes into the shade.

The Diveria, at a fearful depth, hurls itself against the mighty fragments, which the convulsions that rent this awful gap have cast into the bottom of the abyss, and the great cascade of the Alpeinbach pours its foaming tribute to the depth. Here you traverse the gallery of Gondo, pierced for six hundred and eighty-three feet through the angle of the mountain, and emerge to the same oppressive seenes.

The roar and gush of waterfalls, and the beauty of the continual silver bands that glisten on the opposite side of the chasm, relieve in some degree the oppressive solemnity of the vast, dark, silent masses of rock, towering up almost to shut out the heavens, and bearing on their gnarled and distorted brows the fiery marks of their convulsive birth.

The Diveria is crossed by several fine bridges, one of which, near Crevola, ninety feet in height, is a beautiful structure of two arches, and gives once more a glimpse of the profound recesses of solitude and gloom from which we have emerged.

No contrast can be more striking than a passage from such a majestic scene as the valley of the Gondo, to the soft, smiling landscape which greets the eye a few miles farther down the valley. Fertile plains, rich with crops of corn, dotted with fruit trees or shaded by chestnuts, with here and there glimpses of white villages, fill the blue distance, and we sink rapidly from the fresh, pure, bracing air of the Alps, to the heavy, lifeless atmosphere of an Italian valley.

We arrived, at night, at the town of Domo d'Ossola, (we passed the Italian frontier at Iselle,) where we made our first experience of an Italian hotel; and truly, if that pestiferous dog's hole were to prove a fair type of the rest, we should soon bid adieu to la bella Italia. The rooms were very large, floored with stone, or some concrete of a stony nature; the sofas like beds, and the beds like bed rooms; but the house, according to Italian custom, was built around an inner court, the windows of the rooms opening upon a stone balcony which overhung the quadrangle; and when the court proved to be only a stable yard, with all its paraphernalia and occupations, the effect upon a hot summer night may be more easily conceived than described. Eager to escape from such a den, we took carriage as early as possible for Arona, and the drive was like a leaf out of a fairy tale. The plain is rich and cultivated; the vine, a plant of low growth in Switzerland and Germany, is here allowed to twine itself, in all its native grace, about the low trees and trellised arbors. The magnificent chestnuts spread their broad arms, laden with golden balls; corn stands ripe upon the sunny fields, and figs droop beneath their broad leaves. Pearly clouds float lazily across the soft, warm sky, and one feels indolence creeping over him at every breath.

Yesterday we drank of streams dripping from eternal ice; to-day we scare the lizards from the hot wall along the lovely Lake Maggiore. This beautiful lake stretches from the foot of snow-clad hills to almost tropical verdure. Its blue depth, bordered by grand mountains, and studded with the beautiful Borromean isles, presents a scene of the most charming description.

We passed, upon our way, immense quarries of white and red granite and marble, but as we descended to the level plain, we found the lake bordered with elegant villas, with every charming variety of garden, pleasure ground and fountain, and all that enters into the most fascinating pictures of Italian scenery. It is a favorite summer resort for the rank and wealth of Italy, as well as for foreigners, especially the English. The road beside the lake is superb, built upon massive granite foundations, and edged along the lake, as upon the sides of the mountain, with battlements of solid mason work. We stopped for dinner at Baveno, the most picturesque point upon the shore, nearly opposite Isola Bella.

This island is a wonderful instance of the victory of wealth and labor over the disadvantages of Nature. Here, more than two hundred years ago, the proprietor, one of the family of Borromeo, built a chateau, and caused soil to be transported to the barren rock, upon which he built terraced gardens, planted with the growth of all climates, fruit, shrub and flower. The same design has been furthered by the possessors ever since, and the chateau and gardens are now the daily resort of travellers.

We made our journey, still beside the beautiful waters, so far as Arona, nearly at the bottom of the lake, a pretty place, where we spent two days; but as my own views were limited to the hangings of my bed, I can say little of its attractiveness. I lay, with the summer air floating in from the lake, and listened to the soft musical Italian voices of the children at play, or the women at work under my window, and was charmed with the liquid utterance which transforms the stately old Roman tongue into the loving, tender tones of the sweetest language in the world.

CHAPTER X.

ITALY.

Milan — Venice.

FROM Arona we came by rail to Milan, a truly splendid city, through a country essentially American in all its features; corn and peaches, and even pumpkins, reminding us of a fair land many leagues away. We passed through the battle-field of Magenta, seven miles in length, and by a field filled with the buried heaps of dead. Milan is all alive—for Victor Emanuel reviews here the troops of United Italy to-morrow.

Sept. 25. The morning opened inauspiciously for the grand parade, nevertheless the streets were beautiful as a picture. The windows and balconies of the elegant buildings were decorated with banners, and with scarlet and crimson hangings, and bright with gay groups of well dressed people. The pavement was thronged with pedestrians, among them remarkable the beautiful women, with their graceful head-dress of black lace, and, almost as numerous, the priests in long black garments and queer beavers.

The grand cavalcade through the streets commenced about noon, and lasted for two hours. The troops were fine, dark, soldierly men, in the early prime of manhood, well equipped and handsomely uniformed. Most of the officers, and many of the rank and file wore medals which bespoke acquaintance with active service. The cavalry had been reviewed on Monday at Soma, and these troops consisted of infantry and artillery. It was altogether a striking display of soldiery, and for the number and rare beauty of the horses, all apparently in military training, I presume it could not be surpassed in any country. We saw not less than four thousand, and among them were the finest specimens of steeds I ever saw. The dainty, delicate-limbed creatures seemed to enter into the spirit of the pageant, and paced proudly through the thronged streets, as if aware of their claims to admiration. Their riders wore the military air to perfection.

The artillery consisted of three hundred and seven pieces, officered and manned in batteries of six, each piece drawn by five horses, and each caisson by four or five. Victor Emanuel, with the royal guard, brought up the rear. He is a stout, dark visaged, bewhiskered man, and touched his chapeau with grave and courteous salute, in return to the acclamations of the multitude, as he pursued a tedious way through the long streets to the place of review without the city gates. Conspicuously, in his immediate company, rode a jet black dignitary, evidently of no mean rank, attired in a costume as gorgeous as scarlet and jewels and broidery could make it; his bearing among the nobles, quite unconscious of any inferiority arising from color. It was a beautiful picture —the vista of the magnificent street closed by the wonderful Cathedral.

Helmets glittered and plumes floated above "the tossing sea of steel" that poured its steady tide along the crowded way; and the whole air of the martial throng was that of no holiday pageant, but as if composed of men wonted to conflict, who had faced the dangers and wore the honors of deadly combat.

Altogether we felt ourselves to be very fortunate in having an opportunity of witnessing a parade, at once so warlike and so royal—and that, too, within the walls of the ancient and superb city of princes—Milan.

There was an undertone running through all the pleasure of the display for me. I tried to see it through the eyes of one who came back to his native city last night, from an exile of forty years. My heart was touched with the eager joy of the stately old man, as he welcomed the sight of the proud city; for, after forty years' wandering in foreign lands, in the restless life of a proscribed man, what could remain of the tender ties and intimate friendships that make home and country worth having; and I wondered if, to the long exiled, gazing apart at this splendid show, the joy or the anguish of the return were the keener.

We have visited the wonderful Cathedral, but to my great regret I was obliged to take the beauties of the roof at second hand, and was unable to explore half the wonders of the interior. There are some remarkable combinations in this edifice, which distinguish it from all others. The first noticeable feature is, that while it is a structure of vast size, its architecture is of such airy lightness and grace as to destroy the effect of massive solidity which usually belongs to buildings of grand proportions; and it seems rather an ærial fabric, such as the fancy frames of the summer clouds, than a gigantic pile, fashioned by the chisel and wrought by the hammer.

Its snowy purity, too, as it sleeps beneath the soft blue Italian heaven, charms the eye, hitherto accustomed to associate dark weather-beaten walls and ivied towers, with architectural antiquity.

Another wonder is, that, while every part of the vast edifice is in perfect harmony with the whole, each part is finished in a design peculiar to itself, and different from all its correlatives. From cope to foundation, upon column and buttress, tower, flying buttress, window, turret, pinnacle and spire, neither statue, leaf nor flower is reproduced; no design repeated. I doubt if another such instance of imitation of the divine creation, in countless variety, subordinate to perfect harmony, can be adduced among the works of man.

I was especially astonished and delighted with the exquisitely wrought pierced roof, and still more astonished to find afterwards that the whole was a marvellous painting in fresco. The roof is supported on thirty-six magnificent columns, whose capitals are finished in the same endless variety before mentioned.

The church is filled with sculpture, some of it of colossal proportions. One remarkable statue represents St. Bartholomew wearing his own skin as a mantle, after having been flayed.

We were shown into the sacristy, to examine the treasures bequeathed to the church by San Carlo Borromeo. They are preserved in tall cupboards which line the sacristy, and whose massive doors are opened by means of a windlass.

It is impossible to convey any idea of the wealth of gold, and silver, and jewels, which is here enshrined; the Sacristan, of whom we inquired its value, said it was many millions, but beyond any power of accurate estimate. Great solid gold and silver crosses and crosiers many feet in height; candlesticks, patens, bowls, books, boxes inlaid with jewels; emeralds, rubies, sapphires of a size to make one think the Arabian Nights a record of real existences; every device that could be wrought for a church dignitary out of the most precious gems of the earth are here deposited; a vast mine of utterly unused, profitless riches. One large box has for its cover a splendid mass of rock crystal, in its natural state, taken from Mont Blanc, bound and cased in gold.

From the sacristy we descended to the crypt before

the High Altar, which contains the chapel of Cardinal Borromeo. The walls, except where they are interpaneled with rich hangings, are of solid silver, wrought into many exquisite designs; and pictures in alto relievo of silver surround the chapel, representing scenes in the life of San Carlo from his birth to his beatification.

They represent him in acts of munificence to the poor, for which, indeed, he seems to have been distinguished, if there be any faith in tradition.

One figure symbolizes his liberality by a cornucopia, out of which is pouring a mass of real silver dollars. The great wonder of all is the sarcophagus of the saint. It is of rock crystal, pure and transparent, from Brazil, the gift of Philip the Second, of Spain. Within lies ghastly the embalmed Borromeo, in full canonicals, covered with jewels. A cross presented by Marie Therese is pendent in the coffin, made of diamonds and emeralds, and valued at a million of francs. The elaboration of the whole chapel was a gift of the artists, so that, in calculating its value, only the intrinsic worth of the precious stones and metals is regarded; and the chapel is estimated at six millions of francs.

I regretted exceedingly not being able to ascend to the roof of the Cathedral — as my friends assure me that a nearer view of the statues, and the wonderful designs of the pinnacles and flying buttresses, greatly enhances the admiration of the beautiful structure.

From the Cathedral we went to see the Last Supper, by Leonardo da Vinci, in the refectory of the Church of Santa Maria della Grazia.

The profane have invaded the sacred precincts of the church, and the ancient cloisters are now desecrated to the uses of a stable. But the room containing the picture still remains devoted to its exhibition. It is painted upon the wall, and occupies the entire width of the room. The figures are almost colossal, but their great size does not immediately strike one, from their perfect proportion. The picture is greatly defaced, but the wonderful beauty of the face of the Lord shines fair through all the harm that time and restoration have done to the rest of the painting, and shows the hand of the almost inspired master. What a pity that the great painter could not have had a foreshadowing of his own fame, and have painted his picture upon less perishable materials.

Sept. 26. Left Milan in the afternoon for Venice. Were stopped at Peschiera, a name of which the Yankee "pesky" is an undoubted corruption. We had counted upon the hour given in Bradshaw for rest and refection; on the contrary, we spent it in awaiting the slow progress of the investigations by which our luggage was at last declared to be peaceful. The examination was courteously conducted, and not unnecessarily minute; but the use of the passports was not quite clear.

One is in the habit of supposing that peculiar

institution to be a means of identifying the traveller as the innocent individual accredited by his own government to the good faith of all others. That view of the subject turns out to be a mistake.

The officer received the passports, en masse, on our alighting from the train; it is the first time that we have produced them. After the examination of the luggage, a great rush ensued, all the travellers gathering as closely as possible to the counter of the pen within which we had been hitherto confined. A clerk entered with a huge pile of passports under his arm, and proceeded to cry the names thereto affixed, to the best of his Italian power. The individual was fortunate who could see his own passport as it was held up, as he could then interpret the next cry into his own name, and reclaim his property.

They were, at last, all delivered, duly vised, but whether our eyes and noses correspond to the declaration, or we be adherents of Garibaldi in disguise, the Austrian government will never know. We passed through Vincenza, Padua and Verona, with a strange sense of familiarity thrilling us from the old Shakspearean associations; but notwithstanding the ciceronean assurances of some of the party, we did not see the tomb of Juliet. Arrived at Venice about half-past ten, and rowed up the Grand Canal in a floating omnibus, which brought us at last to the Hotel Victoria, once the Molini Palace.

I was awakened in the morning by the plash of oars, and the sharp warning cry of the gondoliers, as they rounded the corners of the buildings into the various canals. Our windows look upon a narrow canal, heavy and green, upon which float all kinds of tribute from the Venetian kitchen. According to our usual custom we had ordered rooms as low as possible to avoid the necessity of superfluous climbing. They were readily accorded us here, but as we were ushered up to the fourth story to the dining room, it was not so great an advantage as we had supposed.

We land from the gondola at the threshold of a spacious and lofty hall, with marble floor and seats, from which open the booking office and the various bureaus of such an establishment. A kind of gallery runs round the upper part of the hall, with windows by which it is overlooked from the first story.

In the conversion of palace to hotel, the spacious saloons have been subdivided into bed rooms, eating halls, &c., and the fanciful patterns of the concrete floors are deprived of their designs by the utilitarian divisions.

We had been recommended to this hotel as being upon the square of St. Mark, but except that it is built upon the same little island with the square of St. Mark, that is a mistake.

After breakfast, we sallied forth to visit the square. By means of a slight balcony that overhung the canal, we reached a narrow passage, damp and dirty, very like the side alleys by which one may reach back entrances in some of our cities. In this, and many others, it is possible to touch the walls upon both sides at once. The larger streets are seven or eight feet in width, filled with shops, long, dark and narrow.

After turning sundry corners in these dismal lanes, we emerged, at last, through an open vaulted court, into the veritable square of St. Mark. It has around its sides the Church of St. Mark, the Ducal Palace, and the public buildings. The Campanile is here; indeed the square is the centre of interest in Venice. Long colonnades run round the open space, filled with tempting shops, gold and silver work and jewels constituting the greater part of the display, and on one side are multitudes of cafes.

The custom of begging by means of merchandise is here carried to great perfection. We were pursued by most pertinacious venders of articles of every description, from the pretty shell ornaments peculiar to the place, down to a live mud turtle, the proposed use of which did not appear.

The Church of St. Mark is singularly brilliant in effect, albeit it is so unlike ordinary church architecture, that we were at first in doubt as to its character. It is adorned in front with large pictures of mosaic, brilliantly colored and gilded. Above the entrance are bronze horses, said to be very perfect, which have undergone various mutations of fortune, having been brought among Venetian spoils from Constantinople, carried to Paris by Napoleon, and finally restored by the French. The interior of the church is wonderful, in being of mosaic from floor to dome. The pictures of the walls, the entire ceiling—in fine all that is usually accomplished in ornament by painting, is here done by mosaics. The tesselated floor has sunk in many waves from the yielding of the foundations. Indeed the only wonder is that such heavy edifices are not prostrated by the slow sapping of the seas, during the ages in which they have poured their sluggish tide through the long rows of piles upon which they are built.

This church was erected in the ninth century, and was constructed and enriched by the spoils of Byzantine architecture. The Baptistery, which is the oldest part, is entirely Greek; the font is of porphyry upon a marble pedestal. A tomb in the chancel is said to contain the relics of St. Mark, brought from Alexandria and deposited, with great pomp, in this shrine. Behind this tomb are several slender pillars, which tradition affirms to have been originally brought from Solomon's Temple. A lighted taper behind them showed them to be translucent.

Some of the doors are of Corinthian brass, or, as we should call it, bronze, of great antiquity, magnificently wrought, not by casting, but by the chisel and hammer. These are also Greek spoils. There is shown, in one of the chapels, a stone which, as the guide related, has the legendary importance of having been brought from Mount Sinai. Our cicerone was an intelligent person, belonging to the church, and was particular in his statements; and when he related sundry traditional miracles, he took care to prefix "the tradition says;" on being questioned as to their authenticity, he shrugged his shoulders in a manner which showed that he laid the responsibility of credence upon those of his hearers.

From the church we went to the Ducal Palace, the mysterious seat of the doges, of whom we have read and dreamed so much, and, I think, with about as much sense of their living reality as if they had belonged to a fairy tale.

A broad flight of marble steps leads up to the corridor, which runs along the front of the palace. From that ascends the golden staircase, trodden only by sovereigns, at the top of which the doges were crowned. We, albeit sovereigns in our own right, were shown a plainer way into the magnificent halls, written, to the spiritual eye, with histories more splendid and more dark than crowd the page of any other nation upon earth — Rome excepted.

The walls are covered with the paintings of Tintoretto, Bassano and Titian, fresh and gorgeous as if wet from the brush of to-day. They are both allegoric and historic, representing the power and the conquests of Venice in her splendid ages, with portraits of all the doges and many senators.

Besides the grand state apartments, we saw the council chamber and ante-chamber, the inquisitors' chamber and its ante-room, which sent a chill through my blood at the thought of the invisible record upon those walls, awaiting the fiery summons which shall call it into legible and fearful openness. There were also exhibited the doge's private apartments, all adding to their historic interest the unfading lustre of art. The Austrian government turns the splendid palace to account by making it the depository of a library and a museum of art.

We were attended by a poor old guide, whose occupation is evidently almost gone. He paced hurriedly along these charmed halls and lofty staircases, restlessly conning, in a whispered utterance, the tale of history or explanation which he was to recite at the next stage of exploration.

After traversing the palace we went to the Bridge of Sighs, which connects it with the state prison on the other side of the canal. It is a closely covered handsome stone bridge, high above all possibility of scrutiny from below — through the openings of whose ornaments, the condemned caught his last glimpse of the outer world.

The business-like haste of the guardians of all places of such profound interest, leaves you no opportunity of surrendering yourself to the spirit of the place, and gives you continually a sense of unreality; in consequence of which you often enjoy the remembrance of an interesting spot, with a keener relish than in its actual presence.

We returned to descend into the palace prisons. One dark narrow cell is styled the "merciful," having a pallet, and a window, not, indeed, opening to the light of heaven, but into the lighted passages. Here the prisoner passed the interval between accusation and condemnation. I doubt if any interval was wont to elapse between condemnation and execution, we saw no place allotted to it, but a small space deeply enclosed by double doors, where secret criminals were garroted.

Thank God for the nineteenth century! I do not belong to those who worship an ideal past.

As the traveller, in gazing at a long range of fair mountains upon the distant horizon, catches only the undulating outline of the sunlit peaks, and sees nothing of the dark chasms and fearful depths between; so the dreamer, surrounded by the evil and folly and pettiness of to-day, turns longingly backward to the far vision of the centuries, where he can dimly discern the splendors of military prowess, the grandeur of art, and the magnificence of almost fabulous wealth; forgetting the savage defiles of crime, and the dark secrets of abomination, and woe, and cruelty that cursed the earth through all those barbarous ages, when, wherever the palace rose on high, the dungeon lurked below. It is only when one looks down from above, that he can take in the true proportions of nature or humanity.

After lunching, as one should in Venice, in the open air, we took a gondola for the Academy of Fine Arts, on the Grand Canal, where we enjoyed a great treat. One never ceases to regret that so much of the genius of the great masters was employed upon subjects in which we cannot sympathize.

But in looking at such a picture as Titian's Assumption, we forget all dislike of the subject in admiration of the painting. There is another great picture of Titian here, the Entombment; but heterodox as it may be, I much prefer Rubens' Descent. I have no doubt that the highest appreciation of art places Titian almost at the head of painters, but I am not equal to his pictures, and found far more pleasure even in such a picture as Raphael's Julius Second. There is a splendid modern picture in the Academy, of Nebuchadnezzar Receiving the Prophetic Warning of Daniel.

We left the Academy reluctantly at the hour for closing, and spent the afternoon in floating upon the Grand Canal, listening to the continual chime of the musical bells, and hearing names familiar to the lips of the gondolier, which have seemed to us to belong only to the realms of fiction.

We passed palace after palace, once adorned by wealth and rank and beauty, but now inhabited only by domestics, or let to foreigners; while their noble heritors either suffer forced exile, or endure voluntary expatriation in preference to the Austrian yoke. The hate of the Austrian rule is very apparent, but fourteen thousand Austrian bayonets within the decaying city are strong arguments to patience.

The Grand Canal is three hundred feet wide, winding in a serpentine line through the midst of the city, and spanned in the middle by the bridge of the Rialto.

We rowed, the next day, about the lagunes and among the beautiful islands, of which there are more than seventy making up the city.

The only way to see the beauty of this ancient realm, is to recede to such a distance upon the waters that the view can take in dome and tower and column and palace, the strange picture that "floats double," city and shadow, upon the still waters of the Adriatic. And, circling ever about the silent city, it seems ever at the same dreamy distance; and you wonder always what may be within its heart, if you could only get at it, and what is now the life within the walls of the Foscari and the Contari.

You have always known that it was a city whose streets are water, and in which the sound of wheels is never heard; that it is filled with palaces and churches, and that the doges held a mysterious fearful sway within these walls; and that is all you know now, and it seems as much of a dream as ever.

These dark green waters are as near an approach to the wave of Lethe as one will find in modern times; and as you float lazily, amidst the soft breath of the Venetian sky, which envelopes you like a bath, it is no very easy thing to bring your thoughts to the sharp edge of a business world and its every day affairs. Nothing about you invites you to do so. Boats lie upon the water laden with fruits and vegetables which the owners seem in no haste to sell; others, piled with grapes, go trailing along to the wine-press; here is a gondolier fishing, and there another basking at full length in the sun. Nothing seems alert upon the waters; and as you watch the noiseless dip of the long oar, you feel the Yankeeism oozing out at the finger ends; and grow as dreamily indolent as if you were to the manor born.

The avocations of the inhabitants are, in no degree, of an industrious aspect; but there is one profession there, which seems to me the sublimity of the dolce far niente. The stock in trade consists of a slender pole, pointed with a rusty nail, usually the possession of a squalid old man, who applies the nail to the side of your gondola, as it touches the step of the pier, and then holds out his unsightly cap for a recompense.

I could fancy Venice to be a far better place to visit with a traveller's enjoyment than to live in. The canals and lagunes are full of the associations of fiction—and they are full of many other things also; and if one had ever harbored the intention of suicide by drowning, it is not in Venice that he would choose to carry it into execution.

And then the mosquitoes! they make night as well as the face hideous, and the traveller is fairly driven out of the domain of the Queen of the Adriatic by a tiny weapon more potent than the Austrian bayonet.

We left Venice in the soft gray dawn of a cloudless morning. The moon shone full and fair upon the deserted waters, as we floated down to the railway. No sound of step or hum of voice arose from the noiseless city, which slept upon the waves as if it had been the city of the dead; and as we sped along the causeway through the sea, we seemed to be awaking from some oriental dream, rather than "doing" a city in the business-like fashion of the nineteenth century.

CHAPTER XI.

ITALY.

Padua — Bologna — Appennines — Florence —Pisa — Leghorn — The Mediterranean — Civita Vecchia.

SEPT. 29. We arrived early at Padua, which brings up Shakspearean memories, despite our actual experience there.

It was the first time that we had learned the utter helplessness of a mute traveller. Not a soul knew any thing except Italian; and as that mellifluous language happens to be lacking in the gift of tongues with which we are clothed, they had it all their own way, and an Italian way is sure to be a bad one, so far as order or system is concerned.

However, one learns language rapidly under the discipline of necessity, and we did obtain, even at Italian hands, a cup of tea and a piece of bread, besides a seat in a carriage to Ferrara. We had a note of commendation from our Boniface at Venice to the landlord of the Croce d'Oro, at Padua, but it seemed to avail us nothing, except, perhaps, the ensuring us a passage to Ferrara instead of the regular stopping at Ponte-lag oscuro. The crossing at the latter place was a contrast to ordinary travelling. The swarm of vehicles brought up suddenly from a prosperous journey, at a very Styx; the Charons of the rude ferry boats urged their craft slowly along the shore, culling their fare from the impatient crowds of mingled nationalities upon the bank, and rowed us leisurely across the sluggish waters of the Po, amid surroundings which seemed to have been unchanged for a century.

The journey was a drive of nine hours, including two hours' detention at a wretched roadside inn; where dinner was served by a sort of industrious man of all work, to whose garments adhered the dust, hay, cobwebs, feathers, and odors which denoted the multifarious duties of his calling.

It is impossible for an American to comprehend, without having seen, the amount of time, vociferation, quarrelling and blunders necessary to get a diligence under weigh in this land; to say nothing of the "lookers on in Vienna," who have nothing earthly to do except to add to the confusion and beg.

The drive was through a perfectly level country, upon a superb road, smooth as a floor, and stretching as far as the eye could reach in either direction, between rows of tall poplars, bordered by fields of tolerable cultivation.

The poplar of Lombardy is quite a different affair from its namesake on our side of the water, and a really handsome tree. The vine, which is here apparently only an incidental crop, is festooned along low trees, forming a kind of hedge about the fields, without, however, shading the growth below. The wine of the country is harsh and crude, partaking largely of the nature of mingled ink and vinegar.

The cattle are remarkably fine; large, well-made creatures, nearly white, with wide, spreading horns, retaining some of the characteristics of their Alpine neighbors.

After the custom of these countries to turn every thing feminine to useful account, the cows are employed in labor quite as much as oxen. A very good type of the civilization appears in a team whose motive power is, conjointly, a woman and a cow.

The women of the peasantry throughout the continent strike one painfully; there is nothing womanly about them; they look harder and uglier than the men, and it is difficult to see how they could ever have been attractive.

Then, the beggars spring up at every step of the way, like grasshoppers. The little child, just able to learn the whine of the mendicant; the sturdy lad who makes a cartwheel of himself for your especial edification, or clings to your carriage step with a doleful story about his "povre padre" or "madre;" the little girl, who wails forth a forlorn ditty to remind you that you are in the land of song; the mother with her baby in her arms; the gray-haired old woman who improves the intervals of begging by spinning on a portable distaff; the bleared, squalid old man, with his greasy cap under your nose; and worst of all, the veritable lord of creation himself, who touches the strap of your portmanteau, and stands inexorable as fate for something which sounds like zecchi; all hasten to swarm about the doomed traveller, as if his only object in travelling were to dispense money by the way side.

It is intolerable, to find your heart growing indifferent to the tokens of want, or harrowed by the incessant sights and sounds of a loathsome humanity. This beautiful country needs nothing but the people to make it smile into Paradise, but at present a sense of disgust is interwoven with all that it presents of attraction.

After being ferried over the river at Ponte-lag oscuro, to the evident disgust of the commissioner who accompanied the long train of carriages, we were driven to Ferrara, and interpreting our ticket literally, he carried us two miles beyond the railway station, which was our proper destination, to the city of Ferrara, how degenerate from the splendor which the name calls to mind. However, after some vexatious delays, we arrived safely at Bologna, a very ancient city, whose sidewalks run through arcades beneath the upper stories of the dwellings. It seemed to me to bear a Moorish aspect, and is just now remarkable for having been the last place of Northern Italy wrested from the papal dominion.

We had rail from Bologna to Vergato, and thence a most charming route, by diligence, across the Appenines to Pistoja. The carriages were easy and well appointed, and the long cavalcade of diligence and voiture swept along the smooth road like a whirlwind. The road lay along a valley, or in easy undulation for about half the way, and a railway, in process of construction, followed the same route. Then additional horses were attached, and we toiled, although still rapidly, up a veritable mountain pass, the same splendid road winding through the difficult ways, and bridging the narrow gorges.

The scenery, without being grand, is wild and picturesque; the hills often crowned with chateau and village, and, even with the Alps by heart, some of these were very respectable mountains.

In this part of the way the railway exhibits magnificent engineering. The road makes straight through the depths of the mountains by tunnels, which are beautiful in their solid strength, and in one place is carried over a long gorge upon a set of massive arches, which will challenge the admiration of many generations.

Through all this beautiful country, with the tramp of Roman legions ringing in your ears, there is the same literally running accompaniment, the same eternal whine. You cannot give the friendly look of recognition which was so heartily returned in Germany, for it makes you ashamed of your race to find the return only an application for money. We have never seen a peasant in the country clad in a new, or clean, or whole garment; as for the children, they, happily, do not suffer in this climate by the grievous lack of any.

We thundered down from the hills at a rate like the travels of the great Napoleon, and whirled through a most beautiful plain, cultivated and ornamented. The mountains had been covered with grand chestnuts, the plain was filled with figs, peaches, vines and olives. The charming scene made one long for the time when the iron heel of tyranny and priestcraft shall be lifted from the down-trodden head of knowledge and industry, and the people and the soil be permitted to develope resources which will make Italy the garden of the earth. There is much in the soil and productions of the country to remind us of our own country.

From Pistoja we came again by rail to Florence, and have been watching the dying tints of sunset upon the still waters of the Arno.

Sept. 31. We made a short tour of exploration among the beautiful mosaics of Florence, a work of art of which the city is jealously proud—and then went to the Uffizi palace.

It does not become me to speak of the merits of such a gallery. I can only mention some of the things that particularly interested us; among which, of course, stands pre-eminent the Venus de Medici. It is a wonder of beauty; the figure and limbs outstrip rivalry, but to my poor taste, Powers has more than once surpassed it in feature and expression. I suppose it is entirely in keeping with the different ages, that the centuries in which life was mainly material and sensuous, should produce its highest perfection in the delineation of merely physical nature, without much regard to that soul beauty which constitutes for us the highest type of loveliness.

Of the paintings, I liked best two demi-figures of great beauty—a Magdalen by Dolci, and La Vierge des Douleurs, by Salvi. There were, also, among the most valuable pictures, two by Rubens, Silenus and a Satyr, and a group of Bacchanals; a Magdalen and a St. Francis, by Allori; a Virgin and Child; The Virgin of the Well; St. John in the Desert; a portrait of Charles the Fifth, and another of Julius the Second, all by Raphael. A head of Medusa, by Da Vinci; a head of St. John, by Corregio, a splendid picture; San Carlo Borromeo and the Sufferers by Pestilence, by Bonatti; a Virgin and Child, by Titian; Judith and Holofernes, by Artemisia Gentilischi; St. Zanobi restoring a child to life, by Ghirlandajo; and a beautiful Cascade of Teverone, at Tivoli, by a French artist, Tierce.

One small room was filled with exquisite sculptures in bas relief, of which two were especially beautiful, the death of the wife of Francis Tornabuoni, and the recluses of Vallombrosa attacked in the choir by the Simonites. Many of these charming sculptures have been mutilated by soldiers lodged in the monastery of St. Salvi, where they were preserved.

One room is filled with gems and vases of great price. Among the most interesting, although perhaps not the most appreciable things in the immense collection, are sketches and studies by the great masters of art, Titian, Raphael, Guido, Da Vinci, Salvator Rosa, Poussin, and many others.

In the same palace is a library, in which we saw the manuscripts of Tasso, Dante, Boccacio, and Virgil; also illuminated books, printed on vellum, and adorned with exquisite designs by pen and brush. Splendid vellum editions of Homer, Virgil, and Dante, and illuminated missals of great beauty testify to the perfection to which both the arts of printing and painting were carried in ages which we are apt to dispose of summarily, by considering them as little removed from the middle darkness.

The gallery of the Pitti palace contains far more of interest than that of the Uffizi. Here were some magnificent portraits by Raphael, Da Vinci, and Tintoretto; marine pictures by Salvator Rosa; a Venus and Vulcan, by Tintoretto; Narcissus, by Curradi; a Virgin and Child, by Murillo; the Hospitality of St. Julien, by Allori; Diogenes, by Dolci; St. John, by the same; a grand St. Peter, by Guido; a very fine Cromwell, by Lely; Leo the Tenth, by Raphael, with countless repetitions of the favorite sacred subjects, by the masters; all striking for some peculiar excellence.

Not being able to make such a stay in Florence as would enable us to study these splendid galleries, it became necessary to pass by numberless pictures of interest, and to fix the attention upon the few most pleasing to our individual tastes. And a great pleasure it was, but one more easily garnered up in the memory than described by any thing short of a catalogue.

Scattered about the saloons were tables of great beauty, mosaics of precious stones, one of green malachite, very like the splendid table at Chatsworth.

We came away unsatisfied, with a deepened reverence for the power of the few masters whose works, even amid so much genius, stand out pre-eminently and unapproachably, the acknowledged sovereigns of art. We still look back to the Descent from the Cross as first among the pictures that we have yet seen, although I doubt if Rubens would have the first place if judged by his other works.

Oct. 1. Visited the Duomo, but did not find its interior present unusual interest. It is filled with busts and statues, and an unfinished Pieta, by Michael Angelo himself, stands behind the High Altar.

The exterior is of black, white, and green marble, and beautiful indeed. My friends went to the top of the Campanile, but I contented myself meanwhile with a stroll, in the course of which I went through a market, filled to profusion with fruits and vegetables, tomatoes, peaches, lemons, and huge bunches of grapes that reminded one of Eschol, and all at prices ludicrously small.

There is something very fascinating in the vagabond life which, by common consent, the traveller may live in this luxurious climate; supplying his own wants how and where he will, and roving at pleasure among the choicest works of ancient and modern art. We went to the Church of San Lorenzo, but found it closed, to our great chagrin. It contains the tombs of the Medici, and the great statues of Night and Morning, by Michael Angelo. We visited also the home of this great artist. The splendid suite of apartments, once the scene of his labors and enjoyments, is kept in beautiful preservation. The walls are covered with frescoes or hung with paintings, some of them by the master himself. Here are some of his own works in bas relief, and studies and models of his great work at Rome. His own furniture still occupies his library, and the tiny cabinet is unchanged, in which sprang into being the wonderful creations which he afterwards embodied for the world, and there still remains his own portrait, painted by himself. The house is still in the possession of the Buonarotti family, and they do honor to the great name, by the sedulous care with which every relic of the painter is preserved fresh and inviolate.

We passed the Casa Guidi, the home of one who loved Italy with her whole great heart, and went to Powers' studio. The New World has vindicated her claims to genius, even beside the undying memorials of Grecian and Italian art.

Mr. Powers has certainly the power of transfusing the ideal or the individual into his marble heads, as the ancients did not often do, perhaps because there was not so much to delineate in the faces of their models, but his figures must yield to the beauty of the

Greek. One may study sculpture in the streets of Florence. Art, here, bestows her charms as prodigally as nature showers the abundance of her riches. Statues are every where. I could not help wondering how long the Perseus of Benvenuto Cellini would have remained unmutilated in the line of great thoroughfare in the cities of our own land.

We drove home by the Uffizi, by the portico of statues, where stand, in stately order, beneath the colonnade, statues of men whose names may well make Italy proud, for they number among them the pious, the learned, poets, painters, and sculptors, at whose feet the world does homage.

Florence is a truly beautiful city, and a most enticing place of residence for a foreign winter. It combines the charms of art, society, and climate, in no ordinary degree, and the government wisely throws all its attractions open to the population of strangers which resort hither. The garb or the speech of a foreigner is a passport to palaces and galleries, which are quite inaccessible to the native inhabitants.

We leave Florence with great regret that our plans of return to America forbid a longer stay amid so much attraction which we long to explore, and so many works of art which we long to revisit.

Oct. 2. Left Florence for Pisa; meeting in the railway carriage friends from America, whom we are to rejoin at Rome. We were unexpectedly delighted at Pisa. The leaning tower is a beautiful structure of marble, well rendered by the many pictures which we have seen of it. It is surrounded by columned galleries, upon which the broad inner staircase emerges; of marble so polished that one hesitates to trust his footing upon the undefended space, especially in such a wind as was blowing when we adventured ourselves upon the task.

The ascent is rendered rather fatiguing by the continual change in inclination, which disappoints the foot; and there is something nervously suggestive in the vast hollow depths into which we look from above. My own head fairly refused the narrow outer staircase of the last division, and I climbed, instead, a slender perpendicular iron ladder, let into the inner surface of the wall. There is a chime of seven bells upon the top, so arranged that the heaviest shall assist in counteracting the inclination of the tower.

The cracks in the marble staircase point conclusively to the solution of the question whether the inclination be intentional or accidental.

The tower is evidently unfinished; perhaps in consequence of the sinking of the foundation. It is a beautiful construction, the spiral colonnade giving it a very pleasing effect. Adjacent are the Cathedral, the Baptistery, and the Campo Santo; all of great interest and beauty.

The Cathedral is of the eleventh century; it is surrounded by a flight of steps, and is built of alternate layers of white and red marble. It has suffered like the Campanile, from the sinking of the foundations, but the irregularity does not strike one on a cursory view. The High Altar is very elaborate, built of marble and lapis lazuli. It has also sunk to such a degree as to have required a renewal of the front.

The church is filled with paintings, which, in general excellence, surpass those of any church that we have visited. Others have had fine paintings, but here are many, not one of which is destitute of great merit; and in coloring they are magnificent.

A beautiful head of St. Agnes, by Del Sarto, enriches the church. An immense alto relievo of one piece of marble represents the Temptation, with figures of Adam and Eve, of more than life size.

The serpent is represented with the head of a woman; which circumstance the guide apologetically assured me resulted from the ignorance of ancient ideas upon the subject.

There are here two other fine pictures by Del Sarto, whose paintings possess a great charm for me; the Virgin, with St. Thomas and St. John; and a St. Francis. Del Sarto died while engaged upon the last picture. There is a fine Judith by Allori; a copy, or rather a duplicate of the one in the Pitti Gallery. The church is filled with statuary and costly shrines; and the ornaments of the architecture are rich and varied. We were quite unprepared for the closing of the cathedral at the early hour of noon, and were, in consequence, deprived of the pleasure of dwelling with more minuteness upon some remarkably fine modern pictures; among which was one especially interesting, the Reception of Cœur de Lion at Pisa, during the Crusades.

Being excluded from the cathedral, we took refuge in the Baptistery; a circular building of Byzantine architecture, richly ornamented.

It contains, in the centre, an immense Greek font, surrounded by exquisite carvings in sixteen slabs, brought from Constantinople; each slab wrought in some curious device, different from its fellows.

The great curiosity of the place is the pulpit. It is a marvel of alto relievo; both the preaching and the reading desks are wrought in carvings of great delicacy, representing scenes in the life of the Saviour. One of the desks is in the form of a book supported by an eagle. The great rotunda gives a fine echo, which was put to the test by an attendant with a musical voice, who sang low chords, and they were returned with great precision and beauty.

The Campo Santo is a kind of spacious cloister around a green court, containing monuments, sarcophagi and statues. The walls are frescoed with numberless pictures, chiefly from sacred subjects. The most remarkable sarcophagus is that of the Countess Beatrice; there is another of the Emperor Hadrian; and many curious monuments of the ancients, exhumed in the vicinity of Pisa, are here preserved. The green plot in the centre contains earth nine feet in depth, brought from the hill of

Calvary, in fifty-three ship loads, during the Crusades. Altogether, Pisa is a place of unusual interest; although as a city, it wears an air of desolation. In the broad day we scarcely encountered a person in the streets, and the wide quay along the Arno was as silent as a Sabbath day.

From Pisa we proceeded to Leghorn, which we did not attempt to explore; and after the most vexatious experience of extortion and bullying, we found ourselves on board the little Italian steamer, bound to Civita Vecchia. The steamers do not come to the wharf, but lie along the mole at a considerable distance from the shore. We were on board an hour before the time of sailing, and it was amusing to watch the embarkations, and see the various ways in which the unlucky passenger, who hugged himself with the belief that he had made a secure bargain, was cheated or abused. We paid ten francs from the station to the steamer, where the officer comforted us with the assurance that it was seven francs too much.

However, we were on board, and the time for the departure came. It blew a stiff breeze, and the little buoyant boat rode the tossing waters like a bird, the only difficulty was that its occupants were not constituted like waterfowl. One after another the visages grew pensive, then serious; some quietly disappeared, others silently devoted themselves to a contemplation of the depths of the sea.

For my own part, I summoned all my intellectual resources to keep down the rebellious spirit within;

but there came a time when resistance ceased to be a virtue, and I gave in — unconditional surrender. The gale freshened, and the waves came sweeping over the deck; but nobody seemed to mind it, so long as he had energy to keep upright. At length the deck was deserted by all except Mrs. R., myself, and a pale young priest, who sat helplessly upon the planks, and smiled a ghastly sympathy at us in his better intervals. It grew wetter and wetter; there seemed no possibility of weathering the night on deck; we heard the sailors prognosticating a stronger blow, and it soon became apparent that we must betake ourselves to the confined depths below. But how to get there was a question.

The boat pitched like a see-saw, with a lateral roll superadded, which precluded the possibility of keeping our feet. The difficulty was solved by two sailors taking us each in their arms, and, watching their opportunity, they staggered with us across the deck to the gangway. Here dispossessing a score of sick outsiders, they lifted us down to the cabin. There the homme de chambre did his best to help us, but we were past help. My friend betook herself to her berth, and bore it bravely, but I lay upon the floor in a state of helpless abandon for which I have no name; not even the fleas moved me to resistance, nor could I bestow word upon friend or foe.

It was well that nobody was hungry, for the kitchen was upset in the beginning of the blow. My prevailing thought during the night was of our projected return from Naples to Marseilles by sea, and my heart sank and my stomach rose inversely. One consolation only mingled with it all—it could not last forever, and with the morning sun we dropped anchor at Civita Vecchia.

One would suppose that the next thing would be to land, but things are not done in that cursory way in the dominions of His Holiness. Rome has been threatened by sea before, and one never knows what may happen again.

The captain went on shore with the passports which we had given up at Leghorn, and after an absence of an hour and a half, he returned, accompanied by two or three small boats.

A man presently made his appearance on deck, with two bits of paper in his hand, from which he read the names of our own party. This turned out to be a permission to land, and we gladly proceeded to take our places in a boat, and rowed away.

It seemed ludicrous to leave the small number of passengers, innocent looking voyagers, ruefully awaiting the moment when the safety of the state should permit them to follow us. Our protector professed to be a commissioner under the especial auspices of the American Consul; and, having seen our passports, he had hastened to secure for us the earliest permit. Our citizenship stood us, for once, in good stead, for, in the examination of the luggage, the word American acted like magic, to close lock and strap upon a very respectful research.

We were duly accredited and seated in the railway carriage before the next detachment from the steamer made its appearance. As for those of the passengers forced by this delay to wait for the next train, one could easily imagine their disgust after such a night.

The train proceeded to Rome, a distance of forty-five miles, in three hours and a half, stopping at frequent intervals, sometimes in the midst of the desolate Campagna, without any apparent reason, perhaps to prepare the Pope, by degrees, for our approach. At last the long, low line of city, surmounted by dome and tower, rose to view — Rome, the city of the Cæsars — I cannot yet comprehend it.

We are established in the Bocca di Leone, near the Pincian Hill, and the associations of ages come surging over the petty present, and almost appal the thoughts. However, even in Rome one must rest, and we went to bed without bestowing many thoughts upon the Cæsars.

CHAPTER XII.

ITALY.

Rome — St. Peter's — Vatican — Capitol — Forum — Coliseum — Naples — Herculaneum — Pompeii — Museum — Chapels — Pausilippo.

OCT. 4. We strolled down to the "yellow Tiber," crossed the classic river in a ferry boat, certainly not less rude than that which carried Cæsar, followed a long dusty footpath, as lonely and uninteresting as any by-way in New England, and passed under an arched and sentinelled gateway, into a silent street, which led to the great colonnade in front of St. Peter's.

This wonderful edifice, like the mighty works of Nature, needs time to comprehend its vastness. It covers two hundred and forty thousand square feet, and is four hundred and forty-eight feet high. I think, however, that it is impossible, by statistics, to gain any conception of St. Peter's.

The disposition of the noble porticoes which lead to it, the immense façade which effectually conceals the height of the great dome, the wide rectangular columns, the breaking of the outline between the roof and the columns, and the colossal size of figure, both in painting and sculpture, all tend most artfully to diminish the proportions of the mighty structure, and it requires a continual effort to remember that it is the greatest of all Cathedrals. Perhaps one of the best proofs of its immense extent is that you are continually forgetting it, and stray about the aisles and chapels to gaze upon the works of art within them, as if you were under the open air of Heaven.

I do not think there is any point of vision in the interior from which we may gain an adequate idea of its size as a unity, as can be done in the cathedrals of Northern Europe.

We traversed the wide space in front of the church, and found that, also, altogether deceptive to the eye. In the middle stands the great obelisk of the Vatican; one of those brought from Heliopolis, and erected upon its present pedestal in the sixteenth century.

I do not propose to attempt any description of St. Peter's; or to do more than glance at a few of the most striking features of its interest. If one should write a volume, there would still be something left; and, so far as impressions go, I know, by experience, how impossible it is to convey them to others, upon a subject like this.

We found High Mass in progress of celebration, with all the mummery of priest and host, procession and torches. Several masses were said in different parts of the church, while we remained; and a score might go on at once without interference. The distant chants strive against the overwhelming space — and die.

In the first chapel to the right of the entrance, is a

famed Pieta, by Michael Angelo, inscribed with his own name. Sculptures abound every where, chiefly monumental; some very fine, by Canova. I believe his tomb of Clement the Thirteenth is considered to be, not only the finest sculpture of St. Peter's, but the most distinguished of his own productions. The Pope is a majestic figure, in the attitude of prayer, supported by two figures of Death and Religion. Two enormous couchant lions lie at the base; one of which, represented sleeping, is a splendid work. A bronze statue of St. Peter sits in the nave, not far from the High Altar, and thither came the devout, in almost continuous procession, to kiss his toe, which is suffering materially from the devotions of ages.

Before the High Altar, a circular marble balustrade surrounds a sunken space, to which descends a double flight of marble steps; and there, immediately under the dome, kneels a figure of Pius the Sixth, before the crypt which is supposed to contain the relics of St. Peter. A hundred lamps shine, night and day, around this sacred enclosure; a transfer of the Vestal fire well calculated to win favor in Roman eyes; and above the most consecrated altar hangs an elaborate canopy, or baldacchino. Higher up, the eye seeks the majestic dome, which almost seems the vault of heaven brought down to earthly eyes; and in its apex is a representation which chills a Protestant heart; the Jehovah himself in visible form. In the tribune hangs an enormous chair, said to enclose the identical chair in which the Apostle was crowned.

The mosaics of St. Peter's are far finer than the sculptures. Three especially seemed to me to surpass all the others; the copies of Raphael's Transfiguration; Domenichino's Sacrament of St. Jerome, and Guido's Crucifixion of St. Peter. The Incredulity of St. Thomas, by Cammuccini, is also very fine.

We returned by the bridge of Hadrian, at the castle of St. Angelo; a fort, which if all tales be true, could speak volumes as to the craft and cruelty of the papal system — even at the present enlightened day. How enlightened this may be, one may perhaps judge from a tract put forth during this very year under the authority and signature of the Pope himself. It purports to have in view the comforting and strengthening of the faithful in these times so disastrous to the true church, by refreshing their memory with a history of a miraculous picture of our Lord, recently exhibited to the public. This portrait is averred to have been sketched by St. Luke, I think the night previous to the Crucifixion. In the morning the picture was found miraculously completed. It was preserved with great care among the most sacred possessions of the eastern church, until the city in which it was deposited (I do not remember where — possibly Damascus) was in danger of pillage. The brethren, in their anxiety lest the precious picture should suffer violence, sought divine direction with many prayers and tears; and being supernaturally advised, they went down to the sea and committed it to the waves. The picture set forth upright, upon its seaward journey, and the brethren returned to pray for its safety. Meanwhile the Pope having been warned in a dream, repaired, with the college of cardinals, to the mouth of the Tiber, there to await the developement of the mysterious command; when they saw this picture approaching, which leaped, dry and unharmed, into the arms of his Holiness, and was carried in great joy to Rome; having made the passage of the Levant, rounded the peninsula, and sailed up the Sicilian coast, if I rightly remember, in about thirteen hours.

The degree of enlightenment, in which the highest authority of the church can gravely put forth such a statement to the people of the nineteenth century, scarcely admits a comment.

Oct. 5. To-day have visited in the Vatican, the Loggie, the Sistine chapel, the chapel of St. Paul, and the Museum; re-visited St. Peter's, went to the Capitol, the Forum, and the Coliseum.

I can say little of the Vatican, that one palace of the world. It is difficult to comprehend a structure containing four thousand four hundred and twenty-two rooms, and I bring away an impression of magnificent halls, and porticoes with splendid frescoes; grand staircases; and curious and precious works of art. Among the latter are some elegant vases of Egyptian alabaster and green basalt.

The Sistine Chapel was one of those overwhelming disappointments which I am willing, in all humility, to credit solely to my own lack of appreciation, since the world of art cannot be mistaken as to its excellence. I know it is a terrible heresy, but the famous dicture of the Last Judgment seemed not only disagreeable, but ludicrous. Here, again, is the embodiment of the Divine Father, and the conception of the scenes of the Judgment are material, puerile, and, in some respects, heathen; Charon figuring anew in this sort of baptized mythology.

Of the execution, I have of course no right to speak. The walls are covered with smoke-stained subjects from the life of Moses on one side, and of Christ on the other. The ceiling is crowded with pictures of Scripture history painted in small compartments, and the figure of Eve is faultless, even to ignorant eyes.

We left the Vatican to return again and again, and went to St. Peter's, which immediately adjoins it; and, leaving the wonders to be seen in it for another time, we tried to see *it;* to comprehend its vastness, to watch the perspective of retreating figures, to pace its length and breadth, and to grow accustomed to the height, ever and anon finding our attention rivetted by some charm of art, unseen before, and resting with increased admiration upon the St. Jerome and the Transfiguration.

Then we went down the Piazza again, and made our way through the city to the Capitoline Hill, and climbed the steps to that august presence, the Roman Capitol. Why is it that the shrines at which we have done mental reverence all our days, should seem such things of course, when we resolve them into the actuality of personal experience? The staircase to the Capitol seemed very like any other flight of steps, even with Castor and Pollux at the top; and the magnificent equestrian statue of Marcus Aurelius which confronts them, compelled a long pause of admiration, even there. It is the most splendid work of bronze I ever saw, and worthy of its noble model.

We found the picture gallery closed for repairs, but had ample food for admiration in the statuary. The bronze Wolf of the Capitol was a matter of legitimate interest. We found here the beautiful doves of Pliny, which are so often reproduced in brooches. The boy extracting a thorn from his foot is one of the most graceful of sculptured works; the engraving is one of my old admirations. The Amazon, the Antinous, the Cupid, and the Fawn of Praxitiles need no description of their faultless proportions. Indeed, in touching upon world-renowned art, any thing beyond the names seems to belittle their dignity.

Pre-eminent in the Capitol, is the Dying Gladiator. I have no words to describe the wonderful power of the round, compact, muscular frame; and the still more wonderful effect of the strong self control of mortal agony fading into dim unconsciousness, as "the drooped head sinks gradually low" in death. It is the only ancient sculpture that I have seen, where the perfection in physical developement is combined with the higher power of perfect expression.

From the Capitol, we descended to the Forum, to me the most profoundly interesting spot of this strange city. Who does not feel that he knows the Roman Forum? Yet here, amid broken shaft and crumbling arch, massive foundation and defaced capital, each one spells out, with difficulty, his own theory of the extent and character and position of the spot which once sent forth the silver streams of eloquence, or hurled the angry thunders of defiance to the echoes of the world. And above the mass of nameless ruins, still stands a fragment of the portico; the silent symbol, eloquent above all utterance, of magnificence and oblivion. No tangled wilderness ever seemed to me so desolate as the Roman Forum.

Then, by the Sacred Way, along which the imperial city was wont to pour its living flood, we wended our almost solitary way, beneath the Arch of Titus, to the Coliseum.

This immense structure has been stripped of its marble exterior to build the palaces of later Rome; but the inner construction still remains, perfect in extent, and, in some places, in its height. It is an immense oval, surrounded by a triple row of arched colonnades, broad and massive still; from which open in frequent transverse arch, the staircases leading to the stalls which overlooked the arena. The amphitheatre rises, story above story, to the height of more than one hundred and fifty feet, its broad colonnades resembling the streets of a city. Below the present level sward lie the dens in which the wild beasts were confined; and one could fancy the scenes of almost forgotten ages again present to the view. Here gathered the imperial purple and the plebeian serge, the haughty patron and the cringing client, to quench the common thirst of cruelty. All watched with eager, cruel eyes, the mortal combat of the gladiators; those barbarians whose animal ferocity was stimulated to the utmost by the applause of the equally ferocious crowd; or perhaps deepened by the long hunger for freedom.

Into that very arena have been thrown delicate women, to be gored out of the shape of humanity; and there have stood Christian men, by thousands, to struggle to the last mortal extremity with savage beasts, until they were torn limb from limb; and the roar of the lion was mingled with the roar of the eighty thousand incarnate fiends that thronged the mighty theatre.

The blood of the slaughtered saints, which cries from that fearful soil to heaven, has not been unavenged. The sentence of retribution is written upon fallen shaft and shattered fane; upon buried palace and forgotten temple; the city sitteth solitary which was full of inhabitants; and the once fruitful Campagna lifts its blasted face to the summer sky, scorched by the fiery breath of desolation. Rome is to me oppressively sad. It seems impossible to identify the imperial city, the mistress of the world, the home of the ancients, whose names make the page of history splendid, with the ruined dust, upon which have arisen the temples of a pagan Christianity, the galleries of almost divine art, the palaces of insignificant despotism, and the substratum of squalid poverty and lazy mendicity.

Oct. 9. If we were disposed to erect a superstructure of vanity upon slight foundations, we might fancy ourselves people of mark, inasmuch as to make an innocent journey to Naples it was necessary to obtain permission of the paternal government of Rome. Then, not content with having satisfied itself that we had brought nothing objectionable into the kingdom, it must needs be assured that we carried nothing out; so we were duly examined and visèd before leaving the Father's dominions. Then, of course, United Italy must protect herself from our inroads, so the same ceremony was repeated across the frontier, a few yards further on. I do not know whether the effect is more ludicrous or wearisome, to be stopped, on a prosperous journey, at some little wayside shed, and watch the process of discharging the vans of all the travellers' gear, without even the satisfaction of seeing the delay justified by a thorough search.

At the frontier between Rome and Naples, there was the usual amount of crowd and begging; one bright little rascal of ten was actually so accomplished as to beg in three languages.

The ragged, dirty countrymen gathered closely about, wearing a dress which is so picturesque in painting, and reminds one of banditti.

The substitute for shoes is primitive. A round piece of hide is wrapped around the foot, and pierced upon the edge with slits, through which a long strap is laced, and made fast by numerous turns about the leg. The women adopt the still more primitive fashion of going bare-footed; or wear the common slipper without heels, usually without stockings.

A large stone station-house was in progress of erection, and women and very young girls carried the heavy hewn stone and the tubs of mortar upon their heads, up the steep ladders, to the masons. We always see Italian peasants laden with baskets of grapes in the world of art; but the reality is of heavier calibre than grapes.

We were not yet done with passports. We must obtain permission at Naples to return; which permission must be again scrutinized on the way; and finally, our credentials were delivered into the custody of the police on our arrival at Rome, to be reclaimed by a fresh application at the bureau on the following day.

The whole operation would seem ludicrous, if it were not both annoying and expensive; but so far as we are individually concerned, the Papa has reiterated reason to feel perfectly at ease.

The route to Naples lies through a country, in some parts very beautiful. The Apennines are bare and barren, but it is surprising to see the luxuriance with which the vine flourishes upon the low hills, whose only soil seems to be the loose ashen debris of volcanoes. The villages are all perched on the summits of the peaked hills:

> "Like eagles' nest, hang on the crest
> Of purple Apennine,"

perhaps as a necessity of safety; perhaps because the air is healthier than in the plains. Still, it strikes one that there is a vast expenditure of climbing in Italy, to very little purpose.

It is very amusing to become suddenly aware of one's own importance by the operation of flying through an Italian village. It requires about five minutes, but, for that display, the horses are put to their mettle, and the whip, unlike any other instrument which bears the name, is tortured into convolutions that produce such cracks as are surely unknown to any other part of the civilized world. The speed and the noise together are something half alarming, half ridiculous, but produce an edifying effect upon the beholders.

One point of remark upon the way to Naples is a convent called Monte Casino, crowning the summit of a high hill, the first convent established in Italy, and said to be very rich in wealth and curious works of art.

I was unprepared to find Naples such a beautiful city, although why a city which has been the abode of a royal court for so many years, should not be beautiful, did not occur to me. It encircles the lovely bay in a sweeping crescent of great extent. Directly before the city, and breaking the sea outline, lie the picturesque islands of Ischia and Capri; and in the back ground rises the double peak of Vesuvius; as peaceful and innocent-looking a mountain as if it were not wont to overwhelm man and his works in deadly ruin.

Naples would seem to one traversing the streets, to be the one point of the earth where the productions of all climates and all soils gather to a common centre of abundance. Fruits, flowers and vegetables are heaped in combinations that cannot choose but be picturesque. Pomona herself could scarcely typify the luxuriant blessings of the country. What is peculiar here is, that the productions of the temperate zone do not disappear, as the earth warms into tropical growth. Apples and oranges, pears and pomegranates, peaches and figs, grapes and nuts, are piled side by side, while the lean, abused donkeys are laden with pyramids of panniers, bursting with vegetables, green, gold and scarlet; spring, summer and autumn, all blended in one.

We took the most respectable and vigorous of commissioners, and drove out, through Portici and Resina, to the strange city, once more open to the sunlight after seventeen hundred years of oblivion. We walked the deserted streets, whose pavements wear the mark of the wheels of two thousand years ago; we stood within the still gaily decorated walls, and explored the penetralia, and trod the mosaic floors of dwellings instinct with life and luxury when the Saviour lived in Galilee; and yet, before even all his own apostles had received the crown of martyrdom, these busy streets, and gorgeous temples, and human abodes were passing into oblivion beneath the ashen waves of that flood which came "when they knew not," and swept them all away. Nearly all the exhumed tokens of life have been removed, and are carefully preserved in the Museum at Naples; but street and house, theatre, temple, forum, and fountain are still as distinctly marked as in any city in the world, and one scarcely knows which excites the most wonder, the completeness of the destruction or the magnitude of the labor of restoration.

I remember one beautiful grotto, around a fountain in the court of a dwelling, which is composed of shells wrought into pictures and colored scrolls, the fine shell-work as minutely perfect as if it had been finished yesterday.

The mosaic floors of the vestibules still welcome us with "salve," or warn us with "cave canem." The dining rooms still wear their bright frescoes of game, and fruit, and flowers, and the leaden pipes are ready to spout water into the fountains and piscinia. The ranges are ready for fire, and wine is still stored in the cellars.

Upon the wall of one of the cellars is distinctly impressed the outline of a human figure, fled to this vain refuge, and even here sought out by the destroying element.

The Amphitheatre is very perfect, showing distinctly the gradations of the several tiers of seats, and the wall is entire to the top. It is very large, and of a slightly oval form.

There remain yet miles of excavation to be made, even after the labor of a hundred years. Still it is easy to comprehend the possibility of the work being successfully conducted at Pompeii, when the superincumbent mass consists of a loose soil of ashes and earth; we tried the hoe and pick ourselves, and found it not difficult; and with care the fine works of art distributed throughout the buried city may be well recovered. But it is a far different thing to go down into the solemn depths of Herculaneum. There one threads lofty black galleries, hewn out of the solid lava, firm as granite, the fiery flood having flowed in and filled every corner of the doomed city. Yet out of these recesses of blank darkness have been exhumed statuary, and pictures, and ornaments, public buildings have been identified and defined, even the books of the day have been rescued, and while the outer folds are burned to a cinder, the inner convolutions have been unrolled, and in many of them the Greek characters are perfectly legible at this day.

The most thoughtless heart must feel appalled within these shades of death, and escape to the abodes of life with a grateful sense of relief.

We drove home through the environs of Naples, where wine was streaming from the presses, and frames of maccaroni hung drying in the sun; the bright gay city in view on one hand, and the sunny bay stretching away into the western distance on the other. The element of mendicity seems to find its highest developement here. The halt, and maimed, and blind, and distorted, throng the streets, and thrust all that is painful and disgusting in humanity under your sight, until, amid all its beauty, the heart sickens at the thought of Naples.

We visited the Museum, which contains the wonderful treasures reclaimed from the depths of the buried cities. They fill many rooms, and consist of mosaics, statuary, frescoes, household implements and ornaments; in fine, every thing that belongs to the busy life of a great city—turned in one hour to the fixedness of the grave. Seventeen hundred Papyri, taken from the excavations, are here preserved, and some of the skeletons which abound in the ruins. The great amount of jewels and household decorations speaks of the immense wealth of these buried cities, yet, strange to say, no amount of coin has yet been discovered. The government is expecting that discovery when the banking streets shall be uncovered. But it would not be strange if the Romans had been beforehand with them, and had made sufficient explorations, after the catastrophe, to possess themselves of the bulk of the buried treasure. The number of the destroyed population has been variously estimated from thirty to forty thousand.

What seems a marvellous feature of the country

is, that beneath the very mountain from whose bowels flowed these desolating rivers of fire, men still build their cities and cultivate their fields. Within the memory of the children of twelve years, the mountain has disgorged its molten flood, and streets in Resina are still blocked up with the solid mass; and there they still live, as if bound by some magic fascination to tempt their fate. However, it is no more astonishing than the parallel in the moral world, which meets us every day and every where.

The Picture Gallery of the Museum is a very fine one, occupying a succession of spacious halls, and enriched by the works of Guido, Raphael, Corregio, Da Vinci, Titian, Rubens, Guercino, Domenichino, Claude Lorraine, and Salvator Rosa.

In one of the rooms sat a little fellow of ten years, the untaught child of the streets, modelling an infant Saviour, his little fingers as deftly expert upon the work of his brain as if he were a practised sculptor. It seems that the arts breathe in the air, and spring from the soil of Italy.

We drove about the city, and visited various churches, some of which contain remarkable works. Finest of all are those of San Severo, a private chapel attached to the palace of San Severo. In a subterranean chapel is a work superior to any thing I have ever seen, a veiled Christ, by San Martino. It is not that the fine outline of the figure has been preserved beneath the shrouding veil, but that the veil itself seems transparent, disclosing perfectly the minute features of expression, not only of the face, but of the sinews, and muscles, and veins of the limbs. It is the only sculpture, representing the Saviour, which has not been extremely painful to me; this, on the contrary, inspires a pleasing, tender awe. In the upper chapel is another veiled statue, that of a lady of the San Severo house, of great beauty, both of face and figure, the veil transparent as in the former statue — both these sculptures were the sole works of their authors. Opposite the lady above mentioned, stands her husband, enveloped in a net, which Cupid strives in vain to remove, symbolizing the retirement into which he fled on the death of his wife. Behind the altar is a magnificent alto relievo of almost colossal size, representing the Descent from the Cross. The chapel is small, but more remarkable than any thing of its kind in sculpture, especially in monumental designs. We visited several other churches, handsome in architecture, and filled with decorations of merit and interest. Some of the palaces and public buildings are very handsome.

We drove out of the city to the summit of a hill, commanding a fine panoramic view of the city and its beautiful bay. While Mrs. R. and myself enjoyed the view from the terrace of a pretty villa, the gentlemen visited the convent of San Lorenzo, within whose holy precincts no profane foot of womanhood is allowed to tread. It is remarkable for some fine paintings.

We were disappointed of a visit to the reputed

tomb of Virgil, by the rain, but drove through the long grotto of Pausilippo; an excavation in the solid rock forty-five hundred feet in length, by which the ancient Roman port of Pozznoli was connected with the more modern city of Naples. With Rome, it was connected by the Appian way, and was not only the southern port of entry, but a summer watering place for the Roman nobility. Here the great Apostle landed on his way from Syria to Rome.

The country below Naples is at present infested with the brigandage of which we have heard so much, and we did not attempt the drive along the shore to Sorrento. It is not a fortnight since a number of carriages were stopped on the return from Castellemare, robbed, and some of the travellers carried into the mountains to be held to ransom. They also attacked and plundered a convent, and maltreated the priests. The Neapolitans are excessively uneasy under the new government.

Accustomed to Naples as the seat of government, they consider their interests overlooked at Turin; while deprived of the advantages of trade which result from the presence of a court, they still feel the evils of the former state of affairs, together with the difficulties of getting a new regime into working order — and the benefits of a free government have to be waited for. So that all the discomforts of their transition state are popularly credited to the new system.

Our clever guide, Mauro, had lived in England, and

comprehended the difficulties and the blessings of freedom in a very sober way for one of his mercurial countrymen. I find that my idea of Italians has been divided between nobles and peasants, and I am perpetually calling myself to account for being surprised at seeing a community of well-dressed, well-bred gentlemen and ladies, who look precisely as if they had just walked out of Broadway. They are a very interesting people to me, with a healthful, genial naturalness, a ready sympathy, and a quick perception, very unlike what I had looked for in Italy. A system of public instruction is getting slowly established, and the thinking part of the people perceive that their hopes for the future of their distracted country, must rest mainly upon this agent of improvement. To those who look only at present results, Austrian Italy is the best governed part of the peninsula.

On our return to Rome, we remarked a large body of soldiery at several stations, where the railway nearly approached the hills; and were told that they alone secure the trains from the successful attacks of marauding banditti, who can make an easy escape thence through the Apennines. The peasantry and servants of the country wear a dress refreshing to eyes accustomed to the respectable sameness of ordinary male attire. They wear a green velvet postillion's jacket, with small clothes, and long white stockings and buckled shoes; while the conical hat is gay with rosettes and plumes.

Among the minor enjoyments of travel, has been an untold amount of education on the subject of currency. It requires a little time to become accustomed to pounds, shillings and pence; by the time this is fairly accomplished, it is necessary to transfer the calculations to the very different, although far easier method of francs and centimes; and we learn, besides, that the French system is the best basis to think upon, while on the continent. It is, therefore, with peculiar pleasure, that we discover that a silver groschen is equal to thirteen centimes, and a Prussian thaler to three francs and seventy-eight centimes; while a silver groschen is two-thirds of a good groschen.

Of course, the absolute value of any thing to be obtained by means of the aforesaid coins, sinks into insignificance, when compared with the importance of understanding the meaning of the money itself. But the groschen must needs be disposed of before entering the confines of Germany; for although it is financially true that five silver groschen are equal to seventeen and a half kreutzer; and seventeen of the same coin with two and one-eighth pfennings make a German florin; yet, practically, they are worth nothing at all, as they are utterly refused.

By this time, the complication of values has arrived at a point which puts a hasty, and at the same time an advantageous bargain out of the question; a fact which the venders of merchandise are not slow at turning to their own account.

And then the travelling accounts! One has need to congratulate himself upon a severe acquaintance with vulgar fractions to be sure of balancing the daily expenditures.

Then the Austrian Zwanziger, and the Italian Lira are each just near enough to a franc to introduce hopeless confusion into my own calculations; to say nothing of the fact that an Austrian florin differs from a German one by three-quarters of a kreutzer. The tornesi, carlini and grani of Naples are disappearing among the clumsy copper coins of United Italy; and it is really comfortable to recognize, in the baiocchi, pauls and scudi of Rome, a close resemblance to our own currency, such as enables one to form some ready conception of a price, without an exhausting demand upon the fiscal education.

It is very surprising that the currency of each small dominion can be so carefully confined within its own limits as to be rendered utterly useless every where else; but the arithmetical exercises necessary to such a tour as ours, are cogent arguments in favor of the universal adoption of the perfect metric system of Napoleon. I, for one, most heartily wish success to that particular aim of the present statistical Congress of Nations.

CHAPTER XIII.

ITALY.

Rome — St. Peter's — Vatican — Villa Borghese — Pincian Hill — Palaces Rospigliosi, Borghese, Barberini, Spada — Churches of St. Augustin, St. John in the Lateran, St. Maria Maggiore, St. Petro in Vineulo, Cappuccini — Scala Santa — Fountains — Catacombs — Columbaria — Baths — Genoa — Turin — Mont Cenis.

Oct. 10. Another day in the wilderness of Rome. We have been, to-day, under the auspices of a valet de place, to the dome of St. Peter's. In no way can one get so thorough an idea of the immense magnitude of St. Peter's, as by an ascent to the roof and the ball.

The way to the roof is by an inclined plane without steps, and the ascent easily accomplished. The roof itself is a broad expanse, flagged with stone, from which rise not only the huge dome, but smaller ones, which would seem imposing any where else.

It affords a fine view of the general scope of the city and the course of the Tiber, and especially of the Vatican and its gardens. No where else can the Vatican be so well seen in all its great extent.

The ascent to the dome is by staircases between the inner and outer walls, built at last in the same zigzags by which we have learned to ascend mountains. From the top of the dome the view is magnificent; the city, the Campagna and the distant hills forming a panorama as striking to the eye as stirring to the imagination. The sluggish Tiber pours its tide between the old and the new city, and my fancy filled the low hills on its right with the Etruscan armies, while the little wooden bridge was crashing to the waves behind the hero of Roman romance; and the buried dust of the ancient city stirred anew with the Fathers and the Commons of that iron time.

From the inner gallery you can examine the rough mosaics, made of large bits of stones, with wide cracks between, that produce such a grand effect from below, and you can gaze into the profound depth, and measure, from above, the height which every where defies your power of appreciation.

Finally, we climbed the perpendicular ladder, and ensconced ourselves within the hot circle, so small when seen from below, yet capable of containing sixteen persons. There are small loop-holes to admit air and light, and from them one can take in a succession of charming pictures, each distinctly framed by the sharp lines of the aperture.

Thence, after another stroll about the aisles of the church, through which it is impossible to hasten, we went to the Vatican gallery, a small but choice collection of pictures; I suppose the best of its size in the world. Among them, those which strike the unlearned taste most forcibly, are those also upon which the world of art has impressed its seal of approbation.

The best in our eyes were that magnificent Communion of St. Jerome, by Domenichino; Raphael's Transfiguration; Guido's Martyrdom of St. Peter; A Madonna and Child, with St. Thomas and St. Jerome, by the same hand; St. Jerome, by Da Vinci; Guercino's Incredulity of St. Thomas, and two splendid pictures by Murillo; The Mystical Marriage of St. Catharine, and The Return of the Prodigal. This gallery is unlike all others that we have visited. In others, even the finest, there have been scores of indifferent pictures, gilded Madonnas, with no merit beyond their age, painful distortions of the human figure, and countless paintings which have merit to the initiated, but which win no favor in the eyes of laymen. But in the Vatican there is no picture which one would not return, again and again, to study and admire.

We went also to the mosaic manufactory of the Vatican, where these great works are reproduced with minute fidelity; a labor far from being simply mechanical, but requiring a truly artistic eye. The completion of these exquisite copies requires from five to twenty years. They are made only for the disposal of His Holiness in gifts to royalty, or for the adorning of the great churches. Besides the knowledge of art necessary to copy figure and color, it seems to me to require great skill to proportion the size of the stones and the minuteness of finish to the distance from which the work is to be viewed. That perfect proportion is one of the chief marvels of St.

Peter's, and demanded nothing less than a Michael Angelo to combine the architect with the artist.

At the Rospigliosi palace, the one great attraction is Guido's Aurora, a picture beyond all praise, beautiful as a dream, and a grateful relief to the eye wearied by Madonnas. One might easily turn pagan in Rome, were it only to soothe his irritated taste for the graceful.

The great masters of sacred art were wont to embody their genius in many painful scenes, marvelously true to life, and all the more exhausting from that very circumstance, but here all is airy grace and entrancing beauty. A perfect realization of ethereal charms floats before the car of day, dropping flowers from her hands, while the exquisite group of the hours follow in their train, leading a dance, in which every attitude is faultless.

It was a charming drive to the Villa Borghese, an elegant country seat without the walls. The casino is a succession of magnificent halls, works of art in themselves, and filled with paintings and statuary. There are some charming pieces of alto relievo from classic subjects, and a grand one of Curtius leaping into the gulf confronts the great entrance. Among the statues is a fine dancing Fawn, discovered in some ancient excavation, and Bernini's splendid group of David and Goliath. But nothing here surpasses Canova's Pauline Buonaparte, and an oil fresco by Gagnereau, of a sleeping Venus, is exquisite beyond description.

We were stopped on our return at the Church of St. Augustin, to see the marvelous display of gifts, in jewels, silver and gold, at the shrine of the Virgin, who sits benignantly, clad in adornings of which the lowly Virgin never dreamed, to receive upon her toe the kisses of the faithful.

Last, but not least, we went to see a fine new piece of sculpture, called the Pompeian Mother, representing a beautiful woman, with an infant clasped in her arms, shielding both herself and it from the fast falling cinders, by a drapery, which she spreads above her head, while she presses on to seek shelter and safety, with a concentration of intentness which leaves no room for the emotions of either fear or horror. I expect to hear the name of Meli among the masters of sculpture before I die.

My ideal Corso, for which I have looked in vain while unconsciously passing and re-passing the real street, has resolved itself into a long, unremarkable street, wide, indeed, for Rome, and dignified as the others are not, by a sidewalk, filled in the afternoon with handsome carriages and riders.

We have been to drive in the gardens of the Pincian Hill, a charming resort, which commands a fine view of the city. The drive ascends the hill by winding terraces, gay with the equipages of all ranks and nations. Mounted sentinels, immovable as statues, are stationed at the entrance of the private avenues, and the gardens are adorned with busts and statues. This elevation gives a fine view of St.

Peter's, which seems to pervade the entire city, and looms up larger and higher as we become accustomed to the distances, and the edifices begin to assume name and form to our recognition.

The mind absolutely refuses to receive, as a type of the severe statuesque Roman matron, the herds of womanhood, neither severe nor comely, who inhabit the ancient city. The vestal fire is quenched; the Penates are not those of the days of Lucretia, and one could enumerate many divinities whose worship is conducted under the open vault of heaven, whose rites are mysterious no longer. And I fear there is less dignity, and no more piety in many of the so-called Christian temples, than characterized the worship of Jupiter and Saturn.

Oct. 12. We have spent the day in seeing pictures, statuary and curiosities, and my not very strong head is tangled with a general complication of saints, martyrs, goddesses, athletes, vases, columns, shrines and sarcophagi.

For some reason or other, my heart was not in sight-seeing, but brim full of individual interests, and I scarcely do justice to the wonders of the day. One thing that has impressed me deeply, in looking at the exhumed treasures of the Museum, is, that Rome is built upon a city as thoroughly entombed, and more wonderful in its riches, than the revived cities of Herculaneum and Pompeii. The very dust upon which we tread is the depository of art and treasure, such as filled the palaces of ancient Rome, or rolled, in floods of riches, along the triumphal way from the Campus Martius.

One grows impatient here. We come to see Roman Rome, and Romish Rome every where treads down the ancient landmarks, and turns the temples and palaces with which we are familiar into idol shrines of far more puerile observances.

One of the most striking features of Rome is the abundance of water. Fountains spout alike from homely corners and ornamented basins. The jets in the piazza of St. Peter's have been playing night and day, for two thousand years, and the long solid arches, which Appius Claudius, of hateful memory, built three hundred years before Christ, still conduct the living flood into the degenerate city.

There are some fountains of especial note; the largest and finest that we have seen is the fountain of Trevi, built against the lofty façade of the Palace Centi. The water rushes in a broad, deep flood, over an enormous mass of rock work, and falls into a vast basin, in which Neptune reclines in his car, surrounded by Tritons. How refreshing is the depth and purity of those waters, and how one lingers to listen to the plash of those crystal streams, one should traverse the streets of Rome to know. The water is clear, sweet, and cold, fortunately requiring no ice, as that is an unattainable luxury here.

To return to the Vatican; the statuary, like the paintings, is of acknowledged and unrivalled merit. I must pass by countless works of art in precious stones, and sculptures of more or less merit, which make the halls of the Vatican a study for years; and note the few which stand out prominently in my memory — which are an Athlete; Meleager and a Boar; The Apollo and Antinous Belvidere; the great Laocoon, a cast from which has haunted my memory from my babyhood; and a Perseus, by Canova, which last, it is safe to predict, will outstrip even the sculptures of the ancients, when posterity shall have reached such a distance as shall give them the same perspective.

In the palace Borghese there are many really splendid pictures. Raphael's magnificent Entombment of Christ; Danae, by Corregio, in its execution, as I think, the most beautiful of them all; the celebrated Cumean Sibyl, by Domenichino; St. Ignatius devoured by wild beasts, by Giordano; Head of St. Joseph, by Guido; a fine Madonna, by Dolci; the Chase of Diana, by Domenichino; St. John in the Desert, by Paul Veronese; Sacred and Profane Love, and Sampson, both by Titian; and a portrait in the Rembrandt style, of Marie de Medici.

In the Barberini is Raphael's Fornarina, and a fine picture of Lucrezia Cenci, by Gaetani; but we had no eyes for any thing except the marvelous Beatrice, the most faultless face — the most spiritual, gentle, resigned, grief-ful face, that was ever put upon canvas. Those tender luminous eyes haunt me with such a beseeching claim upon my pity, that I cannot believe that the original has mingled with the dust of centuries — that the fair young head ever hung ghastly upon the very bridge over which we pass in daily indifference.

In the same room is a picture by Del Sarto, the best of the myriad Holy Families that I have seen. The undeniable tendency of such a superabounding holiness is to make one fatally profane, and one welcomes a real heathen goddess with relief, provided it be not a reiteration of Venus.

St. John in the Lateran is a splendid church. It is the most ancient of the Basilicas, and is the parish church of the Pope. Our guide was evidently scandalized by our indifferent manner of declining a sight of the table upon which the Last Supper was celebrated, but we were not interested in the precious relic, veritable as it is, and wrought of cedar and silver.

The Corsini chapel contains the most splendid and costly curiosities of the whole church, being adorned with an incredible amount of jewels, precious stones, exquisite marbles, mosaics and sculpture. In a subterranean chapel beneath the one just mentioned, is a Pieta of consummate beauty, by Montauti. A Pieta, by the way, is a group of the Virgin with the dead Christ in her arms.

It seems ridiculous and irritating, that such a gem of loveliness should be concealed in this dark recess, and permitted to be seen only by the smoky candle of the attendant. The tenderness of the mother, and the reverence of the Christian, are exquisitely blended in the beautiful figure of the Virgin, while the Christ seems nothing short of perfection.

The largest obelisk in Rome is in the space before the Lateran. It is of red granite, and covered with hieroglyphics.

We encountered here the very best specimen of the genus beggar that we have found in all these begging countries. She was the Irish beggar of the Coliseum, and this was our second interview. The late abundant rain had rendered the Coliseum unapproachable, and she was plying her vocation within the city. Of all beggars, commend me to the Irish for ingenuity and importunity. The gravity of her assertion that she had eaten nothing in five days; the corresponding gravity with which she was assured that, such being the case, nothing could save her life; her baffled disgust at being proffered food instead of money; the respectability of her numerous testimonials, and the Parthian arrow which she discharged at our hard hearts, were truly curiosities in their way, that cost no slight effort to regard with decorum.

Hard by, in a porch of the Lateran, is the Scala Santa, or holy staircase; which can be ascended only upon the knees; where the light of the divine atonement first burst upon the soul of Luther. And here, this very day, we have seen the people of the nineteenth century crawling devoutly up, to claim the indulgences granted to the pious act.

Santa Maria Maggiore is, like many other churches,

famous for its wealth and beauty, and is remarkable for its beautiful columns; but we are weary of churches, and mean to see pagan Rome to-morrow.

Oct. 13. We have been diving into the substratum of this marvelous city to-day, and, with two exceptions, have ignored the Rome of the Pope. The exceptions consisted of a visit to the Church of the Capuchins, to see Guido's famous picture of St. Michael and the Dragon; a picture of great power, which fails signally in any attempts at copy that we have seen. The almost supernatural combination of exquisite spiritual beauty with holy indignation and resistless power, is beyond any conception but that of Guido himself. This church also contains a splendid picture of the Conversion of St. Paul, by Cortona; and one of the Ecstasy of St. Francis, by Domenichino.

The other church was that of St. Pietro in Vinculo, containing Guido's Speranza, which was disappointing; and a statue of Moses, by Michael Angelo. The conception of the great Lawgiver is so just that the mind rests with a satisfaction upon its execution, which is often withheld from great works of art which fail to realize our own ideal. This has finished our pictures.

We have seen besides, the Catacombs; the tombs of the Scipios; the Columbaria of Cæsar's household; the Circus of Marcellus; the Cloaca Maxima; the Silver Fountain; the Arch of Janus; the circus and temple of Romulus; the baths of Titus and Caracalla; the Tarpeian rock; Pompey's Pillar; the house of

Raphael; the porch of Antoninus, and many ruins and fragments of public works; all which bear date far back into the regions of legendary history.

The Cloaca Maxima is among the most ancient of all Roman remains. It was constructed one hundred and fifty years after the founding of the city, or about six hundred years before Christ; and still serves the purpose of a sewer connecting with the Tiber.

This part of the city is the spot where the little cluster of huts built by Romulus, became the germ of the Metropolis of the earth; and here the legend says, the twins were cast ashore, hard by the Palatine hill, crowned with the magnificent ruins of the palaces of the Cæsars.

Near by is the Silver Fountain, at which Castor and Pollux watered their steeds after the battle of Lake Regilius. It is still much resorted to on account of its medicinal properties.

We drove through the Appian Gate, out upon the Appian way, the old wall still skirting that street of tombs, to the great circus of Romulus; an immense amphitheatre for races and games. Adjoining is the temple of Romulus, with the addition of a church, which follows here, of course. All these strong, lasting walls have been stripped of the marbles which gave them their beauty, but the inner structure has still ages of duration in it.

The Catacombs — that dread mysterious, subterranean world — what can I say of them? We wound along the countless narrow streets of that silent abode, peopled with myriads upon myriads of the inhabitants of ancient Rome. These excavations honeycomb the Campagna for miles, and reach down to Ostia. And when we remember what a large proportion of the Roman dead were burned to ashes, and deposited in the Columbaria, or in household urns, these depositories, crowded with graves, speak more expressively of the vast population which had need of this immense work, than any estimate of the dwellings of the living can do. Darker deeds than have stained the pages of any other history, are written upon these black walls. It is estimated that nearly two hundred thousand Christians were slaughtered in these gloomy recesses, whither they had fled from the raging persecutions.

One would think such a living tomb scarcely preferable to a more speedy release by martyrdom; nevertheless, countless families, holy men and women, and tender children sought shelter in these chill dungeons, and here the voice of prayer and praise went up to heaven, and here the brethren brought the remains of the martyred faithful, and left upon their resting places the symbol which distinguishes the Christian from the pagan.

Some of the inscriptions upon fragments of tombs at the entrance struck me with a sudden tenderness of human universal sympathy, which fails to arise in the midst of generalities. There was a "puella dilecta" and an "infans dulcissime" in the ages past, as well as among the babies around our own knees.

From the entrance to the catacombs of Calixtus, one gets a grand view of St. Peter's. The mighty cathedral seems to need a distance like this (of six miles) to be apprehended in its greatness; and the dome swells through the cloudless air, as if it alone were Rome, and the city but its pavement.

The tombs of the Scipios, in which lie all the heroes of that noble race, except Africanus, claimed an interest similar to the Catacombs; but the Columbaria had more the effect of a curiosity. In deep apartments there are built small niches, like the nests of a dove-cote, in which are deposited the ashes of the dead, and inscriptions on the walls mark their identity. We saw, yesterday, the ovens in which the bodies were reduced to ashes.

Nothing has been more calculated to impress us with the elaborate splendor of Roman magnificence, than the baths. The baths of Caracalla retain their walls, some of their beautiful mosaic pavements, and the ruins of such stupendous columns and massive roofs as fill the spectator with amazement. The falling of the roof and upper story has entirely covered the real area of the baths, which held at once sixteen hundred people; while the amphitheatre was decorated with a wealth and luxury, such as scarcely belonged to the palaces. The great statues which we saw at Naples; the Farnese Bull, Flora and Hercules, were taken from the grand oval of these baths. These figures are colossal, and are placed in the Museum in the relative position in which they were found. The central group is a work of great size and beautiful finish. It represents the sons of Antiope in the act of fastening Dirce to the horns of a furious bull, while their mother looks on from a distance. The shrinking, imploring terror of the victim, the powerful strength of the young man who grasps the struggling animal, and the immovable sternness of the mother, are portrayed with painful vividness. The extent of this building was nearly a mile.

The baths of Titus are smaller, but more magnificent. They are, in themselves, a striking epitome of Roman history. We look at Mycenas, and Nero, and Titus, very much upon the same plane—but here is the perspective. Upon the ruined villa of the wealthy Mycenas, Nero built an edifice, which became, in its turn, the substratum of the luxurious baths of Titus; and, one above another, the distinctive remains of each age are to be traced.

From these baths was exhumed the statue of Melcager, at the Vatican, and also a splendid porphyry urn in the Museum.

We contented ourselves with a survey of the exterior of the Pantheon, which is transferred to a new idol worship.

The palace of the Orsini is built above the theatre and circus of Marcellus, and the ancient substructure is perfectly discernible.

One begins after a time to penetrate the intermediate rubbish, and to give local habitation and a name to the ideals of Roman history, and poetry, and mythology. We returned home by the Spada palace, to see Pompey's statue, at whose base "great Cæsar fell." In an alcove at this palace we saw a curious effect of imagination, or rather of perspective. At the end of an apparently long vista of arbor, we saw a statue, as it appeared, of the size of a full grown man; and nothing but repeated experiment could convince the senses that it was scarcely four feet high and but a few feet distant from the eye. The illusion is produced by the rapid diminishing and narrowing of the rows of columns painted upon the sides of the alcove.

We were, by this time, weary; and came home to lay up in our memory the wonders of art and antiquity, of magnificence and desolation, with which the imperial city is crowned and scourged.

Oct. 15. I just began to realize the depth of interest in Rome as we drove for the last time through the ancient streets, past obelisk, fountain, column, palace and temple. The combination of the two interests of art and association tends to confuse the pleasure of a short sojourn in the city. That which is modern and continental overlays that which is ancient and peculiar, and presses itself first and most urgently upon the attention.

I venture to say that, universally, the first visits in Rome are to churches and picture galleries; yet it is beneath all this that the profound heart of the city lies, and one needs to close the bodily eyes, and people his own brain, by the help of the landmarks which he has seen, with the existences of the past. Roma fuit — she wore the purple, and grasped the reins of dominion; she brought to a common focus the art, the learning, the polish of Greece, the gorgeous magnificence of oriental wealth, and the muscle and sinew of the northern barbarians; and then, like Tarpeia, she sank, overwhelmed by the weight of her gifts. Hers was not the genius of creation, either in poesy, oratory or literature, but she possessed the power of elaboration, by which she wrought materials, already created, into shape, for use and transmission. Her era was an advance in the civilization of the world, and eminently an era of law.

But this great moral fungus, which crops out from every spot in Rome, has no share in the great memories of the nation or the city. Rome exists no longer. The papal system, like the foul excrescences which creep over a decaying tree, shines in crimson and gold and silver, and, like them, a touch discloses the decay and rottenness within. We who protest against the corrupt church, have reason to be thankful that she has her seat in the most insignificant nation upon earth. Perhaps it is by a wise dispensation of Providence, that these fountains of evil are pent up within a certain sanctity of position, instead of being scattered abroad to carry their prestige into any other quarter of the globe. However interested in our stay, we bade adieu to Rome with no reluctance; nor will it be with any reluctance that I shall lose sight of the yeasty waves of the blue Mediterranean.

We have passed the day with home friends, who have been also our pleasant travelling companions, upon a French steamer at anchor off Leghorn, which anchorage our former experience here did not tempt us to abandon.

These Mediterranean steamers sail at night, and spend the days in taking on and discharging freight and passengers at the different ports. We have come on from Civita Vecchia, even with the horrors of the former passage in our memory, as our time was too limited for a return by land, as we desired, and we are hastening to France by Genoa and Turin. It has been one of those restful days which are impossible upon land, in a country where there is so much to tax the eye and brain — but it is nevertheless a sea-sick place, and I long for terra firma.

Oct. 16. The rain prevented our doing more in Genoa la superba, than driving a little through the principal streets, visiting some of the shops, and looking up and down the steep flights of steps that connect the streets. The city is beautifully situated upon the crescent bay, and elaborately surrounded by long lines of fortifications, to which the natural defenses of the hills are well adapted. The forests of masts indicate the commercial character of the place, but the shallowness of the water prevents vessels coming to the piers, giving occupation to swarms of boatmen, as at Leghorn; but not to such a grasping race as their brethren at the latter place. A fine statue of Columbus stands opposite the station, with handsome panels of bas relief, representing important events in the life of the great adventurer.

On our way from Alessandria to Turin, we encountered the first detention by accident that has occurred during our whole journey. The train ran over a cow, breaking a wheel, and throwing one of the carriages off the track. However, no one was hurt, and the carriage was soon replaced. The same rain continued, and prevented our seeing any thing more of Turin than that it is a fine, modern-built city, with wide streets and handsome buildings. We came on to Susa for the night, for an early start across Mount Cenis, and staid at a queer inn, with the oddest, out of door effect. The rooms opened upon a heavy stone gallery, which overlooked a court, filled with diligences and various other vehicles; all outside rude and coarse, while within all was comfortable and restful to weary travellers. We went through the usual process of discussion with the proprietors of the possible vehicles, and entered into solemn contract, with printed conditions and penalties, which did not, however, prevent our enjoying the repose of the night.

Oct. 17. The imperative hour for an early departure arrived before the inmates of the inn were astir, and we began to fear the necessity of setting forth on a dim, chill morning, without our breakfast, and that, too, upon a mountain pass, with no possible breakfast upon the way. However, the Italian system prevailed, and we not only waited for our breakfast and enjoyed the steaks, and fagots of delicate Italian bread, but did so without losing our connection with the railway on the other side.

The passage of Mount Cenis, which was the route of Hannibal, is less picturesque or grand than the other Alpine passes which we have made; but while it verified the vetturino's description of "a good road but a bad route," it is not without striking features peculiar to itself. We had expected to travel to Paris, by way of Marseilles, so that it was with a double pleasure that I welcomed again the grave brown range of the Savoys. The pass, though short, is steep, but the road is a broad, smooth construction, magnificently engineered through the rough defile.

Here we found, once more, the rushing beauty of the mountain torrents, and countless cascades, lacing the sides of the mountain in long, slender, silver threads, or drifting in snowy clouds from the summit of the precipices. Unlike the Bernese Oberland, which wears its velvet greenness to the very footstool of eternal snow, the sides of the hills stretched upward, almost barren of turf, but gay with the many hued autumnal foliage of the scanty forests. They are, in general, lacking in great elevations of blank precipice, but near the summit of the pass one mighty head rises square and black, its rugged perpendicular face written all over with the hieroglyphics of creation.

The white crests gathered closer about us as we went onward and upward, until at last we were fairly in the midst of the snows, as truly as if it had been

December in the heart of Yankeedom. Near the summit is a beautiful lake of considerable extent, of which we have often heard as one of the highest bodies of water in the world.

The French side of the mountain is more like our former experience of the Alps; and while our wheels were crushing the snows of the summit, we were overhanging emerald valleys, dotted with town and hamlet, and saw, once more, the unfailing châlets perched in a thousand nooks, and cultivated fields and terraced vineyards clinging to the sides of the brown hills. A broad, beautiful stream rushed down to unite the many streamlets from the summit with the river which flows to the Rhone in the winding valley of the deep gorge, down which we zigzagged in long curves to St. Michel, where we found rail again, by which we came on to Chambery.

Nearly at the top of Mount Cenis, where the gorge of the defile is most precipitous, is a most formidable mass of fortifications commanding the pass, a perfect key to Italy in that direction. Hannibal himself would have made good his retreat had he caught sight of such preparations to welcome his approach. I was about to say that Napoleon would have retired, but that I am inclined to doubt, for he who marched an army across the great St. Bernard would surely have contrived some way of evading the fortress of Mount Cenis — or of taking it.

Chambery lies in a lovely valley, encircled by sharply defined ridges of mountains; they were purple with the slanting rays of the sunset as we set out on our night journey to Paris, and the broad sweet lake which slept at their foot, gave back the glowing sky like a crystal drop at the bottom of an amethyst goblet.

CHAPTER XIV.

FRANCE.

Paris — Louvre — Notre Dame — Hotel des Invalides — Bois de Boulogne — Jardin des Plants — Gobelins — Chapel of St. Ferdinand — St. Chapelle — Luxembourg.

OCT. 22. This is our fourth day in this great, brilliant, cheerful, showy city. The first two days we devoted to rest, and to strolling through the wide streets and wider boulevards, gazing at the countless shops, and enjoying, by contrast, after the dirty narrow streets of most of the continental cities, the broad avenues and splendid gardens of this metropolis of elegance.

It seems to me that it will be difficult to accomplish much sight-seeing while the city itself is so pleasing. Then, too, as a place of association, it means less than the ancient cities, crowded with the interests of two thousand years.

Yesterday we went to the Bois de Boulogne, to see a review by the Emperor. This extensive pleasure ground is perfectly charming. The drives meander through a wide extent, diversified by sweeps of emerald meadow, long forest glades, mounds of flowers and shrubs, shady deer parks, and the most beautiful of irregular lakes, where troops of stately swans sail in the shadow of green thickets, or feed upon the short smooth turf of the margin. Nothing is wanting to make the place a most attractive resort for the pleasure loving inhabitants of the city.

The review took place in a field of such extent that the eighty thousand troops said to be under arms seemed like a picture of an army rather than a living body of soldiery.

There is no need to say any thing of the appearance or organization of French troops — nothing can be more brilliant and perfect, nevertheless, I liked the Italian army better.

We had an excellent view of the Emperor, as he rode within a few feet of our carriage. He is a grave, noble looking man, much handsomer than his pictures, and looks every inch a king. I could not but feel painfully for a man whose finger presses the spring of such a government as France; whose daily life lies amid a network of ambuscade and precedent, which must sometimes shake even the iron nerves of Louis Napoleon. We miss the pleasure of seeing the Empress, as she is at present at Madrid.

The vast assemblage of soldiers and spectators melted imperceptibly away from the avenues of the Bois de Boulogne, leaving only the long line of carriages and horsemen upon their afternoon airing.

We returned past the Triumphal Arch, which commemorates the victories of France, and down the magnificent avenue of the Champs Elysées —

such an avenue as is to be found no where else in the world. The mile which spreads before one, standing at the Arc de l'etoile, has no parallel. It is crossed in the distance by the splendid palace of the Tuileries, and beyond can be seen, here and there, the towers of the Louvre. The street reaches down a gentle descent, growing wider and wider, until it almost loses the character of a street, and becomes pleasure grounds, with trees, shrubs, and flowers upon either hand, and every tempting form of amusement and attraction for children spread out upon the smooth borders of the triple causeway. Half way down it attains its greatest breadth; two large fountains rise on either hand, surrounded by little lawns and flower borders. On the right you diverge to the great glass Palace of Industry; on the left are the charming gardens of the palace d'Elysées. It retains its park-like aspect even to the Place de la Concorde — a wide, open space, directly before the gardens of the Tuileries, which was occupied by the guillotine during the Revolution. In its centre stands the great obelisk of Luxor, and upon each side are fountains and sculptures. Among the latter are two splendid horses, originally wrought for the park at Marly. Between this space and the palace are the beautiful gardens of the Tuileries; on the right the street immediately crosses the Seine, and presents the public buildings of the general government; on the left you look down the Rue Royale to the Madeleine — the finest church in Paris. Still farther down, at right angles to the gardens of the Tuileries, is the Place Vendome, with the column and statue of Napoleon. We watched the lowering of the figure of the General, so identified with the very idea of Napoleon, and the substitution of a civic statue in a Roman toga and a laurel wreath. The destruction of the entire column could not more effectually obliterate the Napoleonic idea, than this new rendering of the personality which has so long crowned the city.

To-day we have been to the Louvre and the gardens of the Tuileries. The gallery of the Louvre does not contain such eminent works of art, as have made many other galleries famous; but here again we find the brilliancy of Rubens, the majesty of Vandyke, the grave solemnity of Rembrandt, the sweetness of Da Vinci, the tenderness of Corregio, the heavy uniformity of Holbein, the rustic naturalness of Teniers, the golden-haired beauties that Titian loved to paint, the life and soul that breathe from the faces of Raphael, and the surpassing spirit and power and grace of Guido — the master who towers above them all; to say nothing of such painters as Domenichino, Guercino, Tintorretto and Del Sarto; in whose paintings are united, in some degree, the coloring of the ancient, and the expression of the modern schools. The Louvre was a sort of general review of the different styles of the great artists, whose works are seen in their perfection in the different galleries of the continent, and are here brought into contrast, each with his peculiar ideality and individual excellence. It was refreshing to find only a light proportion of the Holy Families and Venus.

There are two exquisite modern paintings by the same artist, whose name I have failed to discover; Endymion Sleeping, and The Burial of Atala.

But the grotesque allegorical conceptions of even great painters, especially in religious subjects, strike the mind of the modern beholder with more of the ludicrous than the reverent.

It seems strange, too, when the emotions of the human mind must have been the same in all ages, that students of nature, as all artists are supposed to be, should have failed so often in transferring to canvas any adequate picture of the emotion proper to the subject. Of this the face of the Virgin is an eminent example. Nineteen twentieths of the Virgins wear faces more earthly and expressionless than that of any peasant to be found in common life; while the Judiths, which rival the Virgins in number, have almost invariably a simper of consciousness, which would be fatal to a girl of fourteen. All this, however, is very unlearned and presumptuous criticism. The statuary of the Louvre does not compare with the collections which we have already seen, and, with the exception of the Venus of Milo, did not seem to me to contain very remarkable specimens of art.

Oct. 23. I have another idle day to record. We were abroad from ten to six; and with the exception of visiting Notre Dame and Sainte Chapelle, and getting our luggage from the station, we have spent the day in that sort of operation expressed in America by "loafing;" walking about the splendid streets, and gazing at the brilliant display of wares that make Paris one great toy shop.

Notre Dame is a fine Cathedral of the eleventh century, but not so fine as those of Cologne, Strasbourg or Italy. The wood carvings of the choir, of the fifteenth century, are very good. The Church is not decorated with paintings and sculpture, as is common in the continental cathedrals. One good bas relief represents Archbishop Arf, as he endeavored to quell the tumult upon the barricades, during the last revolution; an attempt which proved futile and fatal, but which has canonized him for all generations.

We were admitted to the sacristy, where we saw various treasures; the gold coronation service of the first Napoleon; a bit of the true cross; some remarkable jewels and vases belonging to St. Louis. In a carefully guarded case is a most magnificent shrine, adorned with numberless jewels; the model of a larger one which contains the veritable crown of thorns, brought from Palestine, by St. Louis, and deposited in Sainte Chapelle, which was built for the purpose; and in which service is performed once a year, for the purpose of exhibiting the sacred relic. At least, to quote our Venetian guide, "so runs the legend." We saw the mantle of crimson, wrought with golden bees, in which Napoleon was crowned;

and the various splendid vestments of the ecclesiastics worn on that occasion; as well as those worn at the coronation of the present Emperor, and at the baptism of the little prince.

The most truly remarkable things in Notre Dame were two silver vases presented by Charlemagne. The attendant told us that in some recent excavations in the course of the present repairs, there have been discovered the bodies of the Archbishop who founded the Cathedral, of Philip Augustus, and of Elizabeth the Second. Behind the High Altar is a Pieta, by Michael Angelo, but it does not compare favorably with the same group by the same master at Rome.

Sainte Chapelle is a small chapel, lined entirely with tall stained windows of the thirteenth century —beautiful, and very different from other church edifices. It is not intended for worship, except upon the annual exhibition of the crown of thorns. Both these churches are upon the Isle, to which there is crossing by many splendid bridges over the brown Seine; and which contains some of the oldest buildings of the city. Sainte Chapelle is adjoining the palace of Justice.

We have been to the Louvre again, and have found another exquisite picture, the St. Margaret of Raphael. It is a relief to find that the glaring tints of Rubens' long series of Medici pictures are supposed not to be the work of the great artist; but of his pupils, after his own sketches.

There is a sweet little child portrait by Velasquez,

the infant Marguerite Thérese. But the gallery is unsatisfying. The beautiful hall adorned with fresco and bas relief, representing the seasons and the zodiac, is admirable.

We have been to the new boulevards, and have admired the magnitude of the works which are converting the irregular suburbs into splendid quarters.

Oct. 26. To-day we have been at the Hotel des Invalides. It is a pleasure to see with what care these remnants of the French army are considered. The house is worthy of its object, and one could imagine the pride with which the battered veterans of the great campaigns of the French army pass their last days beside the ashes of their idolized chief.

The chapel of the Invalides is hung with many a stained and tattered ensign, which must speak volumes to the old worshippers, and which are more touching, even to the careless observer, than any of the paraphernalia of the church itself.

The tomb of the great Napoleon is beneath the dome of the church behind the Invalides. It is a fit resting-place for the man. A superb sarcophagus encloses the remains of the long exiled monarch. It is of red granite, from Finland, massive, yet tasteful, with no excess of ornament. It is sunk many feet below the floor of the church, in a circular space, which is floored with mosaic, and bears the names of his principal battles. The sides of the depository are adorned with figures, representing, allegorically, the results of their battles. The entrance to the crypt is below and behind the High Altar, to which the descent is by white marble steps. There, two dark colossal figures guard the portal, on which is inscribed the famous sentence in which the dying Emperor desired his ashes to rest "upon the borders of the Seine, in the midst of the French people whom he had so much loved." The tombs of Duroc and Bertrand stand on either hand. The altar is beautiful — of green and Egyptian marble; and in two side chapels are sculptured monuments of Turenne and Vauban. It is, altogether, a perfect monument, and adapted to its purpose with true French taste.

Oct. 23. Have visited, to-day, the Jardin des Plantes, and the Gobelin manufactory, and have seen the Hotel de Ville, the Tower of St. Jacques, the Place du Chatelet and Fontaine Palmier, and the Palais Royal. The Jardin des Plantes is filled with plants and animals from all quarters of the globe. We devoted ourselves to the animals. They are admirably provided with proper abodes, each in its own enclosure and cabin. The bears have baths, and dens, and climbing poles, and the clumsy hippopotamus his swimming bath, in which he lies, the very picture of lazy, piggish luxury! The animals of the frigid and torrid zones dwell in amicable proximity, and the beautiful varieties of the feathered creation perch in the branches of the trees, or trip about their yards, as if conscious of their claims to admiration.

We intended to have visited the Conciergerie, but gave it up after an hour of the circumlocution office.

We presented ourselves at the office of Justice for admission, and were told that we must obtain an order from the prefect of police, whose bureau, however, was in the street directly behind the palace.

The bureau proved to be upon the other side of the wide square, but we found it; ascended to the great hall, where we were politely directed by sundry officials to a passage which led back, over a long bridge, to an office, evidently in the very palace which we had just quitted. Here we were as politely directed from room to room, until we arrived at the end of possible directions—the prefecture. Here we found three dignified gentlemen at a desk, who, upon receiving our application, desired us to return by the way whence we had come, to the office of the first division, at the door of "affairs personnels." We retraced our steps, the precious moments of a limited hour slipping away; applied at "affairs personnels," were directed to an inner room, and still another—all in the most civil manner. But the affair began to assume a ludicrous aspect, and it was with difficulty that I could preserve the proper gravity to repeat the question, which had almost lost its signification. The official of the penetralia sent us on our return by the narrow passage which we had already traversed, and, by the way, the whole arrangement resembled some temporary construction in the back yard of a hotel, rather than the access to the most complicated and perfect police machinery in the world. An attendant showed us a narrow staircase, which we mounted, and reached another set of offices, at the innermost of which they directed us to return by the same staircase, and another also, into a vestibule, whence another long passage led down to the real inner den of that mysterious animal—the police, guarded by an ante-room. Here the chief received our application, and in return assured us that it was impossible to issue the desired permission until we had made an application to our own ambassador. This was the result of the long peregrination, and for what?—for permission to visit an empty dungeon, which was directly below our feet on our first request at the Hall of Justice. By this time we had arrived at the conclusion that neither our patience nor our leisure would bear much farther strain, so we shook off the dust of the prefecture from our feet, and departed.

On arriving at the Gobelins we found that we had made another sad mistake, in forgetting our passports, and were peremptorily denied entrance; but I plume myself upon my powers of persuasion in the French language, inasmuch as I did at last soften the heart of the Cerberus in uniform, and we entered.

The tapestry is of exceeding beauty, the pieces exhibited being copies of the best paintings of the masters. Even Raphael's Transfiguration is exquisitely copied. We saw, also, the work in progress. The warp is suspended, the stout threads running perpendicularly, while the woof is wrought in by the workman sitting behind it, with the picture to be copied still behind him. The outlines of the figures are sketched upon the white warp. After the transverse threads are introduced, instead of being beaten up by a beam, they are brought close by a small flat stick, about three inches wide, with teeth that pass between the threads and beat the woof down hard.

The work, when the coarse threads are perpendicular, is called haute lisse, and when horizontal, basse lisse. The pieces now in hand are for the Tuileries and other French palaces, and it is entirely a governmental work. The tapestry is wrought upon the wrong side of the work, but the carpet upon the right, and the threads afterwards sheared closely, like velvet. Among the pictures is a very fine portrait of the Emperor, which it took four years to finish — one of the Empress is still more beautiful. I could fancy that blindness might be the result of looking steadily at colors through the glimmering lines of white thread.

Oct. 29. The weather is unpropitious for lounging, but we have not been idle. We have driven about the city, visited the Luxembourg; the Chapel of St. Ferdinand; the Pantheon; and have seen, in passing, the Artesian well, which supplies water from a bore sixteen hundred feet in depth; and the column occupying the spot where once stood the mysterious prison of the Bastile. And with that sight rises the long succession of histories of undeserved incarceration, of lettres du cachet, of incredible escapes, of lifelong imprisonments and nameless deaths, and finally, of that overwhelming mob that forced the commandant to surrender the keys, set the prisoners at large, and razed the dreaded building to the ground.

We visited the Palace of Industry, which was disappointingly meagre; went to the Pantheon, which, although it has been converted into a church, still wears the temple air, and is a noble edifice.

The Chapel of St. Ferdinand is erected upon the spot where the Duc d'Orleans died, after a fall from his carriage, in 1842. It is a beautiful monument—a gem of a chapel, and contains a fine effigy of the duke in marble, executed by Triquiti. Behind the altar is the sacristy, which contains a large painting representing the scene of his death, with the portraits of the royal family present at the time.

Upon what a slender thread hang the destinies of nations! The restiveness of a pair of horses, in all probability, changed the dynasty of the French throne; for the duke had a strong hold upon the affections of the French people, and might have succeeded his father in peace. Nevertheless, the French need an iron hand at the helm, and they have it now.

We went to the beautiful palace of the Luxembourg; I believe the most ancient of the French palaces. It is now used as a senate house. The halls are all adorned with modern pictures, of living artists, in which the two Napoleons figure as the foreground. The chief room, in size and adornings, is the throne room; a lofty and spacious saloon, gilded and decorated with elaborate art.

The Senate Chamber is a very handsome council room. It has chairs of green velvet, ranged in a semi-circle, rising in rows, one above another; the tribune of the president, and the seats of the ministers directly below it, occupying one side of the room. A small ante-room adjoining is shown as having been used by Robespierre for a prison, during the time of the Girondins.

Last of all, and most elaborate, is the bed chamber of Mary of Medici, the queen of Henry Quatre. Upon the ceiling is a painting of Mary, by Rubens, and the walls are covered with the works of great artists. It has been kept in beautiful preservation, and the attendant said that there had been millions expended upon its decorations.

It is now the place where the civil contract is signed, upon the occasion of the marriage of any of the senators. The gardens are beautiful, but the situation of the palace is any thing but desirable. We have another French palace to visit to-morrow, but I feel a little like repeating the formula by which the Grand Monarque was pleased to be addressed at the morning reception of his courtiers. "Sire, Marly!" But that scene of almost fabulous extravagance has sunk into desolation and oblivion.

CHAPTER XV.

FRANCE.

Versailles — Pere la Chaise — Havre — English Channel.

I SCARCELY know how to begin a description of a day spent in exploring the beauties of such a place as Versailles. The many descriptions of the place which I have seen, have failed to convey to my own imagination any proper idea of its magnificence; and any jottings of my own can only recall to myself the pleasure of the day — not by any means to convey any conception of it to another. We went by rail through a very pleasing country, passing the forest of St. Cloud; a place of much interest as a favorite residence of the first Napoleon, but not at present open to the public, as it is occupied as a summer palace by the present Emperor.

The country is more hilly than I had supposed; the railway ascends continually, and passes through a number of long tunnels, Versailles being two hundred feet higher than Paris. It must be a charming drive during the early summer. It gave me the first real idea of the compactness of population in this country. The whole route, except by the pleasure grounds, leads through a succession of towns and villages, forming an almost continuous suburb.

We arrived early at the gates, and were fortunate in securing the services of Marchand, the palace guide; a former valet to Napoleon; an old man of seventy-seven vigorous years, who has seen eleven different governments in France. He saw Marie Antoinette queen in these very grounds, and, judging from the versatility of the French genius, he may yet add some dynasties to his present experience.

The old servant has been a more discriminating and profound observer of human character and events than many a politician of higher rank, and knew all the points of real lasting interest in the palace and its history. He aptly said, "there are many fine cities in the world, but one Versailles."

It is the most spacious of royal abodes, taking into account the grounds, and the smaller establishments of the Trianons. It is the focus of seven wide avenues of approach, which radiate to the palaces and principal cities of the empire. We enter a paved court of great extent, around which the palace buildings form three sides of an irregular hollow square. The middle, or main building was erected by Louis the Thirteenth, and is distinguished by the introduction of red stone or brick in the façade. Among the buildings of the left wing is an excellent exterior view of the chapel.

In the midst of the court of entrance stands an immense equestrian statue of Louis Quatorze, who completed the splendid edifice, and held his luxurious, almost oriental court here, during the long years in which he lived to oppress the nation, and to draw from it the resources which he lavished upon foreign wars and domestic extravagance. The splendor which so dazzled the world during his reign, has sunk into a darkness from which neither historian nor poet dares longer attempt to extricate it. Around the court are arranged busts of distinguished men, recently transferred from Paris. Directly in front of the great entrance, and looking down the long avenue which leads to Paris, is the balcony upon which Marie Antoinette led her children, in response to the furious demand from the mob, on the fatal day of that terrible outburst. And there, when the same mob, thirsting for her blood, demanded that she should put away the children whose presence was her protection, she put them firmly back, and stood alone, royally brave, in her undefended womanhood; until even that brutal multitude was, for the moment, disarmed, and reserved her, with a cruel forbearance, for a sadder fate.

The unhappy Marie, with the sins of many generations visited upon her fair young head, was the last mistress of this wonderful domain.

After the devastating fury of the revolution had wrought its will, it fell into neglect and desolation; until Louis Philippe restored its noble saloons, and made of its long galleries a museum of art, such as may well attract the admiration of the world; and the magnificent palace and park are now royally kept for the pleasure of that public which was, of old, royally oppressed.

As the palace was not yet open, we made our first visit to the pleasure grounds; and I can do very little towards describing them.

The combination of wide avenues, broad terraces, fountains filled with groups of statuary, smooth lawns, closely clipped hedges and pyramids of yew, artificial lakes and canals, grottoes, copse and forest, is something passing my powers of description.

From the private front of the palace, the view looks down a broad avenue, descending by stone steps to a very large fountain, and, beyond, to another still lower; and the distance is bounded by the pretty sheet called the Swiss Water, shut in on each side by the forest.

The tall dark yews are trimmed in various forms, chiefly pyramidal, and the box forms a broad hedge lining the stone parapets with a continuous arbor.

At every opening a new fountain presents itself, all adorned with sculptures; and the fountains take their name from the groups — such as the Diana fountain — the Neptune — the Latona, &c.

The wide parterres were stripped of their bloom, but the lawns were still green and smooth as velvet; and it needed little effort of the imagination to picture the scene when the waters are in full play, and the flowers in all their beauty.

We went through the stately forest, by paths

thickly strewn with the brown and yellow leaves of autumn, to a charming artificial grotto, called Apollo's Bath. It is adorned with large statues of gods and animals, and the spot is as natural in rocks and water as a dell in the mountains of Switzerland.

The day was unpropitious for an out-door excursion, but we walked miles through the beautiful grounds.

We next visited the Grand Trianon, a summer palace built by Louis Quatorze for Madame Montespan, and afterwards inhabited by La Vallière, becoming finally the possession of Madame Maintenon.

The Petit Trianon, with its Swiss surroundings, built by Louis the Fifteenth for the Duchess Dubarry, we had no time to explore.

Both these abodes, fit exponents of the days of the grand monarch, were given by the better Louis to Marie Antoinette; and the Grand Trianon was one of the homes of Napoleon and Josephine. It is an elegant dwelling, adorned with frescoes, paintings, sculpture and carvings. It was prepared for an expected visit of Queen Victoria, who, however, preferred St. Cloud, and did not occupy it. It still remains as prepared for the expected guest.

The interest of the Trianon centered in the apartments of Napoleon, which remain precisely as occupied by him — his study, with the very table and chair of his habitual use, unchanged — his council room and bed room.

In the council room is a table covered with a faded

velvet cloth, upon which were signed the articles of divorce, which broke the heart of Josephine, the devoted wife and gracious queen, and dimmed the star of Napoleon.

It is eminently suggestive to reflect upon this act of bitter injustice and its motive, under a roof protected and embellished by the royal grandson of Josephine.

From the Trianon we proceeded to the stables, to see the state carriages, which our guide assured us are such as are to be seen no where else in the world. The great state carriage was built for the coronation of Charles the Tenth. It is a most superb affair, surmounted by a crown. The interior panels are exquisitely painted, and the very hammercloth is a magnificent embroidery of massive gold. There was also the coronation carriage of the first Napoleon, and the carriage built for the christening of the Prince Imperial; in all seven carriages of elaborate splendor, with sedan chairs of centuries ago — one built for Marie Antoinette — a sledge hollowed out of a panther for Madame Montespan, and a goat carriage, presented to the present prince by the Sultan.

The spotless oaken floor was polished to the top of its bent for the visit of the grand equerry, which was momentarily expected. Indeed, the trial of the day lay in these polished floors, which made the long miles of traverse as difficult and fatiguing as if we had been treading upon ice.

We reached the palace at last. Its very name

evokes the shades of that half century, which was truly the brilliant cycle of European history. Not only in France, but in Great Britain, were the great lights of literature, of oratory, of pulpit eloquence, of statesmanship and martial glory, burning in such a constellation of splendor as has never risen upon the horizon, before nor since.

If the walls of the old palace could speak, what tales could they relate, of luxury, surpassing Persian magnificence, of beauty, of wit, of intrigue, of tyranny. The centre of the palace contains the royal apartments, and the wings the museum of paintings and sculpture. The King's suites of rooms are on the right, the Queen's on the left.

The apartments of Louis the Fourteenth remain, in all respects except the furniture, as when he inhabited them. Some fine pieces of furniture remain — the bed upon which he died, some clocks, two entresols, and one or two tables; one of the last covered with the same velvet cloth in use during the King's lifetime. The bed is in a room directly upon the balcony of the court from which the death of the monarch was proclaimed as soon as the breath had left his worn out body, and the plaudits with which the succeeding government was hailed, testifies to the character of French loyalty. No silent sorrow, no wail of grief, bespoke a nation's mourning for one whose reign had exceeded the length of most of their lives; and yet no eastern monarch ever received more prostrate servility, more cringing adulation.

This bed room is the most gorgeous apartment of the palace. The ceilings are exquisitely painted, carved and gilded, and the paintings are of great beauty. Next in splendor is the bed room of the Queen; similar in adorning, and, to my taste, more beautiful. The ante-room of the King's bed chamber is a long, elegant room, called from the shape of the window in both ends, the gallery of the bull's eye. This room is famous. In it were gathered the wit, the beauty, the finesse, the ambition, and the greed of such a court as the world has seldom seen. Here the vain King delighted to keep in attendance a crowd of flatterers, and no servility was too cringing, no adulation too gross to please his morbid palate.

The magnificence of all these private apartments of ancient royalty can scarcely be described. Precious stones, curious and costly works of art, paintings beyond price, rare tapestries, time-pieces of elaborate workmanship, give one an idea of what these rooms must have been when they were furnished with a gorgeousness appropriate to the palace and its masters. The palace is filled with portraits of the Bourbons, especially of the family, from Louis the Thirteenth down; of the Queens of the Fifteenth and Eighteenth Louis — beautiful women both — to say nothing of the still more beautiful favorites of the court. We passed, during the day, through two hundred and sixty rooms, and eight galleries.

The history of France, from Clovis down, is garnered up in the pictures and sculptures of Versailles;

and it is pleasant to rest the mind and eye upon historical paintings and sweet, natural landscapes, after the weariness of Holy Families and St. Sebastians.

The galleries are long arcades of elegant architecture, lined with pictures of great merit and interest, depicting the victories, of which France has many to record. The brilliant exploits of the sixteenth and seventeenth centuries, and the splendid achievements of the eighteenth, are here portrayed, with a perfection of art well calculated to stir the enthusiasm of a French heart, since it rouses that of uninterested foreigners.

Horace Vernet has immortalized himself in the power with which he has rendered the splendid history of France. He is one of the few painters who possess the power of painting the human figure in all its spirit, and the animal in its perfection.

There is one picture, covering the entire side of one gallery, which alone should make any man famous. It represents the surprise of the camp of Abdul Kadir by the French troops. In the same room is a splendid picture of Napoleon liberating Abdul Kadir — the latter a grand figure of a man. Besides the pictures of these battles, we find portraits of all the generals who have distinguished themselves, especially those who rose during the republic and the first empire. The Napoleonic presence runs like a thread through all these scenes. The historic pictures of which I speak are a study for a month; there are many charming landscapes interspersed, which we had no time properly to enjoy. These galleries owe their renovation to the munificence of Louis Philippe, than whom there could be no greater contrast to the great Louis. He laid no imposition upon the people for the embellishment of public buildings, but out of his private purse he devoted immense sums for the restoring and beautifying of this palace. One of the finest galleries, that of Battles, which bears also the name of Louis Philippe, is most magnificent. One of the royal apartments of imposing elegance, is the ball room, with a small saloon at either end, called respectively the saloons of War and Peace. They are beautifully painted in frescoes appropriate to their titles. In one of them Marchand pointed to a corner by a window, saying that there Madame Montespan lost at play four million of francs in one night. From such seeds as these sprang the deadly Upas whose poisoned branches overshadowed the empire for many years, and whose roots still lurk in the soil, watered to fruitfulness by the blood and tears of half a century.

Another splendid hall, called the Glazed, is lined on both sides with mirrors set like windows, which reduplicate the objects of the room, giving it the appearance of a triple hall of immense size. It is lighted by a skylight, stretching the entire length of the gallery. The corridors and staircases correspond in beauty and art with the saloons and galleries.

The Salle de Spectacle, a theatre for royalty alone,

a gem set in the midst of these gorgeous galleries, is capable of holding two thousand spectators. It is semi-circular in form; the seats are cushioned with crimson velvet, and rise in gilded galleries, lined with mirrors, which reflect the magnificent lustres with which the saloon is hung.

Among the spectacles which I should like to see, would be this exquisite place of display in full brilliancy of light, and scenery, and music, and rank and beauty.

The chapels, both of the palace and the Trianon, are beautiful—the latter far the prettiest. I think it was introduced in the time of Madame Maintenon. This deserted palace employs the labor of one hundred and eighty attendants; to a utilitarian eye it seems too great a loss to royalty, to lay out of its dwellings the palace which, of all its possessions, is most befitting its abode.

All this conveys not even a meagre idea of the magnificence of this vast edifice—this one Versailles, which crowns the long splendor of royal dwellings with a diadem of riches which scarcely belongs to the home of any other kings in the world.

Oct. 31. Visited Pere la Chaise, which, apart from the fact of its having been the first city cemetery beyond the churchyard burial places in the midst of the population, and its affording a noble view of Paris, possesses less interest than most cemeteries. The largest and most elaborate of the monuments is that of the Russian princess Demidoff; the one most worthy of a pilgrimage is the small temple, where lie side by side, unworthy conjunction, the effigies of Abelard and the unhappy Heloïse.

Most of the monuments consist of small chapels, like boxes, in close contiguity, within which are hung garlands of immortelles, and sometimes of beads. Sometimes beautiful natural flowers stand in pots upon the little altar, and more frequently bouquets of artificial flowers supply their place. The French taste is, for many reasons, more successful in behalf of the living than of the dead, and the cemetery is a stiff one.

The most touching of all the resting places, to me, was a small plot, enclosed by an iron railing, with a hedge — without monument or inscription. By careful inspection one finds, rudely scratched upon the gate, as if by the point of a nail—Ney. It is a text for a volume of sermons.

We looked into the Jews' burial ground, which seems beautifully kept, with a quiet, un-Frenchy seclusion — the monument of Rachel is near its entrance. We saw the tombs of various French authors, and the statue of Casimir Perier, but found an hour or two in the streets of the necropolis a sufficient type of the whole.

Called at the American Minister's, and for the succeeding wet days did little beyond the shopping, which seems here to be never at an end. It is a beautiful, gay, well governed city, and its streets are charming; but Paris has taken no hold upon my affections—not so much as by a hair's breadth.

Nov. 4. We came down to Normandy through a beautiful undulating country, much finer and more picturesque than the route from Chambery. The cultivation seems to be conducted with great care, but the soil does not look fertile. The whole route was a succession of field and forest, village, chateau, park, church and tower. The ancient city of Rouen lies beside the way, with two grand old edifices towering above it; the cathedral, with a still unfinished spire, and the still more beautiful church of St. Ouen.

We enjoyed the day at Havre with kind welcoming friends in the family of our Consul, and went on board the small black steamer at ten.

As we groped our dark way down the steep ladder to the boat, whose smoke pipe was just upon a level with the pier, I cogitated upon what would be the appearance of things at low tide if this were supposed to be high. It turned out that the advertisement was mistaken in the hour, and we did not get out to sea until two in the morning. The passage was excessively rough—the gale which had done so much damage along the coast not having blown itself out. However, we learned that the shorter passages had been much worse, even perilous. We were all glad to come under the lee of the Isle of Wight, and welcomed the calm of Southampton water like mariners of the long voyage. We saw

Osborne house in the distance, and Her Majesty's yacht off Cowes. The country must be very charming; the shore is bold and wooded, and the verdure remarkable for the season. We passed Calshott Castle, at present a rendezvous for the coast guard; saw Netley Abbey, and a fine hospital on the mainland.

Landed at one o'clock, and at three set off for London, through a country such as is to be found no where except in England.

It was pleasant to find that our former admiration of the country was not due merely to the pleasure of novelty, but that it has suffered no diminution after the majesty of Switzerland and the softness of Italy. There is nothing else like it. The natural beauty of the pretty (not grand) scenery is carefully preserved, and superadded is a cultivation which seems to have reached perfection.

The green waves of land roll back upon forests almost as green; the tilled fields, bordered by hedges, are laid down in lines so carefully and finely wrought as to become of themselves beautiful; the great flocks of sheep, which always enliven English scenery, are spread over the downs; and here and there cluster the picturesque villages, with the spires of edifices worthy the name of church; and quiet, snug farm houses, which wear the warm, cheerful air of home, are scattered abroad upon the soft slopes.

Nor is the interest of antiquity wanting. Venerable ruins, wrecks from the dim sea of the past, still cling to the shores of the present, and tell of civilization, and art, and science, in the ages when the wild Indian was the sole monarch of our wilds. At last we are in London.

CHAPTER XVI.

ENGLAND.

London — Madame Tussaud — National Gallery — Houses of Parliament — Courts — St. Thomas, Chartreux — Lord Mayor's Day — Hampton Court — Sydenham Palace — Zoological Gardens — Thames River — Tunnel — Christ's Hospital — Westminster Abbey.

Nov. 6. Our voyage of discovery in the great city has scarcely begun; but by way of commencing at one end or the other of a climax, we have been to Madame Tussaud's. An exhibition of wax-work has always seemed to me one of the very last sources of attraction, but Madame Tussaud has proved herself a real artist, and would, I doubt not, have managed the clay of the studio with great skill. It is truly a wonder in its way, to see the power with which she has rendered the lifelike expression of face and figure, especially in the eye, the feature which, more than all the rest, would seem difficult to imitate.

Her rooms are filled with the celebrities of the past century; the best of all is the Iron Duke as he lay in state, which one can scarcely realize not to be actual life, or rather actual death. It has a reality much more impressive than sculpture.

The most amusing feature of the rooms is the

figure of Cobbett, in Quaker costume, seated upon one of the benches, snuff-box in hand, and spectacles on nose. He turns his head occasionally, with an intelligent scrutiny of the objects around him, and I believe that it is no uncommon thing for people to beg pardon of the old gentleman for brushing too near his person. Madame Tussaud's successor has not inherited her skill; the recent figures are quite imperfect, especially the group of Americans, who would pass equally well for any other characters that might be attributed to them.

Nov. 7. Have been to the National Gallery, to the Houses of Parliament, and various courts.

In the National Gallery are works of most of the masters, but one should see this gallery before going to Italy, in order to enjoy it. The two best pictures that we have seen, by Murillo, are here; a St. John and lamb, which is a picture of exceeding beauty, and a Holy Family, in which the infant Saviour satisfies one's conceptions of what such a face should be, without a fault.

Another gem, which surpasses all pictures of the same subject, is Corregio's Ecce Homo. The great Ecce Homo of Guido is here, but I think no one could fail to feel the great superiority of the former. Indeed, among all attempts to embody the divine spirit, shining through human sorrow and suffering, it stands, in my judgment, pre-eminent.

There are some charming pictures by Turner—especially two landscapes, which by his own desire, hang beside two similar ones of Claude Lorraine; they are four pictures of restful beauty. But it seems to me a mistake to group such a number of pictures by one artist, all in precisely the same style. They are so often repeated that one gets sated with hazy atmosphere — which, I believe, is quite heterodox to say in England.

Rain, Speed and Steam, is exactly calculated to exhibit Turner's peculiar power. I am glad to think that the indistinctness of all these pictures is owing to the want of durability in the coloring; for the engravings from them are very charming.

The Houses of Parliament are in the old Palace of Westminster, and have the quiet, stately magnificence of old English architecture. But their great interest lies in the crowd of associations which throng these ancient halls. When the liveried guardians of such places as these take the customary fee of entrance, they little imagine what trains of dignitaries and notables enter with the silent visitor.

The great state trials, the royal pageants, the important councils, the struggles and the decisions of ages, are invisibly inscribed upon these lofty walls, and the imagination of the beholder supplies the warmth, which brings the mystic characters to light. We took a peep at the four Courts in session, one of which was the Court of Queen's Bench, and one the Nisi Prius. We saw that, of which every one has read, the assembly of the law in gown and wig. The former is a very decorous garb for a court of dignity, but the wig is nothing less than a deformity. It is a close cap of stiff gray horse hair curls; and I fancy it would be difficult to recognize our familiar acquaintances of the legal profession, in such guise.

The sittings were characterized by a quiet, dignified courtesy, but I should think they would sometimes lack the interest of animation. There is certainly one advantage to be gained by the habit of discountenancing declamation — if one may not declaim, he will not be likely to make many efforts at speechifying unless he has something to say.

We saw the Lord Chief Justice, Sir Alexander Cockburn, and a number of judges, who did not need the judicial robes to give them dignity.

The House of Lords is a small room, richly furnished; and the House of Commons surprised us by its lack of size. When one reads of the Houses of Lords and Commons, he unconsciously conceives an idea of vastness proportioned to the importance of the assembly.

It seemed to me a worthy juxtaposition, that the halls in which the great living men of England strive for the great rights of the nation, should stand hard by the resting-place of England's greatest dead.

Nov. 8. Have been to St. Thomas, Chartreux, to hear one of my favorite writers, Dean Trench — now newly appointed Archbishop of Dublin — a worthy successor of that distinguished man, Archbishop Whately. By law of custom, the dean of Westminster succeeds to the see of Dublin.

In the afternoon we went to St. Paul's, to hear Archdeacon Hale. I liked them both very much; it was a pleasure to hear real thinkers preach once more. I liked the intonation less than ever, and fear that I should never learn to pray in cathedral service. I was struck with one idea at St. Thomas'. It is a very common complaint among clergymen at home that there seems to be no way of securing the attention of children in general during church service. This was accomplished here by making the children the most active assistants in the service. They occupied the entire organ loft, and led both chants and responses audibly and reverently. The proper observance of the entire service by the whole body of worshippers is very marked, and might be profitably imitated by our own people.

There is a manliness in the way in which Englishmen show respect to public worship, which impresses us wherever we go — both in England and abroad. They go to church as a matter of course, and read, and sing, and pray, and listen with an earnestness and decorum, which, even if it have no deeper root than a sense of propriety, cannot fail to influence the character for good, in some wise.

Nov. 9. This, the Lord Mayor's day, is the Prince of Wales' birthday as well. The new Lord Mayor goes in state to be sworn at Westminster, and afterwards makes a grand progress through the city; while the day is closed with an immense dinner at the Guildhall, which is just at the foot of our street.

It is a general holiday, and we had a fine opportunity of seeing an English crowd, which, if it differed at all from the same affair in America, did so to its own disadvantage. It was coarser, poorer, more quarrelsome than the masses that I have seen awaiting a spectacle at home.

The procession passed us in the afternoon. It was not much of a display. The troops of the city were represented only by their bands; the main feature of interest being a small band of Knights, in the armor of different periods. The sheriffs were arrayed in furred robes, and the servants in the gaudiest of gilded trappings. The day was chill for the long white silk stockings of the coachmen and outriders; it is to be hoped that they have learned to enjoy it, and to fancy that fashion supplies the lack of comfort. The Mayor's carriage is a cumbrous, rather stately machine, apparently of bronze, drawn by six gaily caparisoned horses with postillions. The new Mayor was attended by his own clergyman and two mace bearers. As it is strictly a city display, there was no representative of the throne in the procession, which was, in itself, not much of an affair.

In the evening, there were elaborate illuminations at the West end in honor of the Prince. Our street was barricaded to prevent the passage of any other carriages than those conveying the guests to the Guildhall; and all night the police were busied in keeping the arriving and departing lines in proper order, and in summoning carriages. How tedious the banquet must have been can be imagined from the fact that the arrivals began before even this early twilight, and it was not all over before four in the morning.

Nov. 10. Hampton Court. Went by rail to Hampton. This is a palace built by Cardinal Wolsey, and afterwards absorbed by his royal master. It was a royal residence during many reigns, and the favorite abode of William and Mary. During their reign the buildings were reduced in number, and a line of grounds, once occupied by a wing of the palace, was planted with shrubs, and trained into a long arbor, called Queen Mary's Walk. The last kingly occupants of the Palace were George the Second and his family. At the present time the upper stories are inhabited by the remnant of several noble families, who have been reduced in estate, and are here provided with home and attendance by the Queen. One could bear some loss of fortune with tolerable equanimity, if it were compensated by the privileges of such a charming abode.

The palace is built around a large court, and fronts upon the most lovely grounds, garden and park, a sweet, perfect picture, in which the repetition of lawn, tree, shrub, flower, walk, forest, gives very little idea of the quiet, picturesque beauty that characterizes this charming domain.

The buildings are massive and rather low, but very extensive. The Hall, a guard room which forms the first of the long suite of state apartments, is adorned with arms of all descriptions, arranged in many curious figures. They represent the mode of warfare of almost all ages. The arrangement belongs to the time of George the Second, and was copied in the similar disposition of weapons in the Tower. The room is wainscoted with oak, and the old oaken floors are every where uncarpeted. The pictures of the guard room are all portraits of admirals, or representations of naval engagements.

From the guard room there leads out a long succession of halls, saloons, bed rooms, banqueting rooms, galleries and private apartments, such as I cannot particularize. They all looked upon some charming view of park, forest, or garden, still green and fresh with the tender verdure which we connect only with the idea of spring. This is one of the perpetual charms of England, and they say that even in winter the fields retain this beauty.

The long ranges of apartments are filled with pictures, many by eminent English painters. The portraits by Sir Godfrey Kneller and Sir Peter Lely, are very beautiful, which is undoubtedly owing, in part, to the wonderful specimens of beauty that were the subjects of their pencil, and which it would seem, should have inspired even ordinary fingers.

There are some fine pictures by Gainsborough; one in particular, a picture of Col. St. Leger, is extremely beautiful. There are several fine pictures by West; several of Titian, among which a Lucretia is one of his best figures. Almost all the Italian artists are represented, and there are some works of Vandyke. Two of the most pleasing pictures are by Denner—two heads, representing Youth and Age, in which the beauty of expression is combined with exquisite coloring in no ordinary degree. Here, too, are the famous cartoons, or paintings upon paper, by Raphael—magnificent pictures of course. They are upon the death of Ananias; Elymas the Sorcerer; Peter and John at the Beautiful Gate; the Miraculous Draught of Fishes; Paul and Barnabas at Lystra; Paul Preaching at Athens; and, most beautiful of all, Christ's Charge to Peter.

These cartoons line the walls of a large hall, built on purpose for their reception. It is difficult to do justice to the paintings at Hampton Court, for the outdoor picture from every window is too enticing for a careful attention to art within.

From the palace we went to the gardens to see the immense grape vine which forms a notable attraction to the grounds. This vine, ninety-seven years old, measures thirty-six inches round its stem; and its branches, in full bearing, cover an area of seventy by thirty feet. The weight of the fruit, now hanging in tempting purple clusters is about eight hundred pounds. The grapes are cut for Buckingham palace after the other graperies are exhausted, and therefore are allowed to hang until January.

Such places as Hampton Court bridge over the mighty chasms of time, and link the present with the past in such wise that history ceases to seem the drama which it is wont to appear, and claims the sympathies of present actuality. To tread the very courts which the ambitious cardinal trod; which the monarch, who lives more for us in Shakspeare than in our real faith, adorned for his beautiful favorite, impresses one with a conception of the sixteenth century which no books can give.

The foggy weather, which so circumscribes the view at this season, deprives us of the pleasure of seeing the far-famed scenery of Richmond.

Nov. 11. It was with no especial anticipations of pleasure that I set out for Sydenham. Every one has said, "You must by all means go to Sydenham," but I fancied it to be much the same thing as our own Crystal Palace, or that at Paris, which had proved disappointing; and we have hitherto gone upon the principle, in our sight-seeing, not to expend our precious time upon things of which we have a fair type at home. We were therefore little prepared for the beauty of the ærial structure, or the still more charming attractions of the grounds.

If I remember rightly, the extent of the palace is sixteen hundred by three hundred feet, and the grounds enclose two hundred acres, with just the variety of undulation sufficient to double the apparent extent.

There are a few pleasing pictures in the gallery, and casts from all the greatest sculptures of Italy, but at present the best part of the exhibition is to be found among the tropical plants and birds, which are numerous and comprehensive, being natives of all the hot countries of the earth. Conspicuous in the wing appropriated to them, is the gigantic tree from California, whose rings mark an age of three thousand years. Its trunk was cut just below the branches, and measures a hundred and sixteen feet in height, the entire distance to the top of the branches being three hundred and sixty-three feet. The trunk measures thirty-one feet in circumference, and the bark is eighteen inches thick. This bark was carefully removed in sections, and reconstructed as it now stands. The conservatory is a wilderness of rare and beautiful plants; from this enormous tree, down to the tender moss that fringes the borders of the basins, every thing is exotic, and the air is heavy with tropical warmth and perfume, and rings with the songs and screams of birds of more than rainbow plumage. There are also here models of the colossal monsters of sculpture which are found in the long-forgotten temples of Nineveh and Babylon — hideous figures, that give one such degrading ideas of the conceptions of humanity in the lower degrees of civilization.

Another curiosity is a pyramid, representing the amount of gold brought to England from Australia, between the years 1851 and 1861. I did not learn its volume, but it towers up, a mass of golden semblance, very rich in suggestion. Various articles of merchandise are displayed throughout the edifice, evidently more for the purpose of advertisement than for profit.

There were two concert performances during our stay, and some very fine organ music. The grounds are tastefully laid out with terraces, fountains, mounds, arbors, lakes, and every variety of miniature landscape charm.

A very interesting part of the grounds, to me, was the quarter exhibiting the geological formations of the earth. It was done under the direction of the late Prince Consort. The regular succession of strata has been carefully produced, and upon an island in a little lake, are huge models of the extinct species, constructed according to the fossils. Here the gigantic saurians gape at each other, in all their stages of advance, and make one devoutly thankful that the species is truly extinct. We had no object in ascending the tower, for the fog was so dense that it was impossible to tell whether the view beyond the grounds were upon city or forest.

Nov. 12. We have visited one of the great parks, which spread their greenness over such vast extent in the very midst of a crowded city like London, that they give the sense of quiet and solitude like that of the country.

And in the midst of these green fields we find a wide area of many acres, devoted to the animals of every quarter of the globe. The exhibition here is much larger, and on a better scale than that in Paris. The creatures are admirably appointed, and are the best specimens of their kinds. The magnitude of the expense, and the stable persistence of such establishments as these, are as remarkable among the things of the old world as its mountains or its architecture, and tell of the slow sifting process of time as truly as its monuments and its palaces.

Nov. 14. To-day we have betaken ourselves to the great highway which runs silently through the heart of the metropolis.

We went to see the monument which stands near London Bridge, marking the spot where the great fire of 1666 broke out; a long inscription records the ravages of the fire, and the fact that the monument was completed in 1677.

The approach to the river landings is blind, intricate, and rendered difficult by the throng of vehicles in the narrow streets near the water side. The boats do not receive and discharge passengers at the same landing, thereby avoiding much confusion, but occasioning considerable inconvenience, and, to a stranger, perplexity.

We took a steamer and went up to Milbank, passing Southwark, Blackfriars, Waterloo and Westminster bridges, and Lambeth Palace, and stopping just short of Vauxhall bridge. The most beautiful of all these noble structures is the Westminster bridge. It rests upon iron arches, with an upper bridge and balustrade of stone.

There is no point of view so fine for many of the London buildings as the river. St. Paul's, the

Parliament Houses, Westminster Abbey, Somerset House, Lambeth Palace, and the Tower are all seen to good advantage.

The sail was full of historic memories. One could almost fancy the gay barges of the pleasure loving nobles, or the swift vehicles of their secret vengeance, among the prosaic boats that now ply their trade under the argus eye of the police. It is far better to lionize among the monuments of the olden centuries, than to have lived, with one's life upon the breath of some capricious mortal, even in the days that seem so picturesque in the distance. I think all real life is in the straight line of prose, until we reach such a distance as shall enable us to take in the mighty curve by which the seeming straight line becomes the line of beauty and grace.

We next went down the river to the Tunnel, the great useless wonder of achievement, by which the miracle of old is verified, and we walk by a dry path through the midst of the sea.

This long arch is a beautiful piece of work, and it is utterly impossible to realize that the waters are tossing, and ships riding over our heads. It is well lighted, and its recesses are filled with small stands of vendible articles, which would seem to be a pursuit of commercial advantage under unusual difficulties.

The great depth of this work, necessitating a descent of one hundred steps on either side, is alone sufficient to destroy the feasibility of the plan; and the difficulty of constructing a carriage approach has proved insurmountable.

However, all is not lost that proves impracticable. The great lessons of practical mechanics are never learned, but by repeated failures; although people are apt to forget that there is as much necessity for learning what cannot be done, as what is truly feasible. Perhaps Brunel has accomplished no unworthy mission in demonstrating impossibilities by the reductio ad absurdum.

We crossed from Wapping to the Surrey side, and were obliged to walk a long distance for some means of conveyance to the city, through streets such as we read of in English books — the very reverse of Piccadilly; most dingy and uninviting; that middle ground between comfort and squalidity, in which a vast number of people must make their habitation; but which is almost equally repulsive to the feelings with utter poverty. I was glad, however, to have seen that phase of London suburbs, which we pass usually by train, and without notice.

Nov. 15. Went to morning service at Christ's Hospital, and afterwards to the gallery of the dining hall, to see the boys at table. It was a place of great interest to me. Christ's Hospital was founded by Edward the Sixth, whose effigy surmounts the inner entrance. Its original intention was, like that of many similar institutions here, the education of poor children; but, like many others of its class, it has passed into an establishment into which entrance must be obtained by influence; and is diverted to the benefit of a rather different class of society from that for which it was at first intended.

The appearance and manner of the boys showed plainly that they belong to no substratum of society. They retain the dress prescribed at the foundation, a most peculiar and inconvenient garb; consisting of a long blue cloth gown, belted with a leather girdle; a yellow flannel tunic like an apron or short petticoat; yellow stockings and russet shoes; no collar, but cambric bands like those of a clergyman, and no covering for the head save the luxuriant protection of nature. Eight hundred of these boys filled the gallery of the chapel and led the responses. In the chancel was a table spread with loaves of bread, which were distributed to the poor at the close of the service. The sermon was preached by Rev. Dr. McCall, a scholarly divine, who has been engaged in the work of revision of scripture; and was in behalf of the Fishmongers' and Poulterers' charity.

After service we brought up the rear of the long procession of boys through the cloisters of the quadrangle, and established ourselves in a gallery which overlooked the dining hall; a long stately room, adorned with paintings and stained windows; with an organ gallery at the opposite end. Eighteen tables were laid in the hall, with long benches for seats; and along these tables the boys clustered, like bees about a hive. A detachment girded up their gowns into their belts, and brought in the huge covered dishes of meat, one to the head of each table, and tall baskets of bread and tubs of potatoes, which were all deposited beside the matrons of the tables, who proceeded to carve the beef. When this was done, a chapter was read from the desk, prayers were said and grace chanted by the boys, accompanied by the organ. How devout the service, would probably depend somewhat upon the appetite. Then the viands were served, the boys still acting as waiters, the bread and beer distributed, and, their dinner being fairly inaugurated, we went home to our own.

In the afternoon we went down to the venerable abbey of Westminster, to enjoy the magnificent service, and to hear the new dean, Dr. Stanley, late of Oxford. Altogether, it was the most imposing service that I have ever attended. The church, or rather that part of it screened for service, was thronged — it was impossible to obtain a seat. The majestic old cathedral, stretching its dim arches above the lofty aisles; the stately monuments of the reverend dead, lifting their ghostly forms in the shadowy aisles of nave and transept; the poet's corner, not only crowded with living worshippers, but instinct with the immortality of genius; the remembrance that we were encircled by chapels, the depositories of the royal dust, and the renowned ashes of ages; the solemn swell of the great organ, bearing the rich deep voices of the choir through the vaulted roof; the prayers, hallowed and mellowed by the memories of the saints and martyrs, who have breathed their holy aspirations in this very language — in which the humblest Christian utters his lowly worship; and, added to the majesty of the service, the sermon — a clear, strong, evangelical unfolding of the character and work of the Saviour of men, plain to the understanding of the ordinary man, yet profound to the comprehension of the scholar — and well worthy the reputation of Dr. Stanley; all this went to constitute a satisfaction and solemnity such as I never felt in any service before. Happy is a church, in which such a preacher can find, in such an edifice, such a congregation to listen to the simple gospel of Jesus!

CHAPTER XVII.

ENGLAND.

London — Hyde Park — Theatres — South Kensington Museum — Guildhall — Oxford — Birmingham — Liverpool.

We have driven about the city, and have seen enough of London to carry away with us some idea of its vast extent, and some satisfactory identification of localities with which we have long been familiar by name.

Among these innumerables, we have seen Whitehall and the Banqueting House, in front of which King Charles was beheaded; Marlborough House, the present residence of the Prince of Wales; Apsley House and the Triumphal Arch; all sorts of statues; have driven about Piccadilly and Belgravia, and the parks; have admired the wide fields and charming views of Hyde Park, and the cultivation of Kensington gardens, and have seen markets and theatres. We went to St. Giles' Cripplegate, where Milton is buried, but were not able to obtain admission. We walked through the by-ways of Doctors' Commons and have driven round more squares, and through more streets than I can attempt to remember. We saw the shop, No. 21 Bow Street, which occupies the site of Will's Coffee House; the Rainbow Tavern, and many other spots of more or less historic interest.

We have paid our respects to the play in London at four theatres, the Adelphi, the Olympic, Drury Lane and the Haymarket. Covent Garden, which is a very fine looking structure, partly enclosed by a glazed roof, we did not visit; not having a fancy for the English Opera, which is its present attraction. I am little qualified to criticise the stage, but the English play is certainly far superior to any thing that I have seen at home. Even the inferior parts were good, and carefully sustained.

Manfred, at the Haymarket, was said to be the finest scenic representation ever put upon the English stage, and I can easily believe it to be true.

The Alpine scenery was wonderful; mountains, waterfalls, and the great Jung Frau itself; while the supernatural scenes were gorgeous.

Manfred was played by a young actor, who, upon the authority of Macready, is destined to achieve great things upon the stage; but the single utterance of "Manfred," by the phantom of Astarte, embodied a dramatic power, of which I had before no conception. None of the theatres were large, but they were handsome and well appointed.

One of the greatest pleasures that we have enjoyed was the gallery of pictures at South Kensington Museum. It is a gallery of British artists, and comprises three private collections—the Vernon, the Sheepshanks and the Ellison. It afforded far more gratification to my taste than the National gallery. There is scarcely a picture there which has not great merit. I cannot remember all, even of those most striking to me, but will endeavor to rescue some of them from the treachery of my memory.

Here are treasured up the works of Hogarth, Wilkie, Lawrence, Reynolds, Gainsborough, West, Landseer, Turner, and, of less universal note, Leslie, Ward, Etty, Cope and many others, who would be distinguished any where except under the shadow of such pre-eminent genius.

We have often sought for some trace of the brush of Hogarth, and have found it here alone; but the series of pictures which here represents him scarcely suggests the bold, strong painting which the history of Hogarth marks as his characteristic. Marriage a la mode is full of spirit, but it does not seem to belong to Hogarth.

Nor are the pictures of Wilkie quite equal to what I had supposed, although some of them are very pleasing; most of them are sketches of village life — the best to my taste is The Refusal.

There is a splendid full-length picture of West, by Lawrence, and another of Kemble as Hamlet, two masterly works. There are lovely real children by Reynolds, and the beautiful picture of Samuel, the parent of all the pretty engravings of infant prayer; but owing to the failure of some of his experiments in coloring, many of his best pictures are faded and disfigured.

West's great picture of Christ Healing the Sick is full of study. I wonder if the president of the Royal Academy were ever perplexed upon the subject of his own identity, as he looked back from London upon the little boy in the wilds of Pennsylvania, who despoiled his cat of her caudal clothing to furnish materials for his prophetic brush.

But, if I desired to go down to posterity with the prestige of loveliness, I should, among them all, select Gainsborough to paint my portrait. His picture of Mrs. Siddons is, among portraits, next to Guido's Beatrice in my reverence. It is said that no painter can do justice to a beautiful woman, but I cannot conceive of beauty that would not be glorified by the touch of his pencil. Near by, another face, that of a young man, looks out from Gainsborough's tints—the same exquisite style is visible in a portrait of Colonel St. Leger at Hampton Court.

There is another picture of Mrs. Siddons at Kensington, by Lawrence; but, fine as it is, it breathes of no such loveliness as this of which I speak.

The wonderful paintings of Landseer are here in abundance; the famous pair of Peace and War—the latter has scarcely a rival; the pictures in which he invests the perfectly executed animal with a suggestive human interest, such as Dignity and Impudence; Town Life and Country Life; Alexander and Diogenes; then the pictures of the mere animals, such as the Sleeping Bloodhound, and, perhaps the best of all, the Shoeing of a Horse.

Most pathetic in its truthfulness and simplicity is the Shepherd's Chief Mourner. The great dog lies in mute abandon of woe, stretching his shaggy head over the solitary coffin with a faithful, clinging tenderness that touches the most reserved sympathy. The Sacking of Basing House shows that Landseer is not of necessity limited to the depicting of animal life.

Among many pictures by Leslie are My Uncle Toby and the Widow Wadman; a charming picture of the Princes in the Tower; Queen Katharine and Patience; a portrait of Queen Victoria in coronation robes, and Sancho Panza and Dr. Pedro Snatchaway.

The fall of Clarendon, by Ward; The Foundling, by O'Neil; a Venitian scene of the Guidecca and the Jesuit's College; and a beautiful picture of the Crypts of Roslin Castle, are prominent among a score of attractive paintings; and there are two which I should like to see again especially. One is a picture of the ante-room of Lord Chesterfield, with Dr. Johnson among the waiting multitude. I do not remember the artist, but the picture is the very embodiment of the old doctor's character and history. The ill-concealed scorn of himself, which mingles with his scarcely restrained impatience and contempt for his own position and his desired patron, is inimitable. The other picture, by Johnson, is one of great pathos; Lord and Lady Russel receiving the sacrament before his execution. The sentinel has withdrawn to the prison window, and the husband

and wife kneel, side by side, before the priest, in whose countenance a curious but sympathetic observation mingles with the solemnity proper to the rite. Lord Russel, in devout attitude and with downcast eyes, is evidently wholly absorbed in the spiritual office — not so the wife. She kneels, indeed, beside her husband, but her devotion seeks no inward shrine; her despairing gaze devours the lineaments before her, as if she would drink in the beloved image and weave it with the very fibre of her being. You can read, in that steadfast, beseeching gaze, the preciousness of the fleeting moments, the tenderness of her breaking heart. Priest, prison and sacrament have no place in her thoughts — "that single spot is the whole world" to her, and your thought outruns the scene, and you forget the unworthy fate of the noble husband in the agony of widowhood that is about to spread its living pall over the wife.

I cannot enumerate half the striking pictures of South Kensington Museum, and have absolutely forgotten Turner, that idol of English criticism.

We came home by that very enjoyable mode of conveyance, the top of an omnibus, a long hour's ride through the dense interminable city. By Oxford Street and the Strand and Fleet Street, up Ludgate Hill, through St. Paul's churchyard and down Cheapside, past the Church where the Bow bells are still swinging, and as we alight we look down the street to the Guildhall. And I feel, as I write these names, that I belong to the past generation, and that Addison and his compeers are still gathered in the coffee house at the corner of Bow Street; or that Goldsmith is reading the Vicar of Wakefield to Dr. Johnson in the sponging house; or that the goldsmiths are negotiating a loan to King James in Lombard Street; or that the scaffold is rising before the Banqueting House; or that De Quincy is fainting with starvation in Oxford Street; or that Mr. Pickwick is learning human nature in the Fleet; and, from all this chaotic chronology breaks forth the idea that this is really London.

Nov. 17. We have been to the Guildhall, the "city building" of London. It has a rather fine effect, as it closes the view of King Street, Cheapside, and has retained its original color better than most of the buildings of the kind. The blackness of London smoke gives an effect which can not be confounded with the venerable, inasmuch as new structures readily acquire the same hue. The principal hall of the Guildhall is adorned with the escutcheons of the various fraternities of the city, and bears panels with the names and dates of the various Lord Mayors. Here are the two uncouth wooden city giants, Gog and Magog. One can not help remembering, by contrast, the sculptures which adorn the streets and porches of almost every town in Italy. These figures are of little higher civilization than the rude sculptures of our own aborigines.

We have been traversing the now familiar streets with lingering and reluctant steps. We have seen some of the objects of interest to the traveller in London, but we feel that a lifetime of wonder and richness lies beneath the surface to which we have grown, in a degree, accustomed; that London itself, without regard to the vast treasures of wealth, and knowledge, and power, and research stored up within her walls, means more to us than all the other cities of the earth.

Setting aside sectional prejudice and party questions, it is evident to the thoughtful mind that this is the fountain from which have gone, and still go forth streams of blessings for these later ages.

The acorn of civil and religious liberty was planted in this cold, distant, wave-defended island by no less than a divine hand. Protected by its poverty, its remoteness and its rudeness, it had nothing to attract the rapacity of the continental hordes, the trampling of whose armies would have beaten down the germ of the mighty shoot, the moment it had lifted its head above the soil. Then, the stubborn phlegmatic race were in no haste to turn their dominion into a hotbed, to force the precious plant to an unhealthy maturity. Thus it grew slowly upward, all the more thriftily for the ploughing and delving necessary to the daily bread of the toiling inhabitants; sometimes watered with blood, sometimes shaken by whirlwind; sometimes checked in its growth, and reft of many a goodly bough, it still grew, for it was of a divine seed, and rooted itself strong and wide, until, at this moment, the nations are eating of its fruit, and reposing under its shadow. And we, who have drawn the principles of our political life, the nourishment of our intellectual power, and the spirit of our religion from this root, must feel bound to this great Saxon heart of civilization by a thousand ties of sympathy and association, such as belong to no other land. Her history is our history; her literature is our literature; and the reading world of our own land is more familiar with London and its associations than with any other subject of history in the world.

The emotions which swell the heart in London are too impressive and too complicated to express or even to analyze. These streets which we pace, musing ever as we go, have been shaken by the tramp of the legions of Cæsar; have rung with the clang of the mailed hosts of the Crusaders; have echoed the tread of the grim battalions of the Revolution; have blazed with Romish faggots, and glittered with Protestant bonfires; have echoed the shouts of acclaim to Saxon and Norman, to Plantagenet, Tudor, Stuart, Cromwell, Orange and Brunswick. And, amid all these changes and chances, the English people have held on, in the main, their steady way; guarding, with jealous conservatism, their ancient laws and customs; maintaining with stubborn independence their legal rights, or those which they fancied belonged to them, against foreign foe and native tyrant; fostering institutions of learning and religion at home, and planting them beside their flag abroad;

spreading the white wings of their commerce upon every sea, and laying the strong grasp of their power upon every land. The finger of England is upon the spring of civilization. That she is proud is very true — too proud even to be vain; but when one has dwelt, even for a little time, upon that which is magnificent in her present, that which is venerable in her past, and glances at the scroll upon which are inscribed names which make illustrious the pages of war, of statesmanship, of law, of science, of art, of letters, of religion — he must, perforce, remember that pride is human, but these worthy objects of pride are English.

We linger still in these streets, resonant with the echoes of centuries, and trace in their dust the footprints of Bacon and Newton, of Shakspeare and Milton, of Addison and Johnson, of More and Russel and Clarendon and Chatham, of Warwick and Marlborough and Wellington; we look once more at St. Paul's and Westminster; we thread again the intricacies about the Bank and the Exchange and the Mansion House; and we write London indelibly and reverently upon our memory. For to-morrow we turn our steps towards the land, which, gathering up the dropped threads of the past from a myriad of nations, weaves them anew into the many colored web of the future — God grant with such a patient and skillful hand, that the fabric may endure the scrutiny of the long ages, and no sleazy thread mar the perfectness of the Master's design.

Nov. 18. We bade, at last, farewell to London, stopping on our way to Paddington to see a stone effigy of the great Earl Guy upon a house in Newgate Street. We soon left the great city far behind, and sped swiftly through the lovely country along the Western Railway—lovely even now, although despoiled of the green and gold of the summer harvest, which glorified the landscape when we last traversed it. Presently the massive outline of Windsor Castle rose bold and sharp against the November sky, with the royal banner drooping from its tower to indicate the presence of the Queen. The broad oaken sea of foliage still ripples at its foot, and the blue haze still curls up from the bosom of the silver Thames, as it sweeps the base of this proudest and noblest of royal homes.

Windsor stirs my heart with a pride akin to that of one who looks upon the towers of his ancestors, even though they may have long since ceased to belong to his own birthright.

The stately vision soon faded in the distance, and we turned eagerly to the gray towers and spires of Oxford. This spot, venerable with associations most dear to the scholar, means so much, and expresses so little, that you feel continually baffled in the attempt to identify your ideal with the actual. You know so much of it, and you see so little, that it seems to be an enchanted castle, which needs only the magic word to open its inner depths and display treasures hoary with antiquity, and precious with the riches of many ages. But the blank, square, impenetrable walls invite no scrutiny, and the stony gloom of the ancient corridors and staircases may well remind one of the days of monastic life.

We went to Christ Church, the largest of the cluster of colleges that compose the famous University. The University College is the most ancient, boasting King Alfred as its founder.

We visited the chapel, the dining-hall, and the library. This last is neither large nor pretentious; but it contains, beside its literary stores, gems of art from the ancient masters, all the more welcome to our recognition for having bidden them, as we supposed, a final farewell. We drove through the streets and scanned the various colleges. Although of different periods of architecture, they all bear the same general features, and it needed an effort of fancy to invest them with the power and dignity of their real importance.

A monument has been erected in front of Baliol College to the memory of Cranmer, Latimer, and Ridley, who perished here.

A few students in gown and cap, loitered about the quadrangles of the college, but we were surprised to see the place so deserted. What was our chagrin to discover, too late, that of all the days of the year, this was the one for the boat-races of the university, and all the world was in Christ Church meadows. To have just missed this event in Oxford life, was inexpressibly annoying.

We went to the Bodleian library—a world of books, ancient and modern, of curious volumes and rare manuscripts. It is next in size to the library of the British Museum, and contains, I believe, over two hundred and forty thousand volumes. There are, besides, models of temples, cathedrals and noted ruins, portraits of royal and ecclesiastical dignitaries, and objects of interest enough to tempt one to many visits. Among the curiosities is the lantern of Guy Fawkes.

There is a picture gallery belonging to the library, but we were not particularly struck by any of the pictures.

We saw there the Princesses Helena and Louise, attended by Dean Stanley, Colonel Ponsonby and the Honorable Mrs. Bruce. They are not handsome, but pleasing and simple-mannered ladies.

We lingered among the treasures of the library, until the bell warned us to retire, and, after driving about the town, we came on to Birmingham, and spent the night at the Hen and Chickens.

Nov. 19. We sallied forth through the smoky town to see some of the establishments that make Birmingham noted at home and abroad. And, among the beautiful things, the handsomest were the elegant bronzes, which I have never seen equalled. The clocks, mantel ornaments, busts, statues, statuettes, were all admirable. We saw the process of electro-plating, and its cognate operations, and were politely received and conducted through the establishment.

The manufactory of papier maché seems more like a magazine of art than a place of mechanical labor. Such beautiful things are done with dull opaque heaps of brown paper as make one wonder at the ingenuity and taste which, besides modelling furniture and household appliances and conveniences out of such unlikely material, afterwards elevates them to the dignity of works of art. There were tables exquisitely copied from Landseer; waiters pretty enough to be framed for pictures; gems of scenery and flowers; sketches of ruins, castles and cathedrals; portfolios, boxes, books, desks, &c., &c., all enticing and useful.

We saw the process of manufacture, from the gluing of the sheets of paper into masses, to the gilding and polishing at the close. Most of the work seemed to be done by women. Indeed there are many avenues of labor and occupation opened to women on this side of the ocean, which ought to satisfy any reasonable advocate of woman's rights.

Women are found in nearly all the booking offices of hotels; they are the book-keepers in shops; they fill positions of respectability as housekeepers, and discharge, with propriety, many offices, such as we bestow upon men, who should be, instead, at the strong armed work of bodily labor.

We spent a day in Liverpool, in rest from journeying, and in preparing for our voyage, Have been about the streets of the city; have seen shops and markets; have been watching the arrivals of our fellow passengers, among whom we have already found some acquaintances, and have been indulging the unusual feeling of having nothing to see, and nothing to do.

CHAPTER XVIII.

HOMEWARD BOUND.

Scotia — Liverpool to New York.

Nov. 21. Once more afloat upon the tossing sea. The good ship Scotia stands first among the means of Atlantic transit, but the Great Eastern has spoiled us for any thing short of a floating hotel, and our accommodations seem narrow and stifling.

The last gleam of sunshine departed as we left the shore and steamed down the Mersey to our ship, and we had reason to congratulate ourselves on taking the earliest tug — for the mail came down in a pouring rain, and one of the passengers, losing heart at the ominous commencement of the voyage, forfeited his passage money, and returned to await better auspices — to the great amusement of his fellows, who, however, learned before the voyage was over, to feel some respect for the good fortune of an individual so true to his instincts.

We dropped anchor the next night in the harbor of Queenstown, and we went on deck to look at the distant lights, and to bid a second farewell to the Old World, and then betook ourselves to our berths, where some of us were destined to remain for a large part of the voyage. We had an unceasing gale to New York, with almost continual storm, and the trip was as bad as it could well have been without actual danger.

My own friends maintained the most upright propriety, holding their position in the saloon in a creditable and seaworthy manner, while I lay in profundis, meekly veiling my bonnet to steward and stewardess, with not even a spar of resolution left upon which to hoist a signal of distress.

But this horrible malady of the sea, while it plunges you in despair as to your own individuality, does not prevent your watching with amusement similar results in the person of others.

There was not even the sense of insecurity, either to intensify or allay the incessant self-consciousness. But as I lay, plunging at every billow, I could feel the stout, firm solidity with which the ship met the shock, and rose buoyant and obedient to keep the unswerving line towards the news boat at Cape Race.

It mattered little to the imperturbable captain that the sea swept the decks; he ruled his floating world, and carved his beef, and read the church service all the same.

I listened to the boom of the breaking waves, and the swash of the returning water, to the rattling of cordage, and the tramp at the heaving of the log. I could see the faces of the few passengers who were abroad, as they stole along the narrow passage, inflexibly set in the determination to persuade themselves and the rest of their world that they were not at all sick.

Then there was the daily fib of the attendants, who assured the patients that the weather was charming above, and that they would be quite well "once they got on deck;" the faint wail in reply; the carrying of some refractory sufferer, vi et armis, into the stormy air; there were kindly neighbors, who, with the touch of sympathy which made that whole world kin, proffered grapes and champagne to ungrateful strangers; and, as days wore on, the most hopeless began to emerge from the lower obscurity, and so at last did I. I crept to the saloon and lay upon the cushions, the only stretch of which my exertions were capable. We assembled in creditable force to do honor to the Thanksgiving dinner, and had a merry time, despite the stormy roar without. We had a brilliant impromptu speech from Mr. Ruggles, who was returning from the Statistical Congress of Nations, and we underwent various political demonstrations; for, albeit in an English ship, we were representatives of almost every sort and condition of American life.

So passed the voyage. We found pleasant companions, not the least among whom was our kind and genial friend of the house of Harper—and the enforced contact of our daily life developed acquaintance into familiar intercourse and intimacy.

We discussed dress and politics, theology and sentiment, poetry and education; compared notes of recent travel and present affliction; we had play and merriment and nonsense—and it was not without a touch of regret at separation, that we stood at last, thank God, in health and safety, upon the welcome shores of our own beloved land.

As I look back upon the enjoyment of the last few months, I am continually surprised that in a journey undertaken, on my own part, specifically in search of health, so much has been accomplished with so little consciousness of exertion or fatigue.

In order to enjoy any success in a short tour, it is necessary to have a definite idea of the main points of interest to be sought, and then to close the eager eyes to many desirable things, which must be omitted, that the main design be not frustrated.

In a reasonably successful pursuance of this plan, we have seen, in part, England, Scotland, Wales, Ireland, Belgium, Prussia, Germany, Switzerland, Austria, Italy, France and—Fairyland. It is evident that in a tour like ours we were to see more of things than of people; for to scan the people minutely requires a long and loitering divergence from the common routes of travel, and a familiar acquaintance with their languages—begging, that one universal language forgotten at the confusion of Babel, and pourboire, by which the traveller is made to supply the missing link between the justice of the employer and the rights of the employed, being the only intelligible communication to the unlearned tourist.

Our pleasure, then, with such knowledge of men

and society as came by the way, lay in scenery, art, architecture, and the associations of antiquity, of history, of poetry or of fiction.

And I would fain gather up more closely the clews by which we have threaded the labyrinth of foreign lands, and brought thence pictures to brighten the chambers of memory for all our after life. These various sources of pleasure are, of course, always more or less combined, in all that we have seen, but, for the sake of distinctness of remembrance, I would classify them in my own mind under their most prominent characteristics.

In church architecture, we have seen the cathedrals of Chester and Dublin and Glasgow; York Minster and Westminster and St. Paul's; of Brussels and Antwerp and Cologne; of Mayence and Frankfort and Strasbourg and Notre Dame; of Milan and Venice and Florence and Pisa — and we have seen the great St. Peter's.

We have scanned the magnificence of noble life at Eaton and Chatsworth and Warwick, and the palaces of Hampton and Windsor, of the Luxembourg and Versailles and the Vatican.

We have seen the ruins of the past in Conway and Caernarvon; in Holyrood and Melrose and Dryburgh; in Haddon and Kenilworth; in the still splendid remains of the castle of Heidelberg, and the countless ruins of the Rhine land; in Herculaneum and Pompeii; and, greatest and saddest monument of desolation, we have seen Rome, whose feet are planted in the ruins of the imperial city, and whose head overlooks the ruins of the Campagna.

We have done homage to the memory of genius at Stratford and Abbottsford and Westminster; at Grasmere and Rydal and Ambleside and Haworth and Ferney and Casa Guidi; we have seen the homes of Goëthe, of Rubens, of Raphael, and of Michael Angelo.

But when I come to speak of associations, there is nothing to do but to measure step by step, the long way, every foot of which is classic ground. There was Chester, full of Roman and English antiquities; Holyrood and the castles of Edinburgh and Stirling; London Tower; the battle fields of Waterloo and Magenta; the tomb of the Invalids; the palace of the Doges, the Roman Capitol, the Forum and the Coliseum.

But this task is fruitless, and so would be the attempt to enumerate the splendid works of art engraven on our memory.

It were enough to have seen the Dying Gladiator, the Apollo, the Laocoon, Moses and the Venus de Medici; the Aurora, and the St. Michael, of Guido; the Transfiguration, of Raphael; the Last Supper, of Da Vinci; the Descent, of Rubens; the Ecce Homo, of Corregio; or the Assumption, of Titian. But these are only the topmost peaks, beneath which lies a world of art and beauty which it would take a volume to describe.

But no art can equal the grand and beautiful pictures of Nature which have marked our way from the Atlantic to the Mediterranean. Old Snowdon looked down upon us, among the green swells and craggy defiles of Wales; we have rocked upon the waves at the foot of the gigantic headland of the north Irish coast; we have seen the clustering lakes, and the heathery moors, and the brown sombre hills that people the horizon at the summit of Ben Lomond; we have followed the windings of the Teith and Forth through the lowland plains, down to the broad estuary which widens to the German Ocean.

We have drunk in the marvellous beauty of Westmoreland, by Ulswater, and Windermere, Rydal and Grasmere; and of the lovely lakes sentinelled by Skiddaw and Helvellyn.

We have climbed the steep ways of the West Riding of Yorkshire; and have seen the flocks upon the thousand green hills of Derby and Leicestershire; we have wound through the quiet lanes and charming fields, and landscape gardens of Warwickshire; and have admired the varied landscape, and the perfect cultivation of the South of England, and the homely comfort of the farms of Kent. We have been upon the banks of the Dee and the Tweed, the Ouse and Derwent, the Avon and the Thames.

We have traversed the low flat country, rescued by Flemish industry from the sea, where the Scheldt pours its slow tide to the ocean; and the well tilled plains of France, and the borders of the brown historic Seine.

We have seen the sun set upon the vine-clad hills of the Rhine, from the "castled crag of Drachenfels;" and we have followed the lovely river of song and story from the rocky fortresses of Prussia to its broader bosom in the plains of France and Germany. We diverged to the sweet valleys of the Maine and the Neckar, and the pretty basin of the Oos.

We floated, humbly and reverently, at the foot of the dark solemn peaks that shut in the unparalleled lake of Lucerne; we looked abroad from the Kulm of the Rigi upon the snowy billows of the Bernese Oberland; we overhung the emerald valleys and the pretty lakes of Sarnen and Lungern; and the wild chasm of the vale of Hasli, from the magnificent road of the Brunig pass.

We watched the line of cascades that leap to the Arve from the long curtain of the chamois mountains of Meiringen.

We have listened to the roar of the Oltschibach and the Seilerbach, the Giessbach and the Reichenbach, by which the waters of the upper world pour their foaming tribute to the sea.

We climbed the rocky pass to the silent sea of ice that hangs forever between the Wellhorn and the Engelhorn; we skirted the sweet lake of Brienz, amid fields greener than even Alpine valleys; we were sprinkled by the feathery spray of the Staubbach, and did reverence to the immaculate Jung Frau from the bosom of Interlachen.

We sailed down lake Thun, under the shadow of

the great Niesen; and over the blue waters of Lake Leman, until Mont Blanc rose like a snowy cloud in the summer sky.

We saw the "arrowy Rhone" shoot forth from the quiet lake, and followed the gorges of the Arve to its courses among the fastnesses of Savoy.

We gazed at the solemn monarch of the mountains with his hoary beard of glaciers, from the pavilion of La Flégère; and watched the Arveiron gushing from the bosom of eternal ice.

We overhung the valley of the Rhone, from the summit of the Forclaz; and traversed the stupendous galleries, beneath the awful glaciers and terrific precipices of the Simplon.

We saw Monte Rosa from afar, as we dreamed beside the blue waters of Maggiore; and we recalled classic memories beside the Po, the Arno and the Tiber. We swept through the picturesque fields of Lombardy, climbed the purple Apennines, and traced the lava hills of Southern Italy to the foot of Vesuvius.

Through all the tour, we learned to repose with confidence upon the comfort, security and facility of the means of travel, and the order and protection of the governments. But beneath the orderly surface of the continent, we could readily perceive the surging of the unquiet people, and the alert, expectant attitude of the rulers — while our eyes turned ever more and more anxiously to the land of our own love, whose destiny hangs trembling in the balance.

May the God, whose hand holds the beam of the balance, grant, that, reading from afar the scroll of the earlier world, she may learn to avoid the errors and imitate the successes which it records.

That, unscathed by the fires of intolerance, unshattered by the earthquake of anarchy, unshackled by the fetters of despotism, and unsullied by the foulness of license, she may yet stand forth, even in her youth, the fair type of that perfect liberty which knows how to restrain the evil, without retarding the good; to repress crime, without oppressing innocence; to cherish independence, without encouraging insolence; to guard reverently the ashes of the past, while she kindles the signal fires of the future; and while she stretches forth one hand to give freedom to the nations of the earth, she may raise the other to swear fealty to herself, and to the God of the Nations!

www.ingramcontent.com/pod-product-compliance
Lightning Source LLC
LaVergne TN
LVHW010152110826
845151LV00002B/499

* 9 7 8 1 4 2 5 5 3 7 4 0 1 *